American
Religious Thought

Chicago History of
American Religion

A Series Edited by
Martin E. Marty

American
Religious Thought
a history

William A. Clebsch

The University of Chicago Press   *Chicago and London*

The University of Chicago Press,
   Chicago 60637
The University of Chicago Press, Ltd.,
   London
© 1973 by The University of Chicago
All rights reserved. Published 1973
Printed in the United States of America
International Standard Book
   Number: 0–226–10960–7
   (clothbound)
Library of Congress Catalog Card
   Number: 73–82911

WILLIAM A. CLEBSCH is professor
of religious studies and humanities
at Stanford University.
His previous books include *Pastoral
Care in Historical Perspective*,
*England's Earliest Protestants, 1520–
1535*, and *From Sacred to Profane
America, the Role of Religion in
American History.* [1973]

To Hans W. Frei,
colleague, comrade, friend

Contents

Foreword by
Martin E. Marty   ix

Preface   xv

Abbreviations   xix

1. Prelude: The End
   at the Beginning   1

2. The Sensible Spirituality
   of Jonathan Edwards   11

   *Theologian and
   Religious Thinker*   11

   *Visible Saints and
   Visible Church*   24

   *The Signs of
   Sanctity*   38

   *The Holiness
   of Beauty*   53

3. Interlude: From Edwards
   to Emerson   57

4. The Hospitable Universe of
   Ralph Waldo Emerson   69

   *The Man and
   the Message*   69

   *Religion and
   Religiousness*   79

   *The Welcoming
   Universe*   99

   A Proffered Hand   110

5. Interlude: From Emerson
   to James   112

6. The Human Religiousness
   of William James   125

      *The Father's
      Humanism*   125

      *The Son's Spiritual
      Crisis*   134

      *Believing and
      Religion*   148

      The Larger Powers   158

      The Atoning Self   168

7. Postlude: After James   171

      Notes   189

      Suggested
      Readings   197

      Index   207

Foreword

The story of religious thought in the American past can be treated in many different ways, and William A. Clebsch could have chosen options other than the one he has pursued in this book. The conventional approach, useful in its own way in works of great length and scope, would commit the historian to setting forth the origins and development of doctrinal discussion in the many religious bodies in America. Most recently Sydney Ahlstrom in *A Religious History of the American People* has panoplied, through hundreds of pages, the varieties of religious thought in Protestant churches, Catholicism, Judaism, and an astonishing array of less established forces. This thought he then webbed into a history of action and organization.

The reader who welcomes access to these varieties will do well to pursue his inquiries by studying Ahlstrom or other full-length chronicles. The danger in such pursuits, when carried on in isolation, is that they can lead to confusion. The main threads of the story can be lost. A society which recognizes over 250 religious bodies and is aware of scores of contending creedal positions within many of these will inevitably confuse those who try to locate the main problems about which religious philosophers or theologians have contended. When the effort at telling the whole story is condensed into a book of the length of those in this series, the confusion is compounded. Had Clebsch chosen the first approach, he could have done little more than

provide a hop, skip, and jump tour through the corridors of
the past. The result would have been a kind of Baedeker for
hurried visitors, a gazeteer and biographical dictionary whose
sequence of proper names would simply overwhelm the student.

Having rejected the idea of providing a miniature reference
work, other choices still remained. A second method, as familiar
as the first, would have led the author to choose several score
representative figures in the churches' and synagogues' past and
treat the thought of these in the course of a page or two each.
The historian can isolate a denomination such as Presbyterianism
and see how its theological positions were fashioned and reap-
praised through the years by notable leaders. Then he can pick
up the Catholic or Methodist threads, and make his way down
all the denominational routes. Or he may choose the "schools
of thought" approach, treating the pragmatists, the idealists,
the historically oriented thinkers and the like in sequence. The
result would be another convenient reference volume. It may
also tell less than one would hope for about how significant
Americans did reason about the reality around them.

Professor Clebsch has chosen a third and in its own way more
ambitious approach. In his three main chapters he makes no
claim that he fully reproduces what everyone in every church
or synagogue was thinking or believing. No one would be so
foolish as to contend that Jonathan Edwards, Ralph Waldo
Emerson, or William James represented more than a rather small
minority of people in their own times. Edwards spoke to and
for New England, and even there his was a distinctive point
of view that was repudiated more frequently than it was accepted.
Ralph Waldo Emerson was and wanted to be an outsider, rejecting as he did most of the opinions of the masses of people,
including churchgoers, around him. William James was a
pioneer and a maverick, drawing upon an arcane resource in
his father's spiritual world, his private religious experience, and
a new scientific approach, to fuse a position approved by few
in his own time.

Clebsch can make his case, however, by showing how thinkers such as these saw what most of their contemporaries overlooked. The popular preachers and crowd-pleasers of their days are forgotten. Few know their names and almost no one reads their works. In their time they could have outdrawn or out-polled these seminal thinkers any day of any week — though one should not underestimate, either, the attractions of Edwards as a popular revivalist, Emerson as a lyceum speaker, and James as a university lecturer. The point is that the lonely pioneer, if he is profound enough, may serve later generations better as an indicator of life in the past than do the many ephemeral celebrity figures whose thought left no legacy for those later generations.

The three figures around whom the basic turns of Clebsch's story revolve are eponymic types. In some modest way or other they gave a name to their generations or epochs. It is not unreasonable to talk about an "age of Edwards," or Emerson, or James. They dealt with what James called "the rich thicket of reality," and with considerable daring and ingenuity cut paths through it, organized its strands, or gave shape to that which it symbolized.

Another principle of choice may have been operative as well in Clebsch's organization of his history. Suppose one were to prepare an anthology of the great religious writing of the Western world through the centuries. Which Americans would deserve inclusion? Certainly not the preacher Henry Ward Beecher, though he commented on virtually everything of interest in the late nineteenth-century world. Nor would most of the Catholic bishops who spoke for so many thousands on the issues of their day deserve inclusion. They and their colleagues left almost no ideas with which later generations have to wrestle in order to come to terms with the reality around them, however important their activities may have been. Yet Edwards, Emerson, James — and very few other Americans — would deserve a place in such an anthology.

In a day when ideas are often being downgraded or devalued,

Professor Clebsch unashamedly affirms them, supporting the idea
that ideas have consequences. The chapters which introduce and
connect the three main turns show that he does not think that
his account is the only one that deserves telling, or that it is
not located against a larger backdrop. Were he making this
the history of high points in the past of American religious
thought, objections from all sides would and should come. I
recall sitting next to a Roman Catholic graduate student during
a lecture on the genius of American religion. The lecturer followed basically the Clebschian track: Edwards, Emerson, New
England, White-Anglo-Saxon-Protestantdom, academia —
these were the landmarks, signposts, and main roads. This student, a product of what he himself would have called the Catholic
ghetto of parochial schools and colleges, said, "This is a very
interesting lecture — about what to me is a foreign country."
He and millions of less literate Americans could put together
a world and live a thoughtful life without much awareness of
this tradition.

While recognizing the foreignness of this account to the ears
of many, it is also important to reckon with the fact that this
tradition did have a privileged position in the past. School children who never heard of some of the spokesmen were influenced
by the world to which these men responded and which they
helped fabricate. The school's textbook tradition grew out of
the writing laboratories of people who were influenced by men
like Edwards, Emerson, and James. A history such as Clebsch's
will help those who unwittingly absorbed elements of that
influence, wittingly to appraise it in their adult lives.

A work of this kind is demanding; its heroes were not superficial. They were difficult because they tried to venture where
others had not gone before. Many of their probes were frustrated
and they often failed. But their false turns are as revealing as
the positions which they came to affirm and defend. The reader
who patiently follows the author through these turns will be
rewarded not only by the presence of a new appetite for the

works of the subjects of the book but also by the development of new knowledge and appreciation for the originality and the surprises in this element in the American tradition.

MARTIN E. MARTY
THE UNIVERSITY OF CHICAGO

Preface

This book concentrates attention on the founders and bearers of a distinct American spirituality, while only glancing at a few of the many American defenders and interpreters of church doctrines. Thus it is called a history of American religious thought and should not be taken for a history of theology in America. That much said, nobody will be surprised by the fact that the book deals closely with Jonathan Edwards and Ralph Waldo Emerson and William James. But anybody could thumb through the index, holding in mind a handful of favorite theologians, and find the names of few, if any, of them. Moreover, the three eponyms of this American spirituality receive the lion's share of the book's attention, for there is no pretense made at exhausting the subject (and much effort is made to avoid exhausting the reader).

The task, then, has been to select, and that means also to exclude. Another author, no doubt, would have selected differently and excluded differently, treating perhaps Philip Schaff instead of Horace Bushnell, or Paul Tillich instead of H. Richard Niebuhr. This author chose as he did in these examples not because Schaff was a Swiss and Tillich a German immigrant, unless their having been immigrants accounts for the fact that their work, on balance, falls more to theology than to religious thought.

The book rests on the thesis that Edwards and Emerson and James (and other religious thinkers) resisted the moralistic spirituality toward which America's chief religious heritage, Puritanism, almost inevitably trends. They resisted not by denouncing moralism but by exploring and affirming another kind of spirituality, which is here called esthetic. In America, esthetic spirituality involved not so much the appreciation of beauty attributed to or inhering in objects of artistic creation but rather a consciousness of the beauty of living in harmony with divine things — in a word, being at home in the universe.

That thesis and its supporting cast of religious thinkers have been, as it were, the plot and the *dramatis personae* of many courses I have taught over the past dozen years, especially since my transplantation from the academic world of theological seminaries to that of religious studies in the university. Steadily encouraged in this work by students and colleagues at Stanford University, I was afforded sabbatical leave in 1971–72 to write this book. The National Endowment for the Humanities named me one of its senior fellows and Yale University appointed me visiting fellow in religious studies and associate fellow of Silliman College for that year. The American Philosophical Society helped me make the transition from Stanford to Yale via England and Scotland, where I retraced the lecture tours of Emerson and James. To the officers of all these institutions Betsy Clebsch and I give thanks.

Members of the faculties in history, religious studies, and American studies; the personnel of the Sterling, Beinecke, and Divinity Libraries; and friends and friends of friends helped us be at home in the universe of Yale. Long, frequent conversations with a very generous colleague there tested my interpretations, prompting me to discard many and refine the remainder; for everything that may be valuable in the book I owe him a large debt, small payment on which is made by dedicating it to Hans Frei. The typescript in its nearly finished form was read by John

E. Smith of Yale, whose criticisms like those of the editor of this series improved many points. Amanda Porterfield Langston gave generous and invaluable aid with proofreading and indexing. The last, but certainly not least, of helpers to be thanked is Nancy Hill, secretary extraordinaire. For faults that persist despite all these good efforts, the blame is wholly mine.

Abbreviations

Allen   Gay Wilson Allen, *William James, A Biography* (New York: Viking, 1967).

Ahlstrom   Sydney E. Ahlstrom, *Theology in America, the Major Voices from Puritanism to Neo-Orthodoxy* (Indianapolis: Bobbs-Merrill, 1967).

Bishop   Jonathan Bishop, *Emerson on the Soul* (Cambridge: Harvard University Press, 1964).

CF   John Dewey, *A Common Faith* (New Haven: Yale University Press, 1934).

Conv.   Jonathan Edwards, "An Account of His Conversion . . . Given by Himself," in Samuel Hopkins, *The Life and Character of the Late Reverend Mr. Jonathan Edwards* (Boston, 1765), as reprinted in David Levin, ed., *Jonathan Edwards, a Profile* (New York: Hill and Wang, 1969), pp. 24–39.

Cross   Barbara M. Cross, *Horace Bushnell, Minister to a Changing America* (Chicago: University of Chicago Press, 1958).

EL   Ralph Waldo Emerson, *The Early Lectures of Ralph Waldo Emerson*, ed. Stephen E. Whicher, Robert E. Spiller, and Wallace E. Williams, 3 vols. (Cambridge: Harvard University Press, 1959–72).

ER   William James, *Collected Essays and Reviews*, ed. Ralph Barton Perry (New York: Longmans, Green, 1920; New York: Russell and Russell, 1969).

FM   William James, *Essays on Faith and Morals*, selected by Ralph Barton Perry (New York: Longmans, Green, 1943; Cleveland: Meridian, 1962).

ISDT   Jonathan Edwards, *Images and Shadows of Divine Things*,
            ed. Perry Miller (New Haven: Yale University Press,
            1948).

JMN   Ralph Waldo Emerson, *The Journals and Miscellaneous
            Notebooks of Ralph Waldo Emerson*, ed. William H. Gilman,
            Alfred R. Ferguson, et al., 9 vols. (Cambridge: Harvard
            University Press, 1960–). In this critical edition of the
            manuscript journals and notebooks, the editors have re-
            produced and flagged both Emerson's cancellations and his
            insertions; I have silently elided the former and included
            the latter.

KGA   Helmut Richard Niebuhr, *The Kingdom of God in America*
            (New York: Harper, 1937).

L   William James, *The Letters of William James*, ed. Henry
            James (his son), 2 vols. (Boston: Atlantic Monthly, 1920).

LR   Henry James, Sr., *The Literary Remains of the Late Henry
            James*, ed. William James (1884; Boston: James R.
            Osgood, 1885).

MS   William James, *Memories and Studies* (New York: Long-
            mans, Green, 1911).

Misc.   Jonathan Edwards, Miscellanies, MS notebooks, Yale
            University, Beinecke Library. Quoted by permission.

NTV   Jonathan Edwards, *The Nature of True Virtue*, foreword by
            William K. Frankena (Ann Arbor: University of Michigan
            Press, 1960).

PP   William James, *The Principles of Psychology*, 2 vols. (1890;
            New York: Dover, 1950).

PU   William James, *A Pluralistic Universe, Hibbert Lectures at
            Manchester College on the Present Situation in Philosophy* (New
            York: Longmans, Green, 1909).

RM   Helmut Richard Niebuhr, *Radical Monotheism and Western
            Culture, With Supplementary Essays* (New York: Harper,
            1960).

RS   Helmut Richard Niebuhr, *The Responsible Self, An Essay
            in Christian Moral Philosophy* (New York: Harper & Row,
            1963).

SP   William James, *Some Problems of Philosophy, A Beginning
            of an Introduction to Philosophy* (New York: Longmans,
            Green, 1911).

TC   Ralph Barton Perry, *The Thought and Character of William James, as Revealed in Unpublished Correspondence and Notes, Together with his Published Writings*, 2 vols. (Boston: Little, Brown, 1935).

UL   Ralph Waldo Emerson, *Uncollected Lectures by Ralph Waldo Emerson*, ed. Clarence Gohdes (New York: Edwin Rudge, 1932).

VR   William James, *The Varieties of Religious Experience, A Study in Human Nature* (London: Longmans, Green, 1902).

W   Ralph Waldo Emerson, *The Complete Works of Ralph Waldo Emerson*, ed. Edward Waldo Emerson, centenary edition, 12 vols. (Boston and New York: Houghton Mifflin, 1903–4).

WD   Jonathan Edwards, *The Works of President Edwards*, ed. Sereno Edwards Dwight, 10 vols. (New York: S. Converse, 1829–30).

WY   Jonathan Edwards, *The Works of Jonathan Edwards*, gen. eds. Perry Miller (vols. 1–2) and John E. Smith (vols. 3–) (New Haven: Yale University Press, 1957–):

           1. *Freedom of the Will*, ed. Paul Ramsey (1957);

           2. *Religious Affections*, ed. John E. Smith (1959);

           3. *Original Sin*, ed. Clyde A. Holbrook (1970);

           4. *The Great Awakening*, ed. C. C. Goen (1972).

White   Morton White, *Science and Sentiment in America, Philosophical Thought from Jonathan Edwards to John Dewey* (New York: Oxford University Press, 1972).

YES   Ralph Waldo Emerson, *Young Emerson Speaks, Unpublished Discourses on Many Subjects*, ed. Arthur Cushman McGiffert, Jr. (Boston: Houghton Mifflin, 1938).

1 *Prelude* *The End at the Beginning*

In a book of history the reader likely begins where the author ended — with a summary of the story about to be told, and with a hint of how the author thinks the past he labors to study can bear on the present he tries to observe and the future he dares to anticipate. Properly done, these ending words at the beginning build a mental window framing the story, not a box containing it. They foretell the story's major moves and suggest the story's significance; they must also respect the stance that reader and author occupy, a locus that is always moving ahead of the history the two begin to share.

To say a little, then, instead of too much, this book shows how a lineage of thinkers tried to divert American spirituality from its natural spillover into moralism by translating the religious impulse into being at home in the universe. The lineage springs from Puritan forefathers who opposed turning the idea of God's sovereignty into the divine right of Tudor and Stuart monarchs. For monarchy these forefathers substituted morality, the rewards of obeying God's will for the advantage of obeying the King's law. These English Puritan forebears begat American progeny equally bent on doing their own thing, on using religion as the means of making the universe into man's hospitable abode.

To trace the lineage of Americans who turned religious ethics into religious esthetics is to write history by selecting data. Every historian chooses the data he writes about. He need not select the way bird watchers take the winter census, recording every observable species and estimating the population of each. He may more profitably select like an affluent shopper, at once following and revising his list, picking out many familiar items and also discovering new and useful ones. Unlike a shopper, the historian publishes his purchase-record. He attains honesty as well as objectivity insofar as he knows and acknowledges the criteria by which he has chosen his data.

In this book America means the United States and their antecedent settlements in North America. Religious thought means something far broader than the denominational doctrines that theologians have certified, whether by appeal to traditional or to novel revelations, and also something more definite than personal opinions about things unexplained by accepted natural laws. Here religious thought means the reasoned, the cogent, and the evocative consideration of ways in which the human spirit of Americans seriously and strenuously relates itself to nature, to society, and to deity.

Here religious thought embraces more than a thinker's description of somebody else's way of being religious. Each thinker's own religiousness — how he involved himself in what he took to be humanity's most momentous exercise — enters the picture. But religious thought is not spiritual self-portraiture. "If men will surrender to the confessional instinct," observed an astute student of spiritual autobiography, "it is not our unavoidable duty to hear them out. The rewards of eavesdropping appear too slight and too unsavory." [1] What a thinker claimed religiously counts to the extent that the claim was lived out and reflected upon, thus making a style of religiousness imitable by others. Significant religious thought is not uniquely the thinker's own possession; it is what he is able to present as potentially everybody's.

How a thinker may have stood with any denomination does not of itself signify for the great trends of American religion.

It counts for more if a person addressed Americans in ways that helped them describe their spiritual hopes and celebrate their spiritual attainments. The Americanness — not an inherent quality unfolding itself through time but something the historian sees in retrospect — of religious thought denotes something at once obvious and elusive. By common sense we can ascribe Americanness to thinkers who were themselves American and were thinking much about the religion of the Americans whom they addressed. On these grounds, despite the brilliance of their insights, foreign observers like Alexis de Tocqueville and Frederika Bremer do not count; George Santayana could be made to count; that Ralph Waldo Emerson belongs to the story there could be no challenge.

Yet religious thought of Americans, by Americans, for Americans may either lack or abound in a style and a content that is characteristically American, difficult though Americanness in this subtler sense is to define. Rather than define it neatly, this book means to exemplify it. Here it is enough to say the religious experience of Americans has been emphatically more voluntary than organic, more diverse than standard, more personal than institutional, more practical than visionary or (in that sense) mystical.

And the thought that has reflected on this American religious experience has typically asked what went on when people acted religiously. It has subordinated strictly theological questions about God to more experiential ones about men and women. Americans like to solve more than they like to concoct problems, and American religious thinkers typically adjusted their ideas of deity to religious experience, not vice versa. Typically they resisted collapsing the significance of the human spirit's earnest exercises into something other than religiousness itself, not psychology or morality, not metaphysics or theology, not doctrine or liturgy, not social or ecclesiastical institutions. Typically they construed religious experience as really saving men and women (however transitorily or permanently) from otherwise insoluble difficulties, symbolized perhaps by Satan, perhaps by spiritual mediocrity, perhaps by divided selves. Typically they avoided extreme intellectualism and extreme emotionalism, rather conjoining the head and the heart as twin seats of religious experience. Indeed, one of them wrote that head and heart "are inextricably tangled together, and seem to grow from a common stem" (L, 1:97). And typically they interpreted religious experience as coming to terms with, not as escaping from, the whole of mankind's environing universe.

The thesis of this book is that certain great exemplars of American religious thought found their universe to be fraught with dark and ugly forces stronger than man's common powers, yet nevertheless fundamentally hospitable to the human spirit. These exemplars shaped a recognizably American spirituality to changing times and needs. They consciously reflected on Americans' religious hopes and attainments, and they tried both to evoke and to realize these aspirations. In doing so they came to derogate, on the one hand, systems of dogma and, on the other, to rise above psychoanalytic debunkings of religious behavior. Thus this book deals more with essayists who shaped the American spirit than with clergymen who built the American denominations. It dwells on three thinkers by way of nominating them as eponyms of American religious thought and experience.

To speak more schematically, the book discerns certain spiritual responses to fateful turns in American history, responses that made persons at home first with deity, then with nature, finally with their own humanness. Our exemplars or founders or eponyms took being at home in the universe to involve overcoming ugly discordances of life by accepting invitations to and gifts of harmony. In this sense, their religious thought like their own shared spirituality was less doctrinal, was less moral, was less ritual, was less otherworldly than it was esthetic.

These American spiritual eponyms were rigorous even though their popularizers have repeatedly made their message seem easy. Certain celebrities, fond of the head and suspicious of the heart,

simplified this reconciliation with the universe by making trite
the discordances that needed to be overcome. Religious rationalists have proposed such a smooth road to every generation of
Americans. Certain others, doting on the heart but leery of the
head, translated the task of finding a welcome universe into
feeling right (or at least tolerably good) about things in general.
Religious sentimentalists as well as rationalists have made their
proposals to each American generation.

But the exemplars or eponyms of our religious striving, to
paraphrase one of them, could not blink the evil without also
blinking the good. To paraphrase another, they tested their
spiritual insights against calamity. These thinkers expressed the
religious quest as a human endeavor requiring all the energy
any person could both evoke from within and invoke from beyond
the self. A happy quest? Yes. An easy one? No! Felicitous in
effect, always. Facile in process, never!

Saintliness brought its felicity to, but came with no facility
for, Jonathan Edwards, whom this history takes as a kind of
summarizer and translator of Puritan moralism. In his generation's experience of the first truly "national" American event,
the Great Awakening, our colonials were forgetting they were
Englishmen living abroad and were becoming, at least in their
religion, what we by looking back can call Americans living
at home in the New World. Moreover, Edwards figures in our
history as a sort of funnel, for his experience and thought mixed
the earlier English-colonial religiousness into a native American
brew. His notion of the soul's immediate inspiration by God's
spirit would have suited an Anne Hutchinson and the early
Quakers. His rendering the conscience in agreement with God's
law would have pleased the stiffest Anglican and the most loyal
Jesuit in early Maryland. Thomas Hooker and Thomas Shepard
would have applauded his analysis of conversion. Calvinists
everywhere would have endorsed his doctrinal orthodoxy. But
none of these predecessors had brought together all these
impulses into a single spirituality.

So our starting with Edwards acknowledges the importance of his forerunners and sets him within a great tradition. But when we discern the new spirituality he erected by transmuting that tradition, we then search long and hard for a true successor to his genius. Did the spirit or only the letter of his religious thought mark that school of divines who (from Joseph Bellamy and Samuel Hopkins down to Edwards Amasa Park) called themselves Edwardeans? Were the revivalists (from Gilbert Tennent through Timothy Dwight and Francis Asbury down to Charles Grandison Finney) developing or diluting the religious thought of Edwards? Or did his emphasis on the affections accurately translate into the religious sentimentalism of Horace Bushnell and Henry Ward Beecher?

None of those probings finds Edwards' true heir. The spirituality that he clothed in his inimitable rhetoric broke out again, hardly imitated but genuinely inherited, in Emerson. To be sure, the legacy of Edwards to Emerson has concerned other historians of the American intellect (like Perry Miller and H. Richard Niebuhr and Morton White), even though this lineage rattles our stereotypes of the dour Puritan and the happy Transcendentalist. Emerson's religiousness in fact shared profoundly in the practice (or ethos) of Edwards' saintliness, however different the doctrines (or world-views) in which the two men positioned themselves. What came to the fore with Emerson is nature, declaring to the soul the universe's hospitality, while for Edwards the declaration came explicitly from God Himself (of course the visible saint could hear its echo in nature).

The human soul at home with nature and God also belonged to human societies and indeed to mankind. A heightened sense of this membership set Emerson's generation to building social institutions that would solve the age-old conundrum of politics: whether to enslave others or to be enslaved, to be ruled or to rule. How human communities could mirror a friendly universe became the preoccupying question for our religious thinkers as well as for our novelists.[2] Emerson and his Unitarian friend

Theodore Parker disagreed over how to answer this question.
So did the elder Henry James and his Congregationalist adver-
sary, Bushnell. But all these thinkers made man's communities
the locus of his basic religious question. The most typically
American answer finally came from a psychologist and professed
individualist, William James: religion sets men and women in
harmony with their humanness and empowers them in social
concert with one another (and with their chosen deities) to
reshape reality. James's proposal set the agenda for the major
religious thinkers in America in the twentieth century.

This book, then, examines a wide range of American religious
thought, arrayed around three eponyms of a distinctly American
spirituality. Edwards found divine things lovely in themselves
for persons whose lives were made works of divine art. Emerson
found nature welcoming persons to the indivisible act of reliance
on God and on the self. James found in humanity itself a companionship open to men and women of strenuous mood and serious
mind. Through different agencies each found the universe, for
all its darkness and calamity, an eminently hospitable home for
the human spirit.

Historians naturally hope the movements they narrate will
prompt the correction and encourage the refinement of present
policies and future practices. To depict an actual past religious
achievement in America is to propose a possible present and
desirable future agenda: can we today and tomorrow combine
the heroic striving and the patient awaiting that enact the hos-
pitableness of our universe? Can we regard as friends and companions rather than as enemies the nature we participate in even
while we transcend it, the deities we choose even while they
transcend us, and the humanity to which we belong even while
we constitute it?

The present age is more "a time of trouble" than "a poised
epoch," and in such an era, writes R. J. Kaufmann, we tend
"either to submit or to rebel or more commonly to submit in
fact and rebel in trivial ways, or conversely to submit in routine

ways and to rebel inwardly."[3] In this present age American spirits groan because the universe seems inimical. Our world seems to require either rebellious resistance or submissive compliance — or yet a third option: to avert our gaze from the universe to the self itself, perhaps hoping to discover in or beyond or underneath our personhood the grounds or the dimensions of a novel universe.

From that terse reading of our present religious possibilities we can identify three kinds of spirituality that are now being urged in the visible forms of American religion. The first form asks fealty to what it represents as God's law, made authoritative by the sanction of Bible or doctrine or special revelation; being loyal to this authority and living by its detailed demands become the soul's only goal. The reward is relief from worry about the individual soul's contingency and the community's uncertain destiny. Life under this religious authority becomes fully and certainly instructed.

The second form, perceiving the transitoriness and imperfection of everything that now exists, invites the spirit to dedicate itself to a certain program of reform. Taking a firm stand against war or poverty or the repression of minorities (or whatever) assures the spirit of its relevant engagement with reshaping the universe. Life under this religious activism becomes an act of sheer assertion, which seeks to establish the rebellious spirit as the acme of creation.

The third form asks for sensitizing the soul to its widest range of feelings either as the core of reality with which it deals or as the doorway to an unknown divine power. To train oneself to be sensitive to one's personhood and personal relations with other human (or transhuman) selves is to fight off the gnawing sense of insignificance and aimlessness that complex social institutions seem to foster. Living under this religious sentimentality leads to investing the self in the feeling and the healing of personal and interpersonal fissures.

The first form means obeying the divine system. The second

means overturning the world's systems. The third means discovering in the self a new personal system. The first finds religious
authority in regimen. The second receives religious assurance
in the intensity with which causes are espoused. The third gives
the soul religious significance as a source of endless self-
fascination, perhaps even as an avenue of approach to some profounder or purer Soul. The first symbolizes the universe by God
as the uncompromising authority, the second by society as the
resistant but reformable oppressor, the third by nature as the
alien locus of personhood. Respectively the forces of the universe,
thus symbolized, are to be obeyed, changed, or fled.

So far as the visible forms of American religion embody these
styles of spirituality, the heritage with which this book mainly
deals would correct them. In this heritage our relations to nature
and to humanity and to God are inseparable. How we position
ourselves with respect to each of these forces or dimensions of
experience establishes also our stance toward the other two. This
is not to say that the universe fits together in a neat unity.
It is rather to say that the self is indivisible and therefore the
universe is open to considerable (but never final) unification.

This unifiable universe can become our hospitable abode not
as we possess it or rule it or overcome it, but as nature and
man and God make up an environment well suited for us, the
fitting inhabitants, the appropriate occupants of a welcoming
home. In such a hospitable world, God is for us, nature is in
us, humanity is our métier. Deity, to be sure, remains "Thou"
or "Other" not as an opposing alien but as a potential aide.
Nature, to be sure, retains its fixed and often calamitous structure
not as a prison confining the spirit but as a paradigm or mirror
of its latent harmony. Humanity, to be sure, continues to be
incomplete and frustrated and yearning but the partialities of
its fulfillment instead of condemning our hopes can encourage
our aspiring and striving.

The fact that historical exemplars in our tradition found their
universe hospitable does not, of course, demonstrate that the

universe truly *was* or *is* or *will be* hospitable. They discovered one of several ways to station the spirit in the world, and their way is possible for us insofar as what the human spirit once did it may once again assay. Surely the only way to test whether the world in truth welcomes us is to act strenuously and seriously as though it welcomes us.

2

The Sensible Spirituality of Jonathan Edwards

Theologian and Religious Thinker

The courage of America's early English settlers in seeking a hazardous new home on earth issued from their certainty that their covenant with the Almighty promised them an abiding home in heaven. But they did not play worldly courage off against otherworldly confidence like alternating moods or compensating virtues. Rather they compounded their daring in the tangible world with their security in the spiritual world by erecting earthly communities made up of visible saints who covenanted with God and Christ for redemption and with one another for ecclesiastical and civil amity.

The actual experience of these first Puritans in New England foreshadowed what would happen to many Americans after them. Their experiment, intending at first to develop a novel mode of living, led them to establish permanent, self-renewing communities. They used the New World as a display-case for the way they wanted life back home to be reformed. Far more intently than the Virginia planters, these New England villagers dreamed of an English church and state modeled on their experiment. But by the late 1640s or early 1650s their beacon was already lighting a westward path; for by then their "errand into the wilderness" became a holy migration to scenes of God's new spiritual outpourings — some even hoped, of Christ's last great works on earth. And a century later that hope produced the postmillennial belief that in America Christ was inaugurating his thousand-year reign.

The grandchildren and great-grandchildren of the pioneering settlers inherited social and political and ecclesiastical institutions with traditions and continuities and momenta of their own; even so, these institutions presupposed a repeated renewal of spiritual sanctity. To sustain a holy society required making people holy; sanctified houses needed saintly inhabitants. The electric currents of courage toward transitory life on earth could be constantly generated only by spiritual confidence about eternal life.

Puritanism

The truly compelling religious virtuoso of American Puritanism, Jonathan Edwards, was wholly a great-grandchild of settlers, belonging to the third generation made in America.[4] He indeed was the intellectual luminary of our colonists by virtue of his unrivaled mental power, his expertness in personal psychology and experimental religion, and his instinctive facility for rhetoric affecting the spirit. Taken singly or together, however, these native endowments fall short of explaining how this timid, rather impolitic divine merged the traditional springs of Puritanism in both Englands into the fountainhead of a distinctly American way of being religious. His talents were tailor-made to solve the peculiar problem of his time: how to sustain and renew the personal virtue that a virtuous nation would require, how to cultivate the moral persons who alone could people a moral civilization, how to generate the personal sanctity without which a holy experiment would be neither holy nor experimental.

Orthodox Puritan Christianity provided the furniture and landmarks, even the very moon and sun, of the world in which Edwards positioned himself. In that world the Christian God ruled over all things, spiritual and material. With intelligent beings He entered into two-way covenants — of conditions and promises; if this then that; quid pro quo — and therefore men and women might rely upon Him. It was just this covenanting, this making sinners into saints, that Edwards pondered in both its scriptural and its experiential manifestations until he was able to say precisely what it meant to have been wrought upon by the Spirit of God in His common or saving operations. So certain was Edwards of his world-view's cogency that he put it up for debate with the five challenges that his contemporaries advanced: with rationalists or deists, whose world brooked no divine meddlings contrary to nature; with Unitarians, who simplified God's character and operations; with Arminians, who made man God's partner in producing true saints; with enthusiasts, who took every pious feeling as a sign of salvation; and with separatists, who set off their pure churches from the general society. Two other sorts of human beings, Jews and heathens, Edwards knew by reputation; he would refute them should he ever encounter them.

If being sure of a world-view can render one ready to discuss it and therefore to be critical of it, if being enraptured by God's transcendence can yield a vivid sense of His immanence, if believing that one has been made righteous in Christ can produce, instead of self-righteousness, a plain and simple righteousness (not a superiority complex but real superiority), then Edwards lived out these paradoxes. And more besides. To protect his parishioners against the sin of professing Christian faith without really having it, Edwards proposed to bar from the Lord's Table many well-meaning, sincere men and women. Indeed, to benefit the children of such unregenerate parents he would refuse to baptize them so they would grow up knowing that they had not "closed with Christ" and that their parents could not "stand them fair" to do so (Misc., # 849).[5] To heighten the power of his sermons, he would teach people how to dwell on their own sinfulness, from which God (through Edwards' preaching) might deliver them. To prove the scriptural and psychological soundness of keeping sinners out of full membership in the visible church, he would labor prodigiously and be dismissed from his pastorate rather than give an inch.

Edwards, of course, inherited the belief that God stamped His image on all He made. Edwards experimentally proved the hypothesis that God would never apply saving grace to an intelligent soul without giving that person a reliable sense of the operation. Only God, to be sure, could know who would be rewarded in heaven or tormented in hell, but nevertheless persons could know (with a slight margin of error unavoidable in the conditions of finitude and sin) whether or not God was regenerating their own souls. If so, their lives would show effects so palpable that other visible saints could reliably tell their fellow travelers from unregenerate folk.

Edwards validated this theory of tangible grace by two authorities. First, he appealed to the Bible in a way that made it, as Clyde Holbrook notes, "a fairly full report of human history as well as the word of God" (*WY*, 3:27 n.). Second, he appealed to selected Puritan divines, whose Protestant inwardness would have made them shrink from the end toward which he carried their logic. By both these appeals, however, he was underlining his intention to identify saints by an empirical method. He subjected to "the most critical observation, under all manner of opportunities of observing" many hundreds, perhaps thousands, of particular persons, varied in age and sex and station, whose religious affections had become lively, vigorous, and sensible (*WY*, 4:472; 2:96–97). Edwards developed psychological tests for telling whether a religious experience originated with the subject's own wishful thinking, in a delusion, from Satan, under God's general graciousness, or out of a saving work of the divine Spirit.

Satan, demons, angels, and the Holy Trinity were no less real to Edwards than were the Puritans whose religious experiences he observed and classified. And precisely by according equal reality to the noumenal and the phenomenal Edwards fathered divergent religious traditions. One tradition, seen best in the theologians who called themselves Edwardeans, actually muted his emphasis on the sensibility of all religious affections and thereby built the symbols of his thought-world into metaphysical dogmas cherished today, if at all, mostly by religious fundamentalists. The other tradition, soft-pedalling Edwards' stress on the sovereignty of God, cherished a religious sentimentalism that measured a soul's religious states by its moods. In Edwards himself there was a theological certainty but no clinging to literalized symbols for the sake of their authority. There was also a naturalism and even a kind of immanentism but no subjectivism of the sort that cultivates coziness with God (or enmity toward Satan) by fanning the emotions. And of course to combine these two distortions into fundamentalist emotionalism, after the fashion of, say, a Billy Graham, only caricatures the two polarities Edwards ingeniously brought together.

To approach Edwards as a religious thinker who, within a framework of theological orthodoxy, developed a psychology of religion at once recapitulating and transforming Puritanism means to press seriously his own inquiry: "What is the nature of true religion?"— which to him was the same as asking, "What is the nature of true virtue?" (WY, 2:84; NTV, pp. 25–26).

First, this approach must situate Edwards in the spiritual and theological world of Christianity. He applied its theme of covenants between God and man trenchantly to individual persons, turning the sense of duty into the sense of beauty. His way of viewing this world, as well as the particular world he took for his own, shines through his confident polemics. He never doubted that intelligent analysis of religious experience, like the study of nature and history, would reinforce theological orthodoxy.

Second, this approach involves asking why Edwards came to insist that only visible saints be admitted to full membership in the visible church. This very practical trend of his career exposed his most radical religious insight: persons who received true religion (=true virtue) would sensibly know and palpably display it. Spirituality would inexorably become outward in practice. By empirically demonstrating this principle, Edwards turned inside out the traditional Protestant emphasis on spirituality as inward, hidden, unknowable, and mysterious.

Finally, this approach asks whether (and how far) Edwards opened the door for true virtue to be experienced *outside* the church — even outside a world-view bounded by Christian theology. This final question leads to asking who were his true successors (if any). Edwardean theologians defending "consistent Calvinism"? Revivalists and emotionalists reducing religion to feeling (and thus setting it aginst thinking)? Or, possibly, still others who translated holiness into the sense of a welcoming universe?

Thought-world

Edwards is best known today for a sermon he preached in 1741 at Enfield, Connecticut, on "Sinners in the Hands of an Angry God." The sermon insisted that every person depended on God, who might justly assign him or her to everlasting torment because, the preacher believed, the Creator constantly recreated every creature. To Edwards any remote or bland, any dying or dead deity was only a god in the hands of angry sinners. Each soul at the moment of death, Edwards believed, went straight to heaven or hell, and, since all eminently deserved hell, the reward of heaven had to be God's free gift. The state of torment or bliss that the soul then entered would continue until it became absolutely intensified when all bodies were resurrected at the Last Judgment. If a man must work out his salvation with fear and trembling, how must he who neglected his salvation quake! Themes of the end of each person's life and the end of the world resounded in Edwards' preaching because sermons functioned in his religion to convict persons of sin and make them thirst for salvation.

But the edifice of his thought rested also on the other pillar — the principle that the merciful God once had made and in every moment was remaking and refreshing His entire creation. This activity of creating and sustaining the world sprang from the very outgoingness of God's inner nature. Just by being true to Himself, God subsisted, to Edwards' mind, in three eternal, divine persons: Father who loved, Son who was loved, Spirit who was love. Fittingly the Son, who mediated between Father and Spirit, also mediated between Godhead and the world; Christ was mediator both as the Logos or Word who fashioned creation and as the incarnate union of divine and human natures in the person of Jesus. In this incarnation God fulfilled His ancient purpose of covenanting with the patriarchs — Adam, Noah, Abraham, Moses. This Christ, the God-man, was the Father's Son and man's Brother. God's Spirit both restrained men and women from doing their worst to wreck creation and also enabled them graciously to do their best by accepting salvation. Now in all this Trinitarian and christological and soteriological thought Edwards held to a Western orthodox tradition normatively stated by Augustine of Hippo, modified by John Calvin to emphasize predestination, and refined by English Puritans since William Tyndale to make covenants the coinage of business between God and man.

God, Trinity, Christ, sin, grace, covenant, conversion, visible sainthood, church, heaven, hell, Last Judgment — these entities were to Edwards every whit as real and vivid as his preaching could depict them —"and that without any hyperbole" (Misc., #280). Three sources attested their validity, in this order of importance: Scripture as God's revelation, the saints' experience as lively and sensible affections of holiness, and the created orders of nature and history as images or shadows of divine things.

But if Edwards assumed these gospel truths in traditional form, he also began a new religious legacy by rearranging them according to a new logic, and he developed a new psychology in which really believing these truths made a visible difference in people's affections. In fact, he made religious experience so

outwardly palpable that these Christian truths and the realities
for which they stood became sweet to the taste, symmetrical
to the eye, harmonious to the ear, pleasant to the touch and
the smell. In a word, they became for their own sakes lively
to the senses, enlightening to the mind, and delightful to the
heart. The emphasis here falls equally on the sensibility of their
loveliness and on their being lovely in themselves — not for
what one might gain by loving them. For Edwards these were
happy thoughts in their own right. Naturally, thinking them
delighted him.

If (it is natural to ask) more than two centuries ago Edwards
brought together the noumenal and the phenomenal, if he unified
divine revelation and empirical experience, how did he escape
the conflict of science with religion? Even more tantalizingly,
did he solve it? Asked thus glibly, the question has to be
answered that he was no modern scientist. Yet he did believe
in an all-powerful God and he did organize astute observations
of spiders and rainbows, sinners and saints, into cogent explanations. His reverent belief in a trustworthy God implied believing
that nature and human behavior, fully dependent on God, gave
clear answers to pertinent questions. Only irreverent theology,
he might have predicted, would foster impertinent science. For
Edwards (as for Newton and Locke) the Newtonian physics and
the Lockean psychology reinforced the reliability of both the
Creator and the creation. Symmetry between force and motion,
action and reaction, faith and morality signified to Edwards that
God stamped His beauty on all He made.

So Edwards' famous boyhood essays examining insects and
rainbows, uncanny as they are for the clarity of his observations,
foreshadowed the grown man's sermons showing that spiritual
things manifested themselves palpably and that nature mirrored
God. Without cracking the eggs of Calvinism (indeed, without
even thinking them fragile) Edwards carried them along a rough
road into the thought-world of the eighteenth century as he
joined together the doctrines of revealed theology with descrip-

tions of sensible experience. Thereby he reasserted a continuity
of grace with nature but not with sin. He reconceived truth
as the consistency of relations between apprehensions of things
rather than as the relations among things in themselves. Gospel
truths comprised for Edwards a world that embraced heaven and
earth and hell, time and eternity, mind and body, spirit and
nature, head and heart, revelation and reason, God's sovereignty
and God's covenanting.

Puritanism in both Englands learned God's will mainly from
the Bible (not from church, tradition, or intuition). Puritans
saw the Bible mainly as the record of God's covenanting with
people He chose to save, of His making promises and decreeing
the conditions on which He would fulfill them. In New England
the leaders had long debated certain questions implicit in this
covenant theology. By Edwards' time the questions meant:
(1) Did God perform *all* the work of salvation, conferring the
covenant's conditions as well as its promises (so the orthodox
Calvinists), or did persons *somehow* meet the conditions and
thereby oblige God to make good the promises (the Arminians)?
(2) Did Christ's covenant only continue and fulfill the old covenants with Israel (the anti-revivalists), or did Jesus initiate a
new scheme of salvation (the enthusiasts)? (3) Did the covenant
bind saints into both a church and a state (the establishmen-
tarians) or only into a pure church immune to political influences
(the separatists)? (4) Did Scripture reveal a miraculous covenant
of salvation (the biblicists), or could one deduce the promises
and conditions of salvation from nature and man's moral sense
(the rationalists)?

Taken only as a technical theologian, Edwards seems to have
sided with the old Calvinists on the first question, ducked the
second, straddled the third, and reinforced the biblicists on the
fourth. This is not an unfair reading. Nor is it the only fair
reading. For when Edwards was thinking about the nature and
attributes of God revealed in Scripture and stamped on creation,
he insisted that God alone could known for sure who was truly

saved and what it was like to experience true salvation. But
Edwards was also a religious thinker, interested in boiling down
the abstruse questions of revealed theology to the very practical
question, What is true religion? As a religious thinker Edwards
focused attention on those aspects of sainthood that humans could
and did know: the lively and sensible effects of holiness on the
minds and hearts and lives of men and women.

As a theologian dealing with questions about God and His
covenants Edwards maintained a conservative orthodoxy. But as
a student of visible sainthood he found the covenant idea, as
Perry Miller asserted, a "rusty mechanism" (but he did not throw
"over the whole covenant scheme").[6] He derusted and rebuilt
the machinery by stressing four points. (1) Visible saints were
those who thanked Christ for the gift of faith by which they
gained the covenanted promises. (2) The covenant whose operations could be studied applied to individual persons. (3) By loving divine things for themselves, a person with true religious
affections would love the old covenants as well as the new. (4) Instructed by their new spiritual sense, visible saints would find
images and shadows of divine things in nature and conscience.

Naturally, when Edwards observed the phenomena of sensible
salvation, probable conversion, and visible sainthood he saw in
the best Christian lives a mixture of sin with righteousness,
of pride with humility, of human nature with new spirtual sense.
Even if God alone wrought man's salvation, the visible manifestations of religious states could be studied and classified. The dili-
gent student of religious experience could distinguish saving from
common works of God's Spirit and could also distinguish these
divine influences from a host of human and demonic ones.
Without questioning the orthodox Christian world-view's symbols, even without adjusting theology to some autonomous science of religious experience, Edwards turned the attention of
Americans to the outward manifestation, the sensibility, the pal-
pability of religious experience in concrete human lives. His
case-history approach to religion brought Puritan theology into

public discourse under a new kind of scrutiny. Looking to the effect rather than to the sources of Edwards' genius, Harriet Beecher Stowe wrote that "He sawed the great dam and let out the whole waters of discussion over all New England."[7] Some Americans who retraced these steps found the study of phenomenal religious experiences difficult or impossible to reconcile with traditional theology. Nevertheless, for Edwards the phenomena of sensible experience expressed the noumena of the theological world. He *did* pay attention to phenomena and he broke *new* ground as a student of religious experience. In Edwards' polemics this new emphasis becomes explicit.

Polemics

Less subtle thinkers than Edwards were saying men initiated their own conversions. Edwards accorded persons no modicum of worthiness for salvation. The Arminians, he contended, misunderstood conversion and gave natural man a subtle kind of worth. They accurately described the *actual* commission of sins by men and women, who were restrained by God's general grace from doing their potential worst. Also accurately, they assigned the *actual* punishments that God meted out for this restrained evil. But then they mistook actual sins for the natural tendency toward evil; they said people deserved only these actual demerits and not the infinite punishments God would apply to unrestrained evildoing.

But, we might ask, if Edwards could only deal with actual, experienced salvation, how could he probe beyond actual sin to natural or ultimate sinfulness? We need not tarry long over this question. God knew who were truly saved and who were ultimately damned. After all, God judged His own creatures. Thus men and women could only identify sensible, visible, overt saints and sinners. But if salvation ran to God, so damnation ran to creatures, who could know their own sin to its depths precisely because sin belonged to them and not to God.[8] Over persons on earth as well as in hell sin raged unchecked by grace. Indeed, some natural persons had numbed, evil consciences that made them revel in sin. Not the milder sinners restrained by grace from their worst evil, but rampant sinners measured the punishment that all deserved. The same God who restrained men and women from rampant evil, alone granted and caused their conversion.

Wearing the theologian's hat, Edwards vindicated God's sovereignty by proving people wholly unworthy of either general or saving grace. He protected God's justice by having creatures infinitely deserve infinite punishment. As a religious thinker, Edwards consistently argued that persons claiming moral worth before God thereby rendered themselves unable to love divine things solely for their own sake. Therefore, the Arminians inoculated people against humility, a necessary fruit of true virtue or visible sainthood. The religious argument, for all its coherence with the theological one, proceeded on specifically religious grounds and rested on its own religious assumptions. To emphasize the cogency of Edwards' religious argument is not to tear it away from his theology. It is to suggest that he advanced a theory of religion congruent with but not dependent upon his theology. For this achievement he may be nominated the first straightforward religious thinker in America. The nomination detracts nothing from the dignity as theologian that he has long been accorded.

Brief attention to other polemics by Edwards may second the nomination. Those rational philosophers and moralists who found in nature and in the conscience all they needed to know about divine things and true virtue, he asserted, generalized the Arminian errors. As a theologian Edwards of course defended revelation against unaided reason. As a religious thinker he granted that reason and conscience, well-instructed but unmoved by saving grace, might approve divine things but could not truly love them. The uninstructed conscience given over to sinful pleasures characterized mankind's raw, natural condition. The best moral instruction would lead persons to desire divine benevolence. Only a reoriented conscience would yield heartfelt consent to God for His own sake. In the work published after he died as *The Nature of True Virtue*, Edwards attacked the deists and rationalists not by a theological appeal to God's revelation but by the logic of religious and esthetic experience. Of course, he was employing reason against rationalism, and he knew the difference. Jesus' own apostles provided the precedent for using rational argument to elicit a consent to divine things that rationalism could not attain. He recorded in his notebook, "Faith saving may be built upon rational arguments or rational arguments may savingly convince the soul of the truth of the things of religion" (Misc. #636). The God who created rational creatures used their reason to convert them, but they could never convert themselves.

Even so patently theological a matter as the Trinity, which Edwards defended against its attackers and made central in his own theology, bore a distinctly religious value, in this way: whoever would deny active love among the persons of the deity made God dependent upon His own creation for an object of His benevolence and thereby hedged God's self-subsistence. More important, Edwards modeled his doctrine of the Trinity "after his psychology of the faith-act."[9] That is to say, the religious experiences of observed converts combined three facets: receiving a love for divine things, relishing the order or the harmony of God in its own right, and consenting to being in general. This three-in-one experience transformed natural virtue into disinterested or true virtue.

Religionists who categorically denounced the revivals because they involved sentiments seemed to Edwards to be robbing God of the fittest vehicles, the religious affections, for making His Spirit's work vibrant and visible in the lives of men and women. On the other hand, what the conservatives rejected in toto their opponents, the enthusiasts, mistook to be univocal signs of the Spirit's saving operation. For the latter, according to Edwards, any heightened emotion or imagining seemed as good as any other; the former would maintain a cold heart and a dull head before the liveliness of God. Against both parties Edwards appealed to religious experience as well as to scriptural norms of God's gracious work.

Separatists thought they could purge from their congregations all alloy of human sinfulness — to Edwards bad theology because it invaded God's prerogative of identifying His own elect. On distinctly religious grounds, Edwards thought the separatists erred by pretending to know more about a person's spiritual state than the person himself could know, which is to say, more than the sensible effects of spirituality. They also isolated religion from political sanctions, which flew in the face of Edwards' insistence that outward institutions guarded and manifested inward states. What most disturbed Edwards, they made sainthood a matter of the subject's *claiming* holiness before fellow believers instead of *testing* sainthood by its fruits in common, palpable, practical, sensible, day-to-day life.

The coherence of Edwards' religious thought with his theology on these crucial matters has double significance. On the one hand, he investigated experiences of divine things by particular persons without diminishing his confidence that divine things were self-evidently real and inherently lovely. Positioning himself in a grandly Christian universe of thought and action, Edwards tested how that universe became manifest in the palpable senses. From this stance he actually measured God's effects on men and women. On the other hand, he used his religious thought and his empirical psychology of religious experience to defend an inherited theology. From this stance he gave American Puritanism a new synthesis, understanding man by examining God's word and understanding God by examining man's religion.

Visible Saints and Visible Church

Edwards brought theology and religious experience — theory and practice, as it were — to terms with one another. As pastor

of the leading church in the Connecticut Valley, he also
eliminated discrepancies between religious theory and practice.
This chief interpreter of the Great Awakening sought at the
peak of his ministerial career to purify his congregation on the
simple principle that the saving work of God's Spirit produced
saints who knew they were saints and who displayed saintliness
to others. Only such persons, he came to believe, should hold
fully privileged membership in the visible church. Any disparity
in church members between the *possession* and the *profession* of
saving faith involved a triple hypocrisy. First, the candidate for
church membership would be pretending a nonexistent salvation.
Second, his children would receive baptism under the parents'
false pretenses. Third, the minister would certify both errors
as true. Northampton's First Church had long received into full
standing members who claimed no saving faith yet joined in
the congregation's professions of such faith. An inexorable logic
led Edwards to manifest outwardly his inward revulsion from
such hypocrisies.

Sainthood

Edwards' autobiographical writings illustrate his genius for consistency between theory and practice. About 1739, just when
he began to think of purging the church, he recorded (for private
use) the three religious changes he had personally undergone,
in effect establishing his typology of religious experiences.

The first change, "some years before I went to college," must
have been prepuberal. For in 1716, just before his thirteenth
birthday, this son of Timothy Edwards, pastor of East Windsor,
Connecticut, entered the collegiate institution soon to be con-
solidated at New Haven as Yale College. Before that, during
an awakening in his father's congregation, the lad became "very
much affected for many months, and concerned about the things
of religion, and my soul's salvation; . . . and it was my delight
to abound in religious duties" (*Conv.*, p. 24). These affections,

his account emphasized, soon diminished and eventually passed away.

Later, after a severe illness during the last year of a precocious and independent-minded college career, Edwards (note the passive voice) "was brought wholly to break off all former wicked ways, and all ways of known outward sin," but although he "was brought to seek salvation, in a manner that I never was before," there was no delight in it. "I felt a spirit to part with all things in the world, for an interest in Christ" (*Conv.*, p. 25). Unlike the boyhood enthusiasm, this concern endured, but at low pitch.

Having graduated in 1720, Edwards remained at Yale for two years to study theology. Probably in February 1721 he experienced "inward, sweet delight in God and divine things, . . . a sense of the glory of the Divine Being; a new sense" that made the sovereignty of God and redemption in Christ "exceeding pleasant, bright and sweet" to him. This feeling endured. The liveliness and sensibility of his religious affections increased. All nature and all grace, so to speak, delighted him. He "had vehement longings of soul after God and Christ, and after more holiness" (*Conv.*, pp. 26, 28). Early in August 1722 (the year Yale's leading lights defected to the Church of England), Edwards became pastor of a Presbyterian congregation in New York City, where these wonderful affections became ever more intense and engulfing. He recorded a resolution solemnly dedicating himself to God. In April 1723 he returned home. After a term of tutoring at New Haven, in 1726 he joined Grandfather Solomon Stoddard in the Northampton pastorate. All this time he was rejoicing in divine things even while his thirst for more of the same went unslaked. He constantly sensed his lowliness among other Christians and before the infinite God.

In New Haven in July 1727, the young clergyman married Sarah Pierrepont who would bear him three sons and eight daughters and follow him in death by only seven months. Then Stoddard died, early in 1729. The apprentice inherited the old

prophet's mantle. Edwards lost no time in establishing a ministerial reputation for his own name. His Boston Public Lecture
of 1731 pleased some Puritan apostles who printed it over their
imprimatur. Edwards assumed the full power of the Puritan pre-
lacy his grandfather had founded. He was prodigious of mind,
persuasive of tongue, confident of a gracious heart.

From the experiences and observations of a mature manhood
Edwards was declaring religiously valid the manifestation of
God's saving grace in certain lively, sensible affections. The
young preacher who was devising this test of grace was also
quickening the affections of thousands, confirming the probable
sanctity of hundreds, of persons in and around Northampton during the revivals of 1734–35 and 1740–42. As he reported the
Great Awakening to Boston and Britain, this sense of balance
between salvation and visible sainthood allowed him to validate
affectional religion while rejecting religious emotionalism and
saintly imaginings. The three types of religiousness he attributed
to his youth framed conceptually the psychology of religion he
poured into the great book of his pastoral career, *A Treatise
Concerning Religious Affections* (Boston, 1746). Parishioners, to
whom Edwards was more the spiritual father than the human
brother, admired his ministerial distinction, responded to his
affective preaching, tried to follow his godly counsel, brought
their infants to his priestly baptizing and their children to his
earnest catechizing, sent their youth to his heartfelt prayer meet-
ings. They were their shepherd's flock — until he changed the
metaphor, made the congregation a garden and proposed to weed
it, using as the hoe his criteria of visible sainthood.

They knew the principles all along. In his first publication,
that Boston Lecture called *God Glorified in the Work of Redemption,
by the Greatness of Man's Dependence upon him in the Whole of it*
(Boston, 1731), there were few hints or implications for being
a saint back in Northampton. But a mere thirteen months after
he won this laurel the home congregation heard a sermon they
chose to print: *A Devine and Supernatural Light, Immediately*

imparted to the Soul by the Spirit of God, Shown to be both a Scriptural and Rational Doctrine (Boston, 1734). The preacher urgently pressed them to test their sensible affections to learn whether theirs was (1) a natural interest in religious things but of no spiritual distinction, or (2) an intensified zeal for or notional knowledge of the gospel which the Spirit's common operation (even the devil's counterfeiting) could engender, or (3) a sensible love for the excellency of divine things in their own loveliness, springing from saving grace. The preacher allowed no degrees of sophistication or ignorance to excuse persons from opening themselves to this divine light. All must examine their lives to determine whether they had received the light. Everybody should seek such enlightenment for its own worth and sweetness and efficacy in the soul.

Looking backward through the subsequent controversies to this sermon of 1733, we can hardly imagine how its hearers could have failed to see the trouble brewing. Simply, blatantly, Edwards equated theology and experience: having taught the piety he practiced, he would surely practice the purity he was teaching. The piety could be sensibly appropriated. The purity of visible sainthood could be rhetorically represented. If they inwardly digested the sermon they must tacitly have classified themselves natural sinners, religious pretenders, or visible saints. By clear implication of the sermon, those who hypocritically pretended the highest status sank to the lowest.

The Northampton churchgoers who were thinking along these lines in 1733 also remembered their late lamented pastor who, wanting to keep church and town rolls nearly identical and despairing over his inability to tell false from true converts, had taken the opposite tack. Stoddard had conferred full ecclesiastical privilege on every sincere, upright person who sought it. Although the privileges of church membership with which Edwards was dealing implied nothing about civic rights, they cut close to the nerve of respectability. He had no notion of expelling from the congregation anybody except notorious evildoers. However, he came to insist, he could admit only visible saints to full standing. Only they would determine church governance, participate in the Lord's Supper, and (the crux of the matter) bring their children to baptism.

Parishioners as well as pastor knew New Englanders had been debating church membership since their first landfall. Edwards shifted the debate to new ground, subordinating concern for church purity to concern for the spiritual health of persons (and their children) who presented themselves before God and congregation as Christians but knew in their secret minds they had not entered the convenant of Christ. It had been one thing to ask how far church membership might be extended. It was quite another to question whether holding membership under false pretenses might damn one's soul. Edwards posed this issue sharply, erasing all shades of grey. "There is no being on Christ's side [against Satan] . . . but with an *undivided heart.* . . . The case admits of no . . . middle sort of persons with . . . such a common faith as is consistent with loving sin and the world better than Christ" (*WD*, 4:334). The harm of hypocrisy in the middling Christian outweighed the good of the church and the solidarity of the town.

Church

However important the new slants of Edwards' position, the problem had a long history involving Northamptonites. When the New Englanders' errand for the reform of England became a permanent American enterprise, some powerful winds began to erode their ideal of the church as God's community composed of persons bearing Christian sainthood and regulating the common life. By scriptural sanction their children, the offspring of saints, received baptism; parents and congregation pledged to apply influences that were expected to bring the new generation into adult sanctity. More often than theory allowed, this program failed. The grave problem arose: what to do with children of parents whose church membership derived wholly from the sanctity of *their* parents? By 1660 the preachers found a pragmatic way to have the cake of a holy church and eat it too — by granting halfway membership to unconverted persons who wanted their children baptized. The scheme changed no qualifications for communion, only those for baptism: persons professing no conversion to Christ, if "not scandalous in life, and solemnly owning the Covenant before the Church, wherein they give themselves and their Children to the Lord, and subject themselves to the Government of Christ in the Church, their Children are to be Baptized."[10]

Few saw as clearly as Stoddard that both baptism and communion were involved in the problem this halfway covenant was devised to solve. If baptized children sailed toward salvation on the winds of their parents' influence, surely the parents should themselves be making for the port of sainthood. Stoddard's own preaching stirred many such adults to excitements bearing the appearances of conversion. On that basis he admitted them to communion. Then for many the "conversion" proved only apparent. But some of these nominal saints sensed genuine regeneration through their partaking of the Supper. How could it harm the congregation, he asked, to open communion to all earnest seekers?

Moreover, Stoddard's pastoral experience led him to conclude that by the best available criteria of sainthood he would admit to the Supper more unconverted than converted persons. Therefore in 1677, finding no scriptural barrier, he opened communion, admitting persons to full membership without asking whether they had saving faith. By 1700, having thought out the implications of this decision, he proclaimed that all ordinances instituted in the church were *intended* by Christ to be used as the means of regeneration — preaching, praying, baptizing, communion alike. Thus everybody who lived *as though* they were Christ's should be regarded *as* Christ's. Granting Stoddard's assumption that no test could reliably tell a visible saint

from a pretending saint, it would not logically harm the church
to receive members solely on the basis of their intention to
become saints. But when you change that assumption you shift
concern from the church to the spiritual predicament of a person
who, knowing he lacks sainthood, pretends it by coming to
communion.

Edwards changed this concern by devising tests to virtually
eliminate the margin of error in identifying visible saints. Using
an instrument Stoddard lacked, Edwards found in the inherited
practice a danger Stoddard could not have spied. Both men
wanted to avoid setting different standards for baptism and communion and both did so, in opposite ways. Stoddard flung open
the doors of church membership to keep the community coter-
minous with the congregation. Edwards narrowed the passage
to save his parishioners from hypocrisy. Edwards was pushing
the problem onto new grounds, not running back behind his
grandfather's practice to the pure-church-equals-pure-society
theories of early American Puritans. The Founding Fathers,
perhaps preoccupied by the new space they were occupying, suffered a lapse in their sense of time. Forgetting how far they
themselves had left the ways of their own elders in England
by becoming Congregationalists, they failed to foresee how far
their own children and grandchildren would fall short of parental
standards of piety.

Edwards observed that children produced few carbon copies
of their parents' piety. He also realized that parents would surely
fail to elicit true piety if they feigned sainthood in an attempt
to produce it in their children. With these concerns in focus,
he proposed closing down Stoddard's Way in favor of a steeper
route, one we might call Edwards' Trail, to church membership.
Whatever we call his program, he meant to encourage sensible
conversions by discouraging the self-deceit and spiritual harm
of acting *as though* converted. Ironically, just when he most
needed support, he would lose by death his most powerful back-
er — his uncle, John Stoddard, Solomon's son — and the con-

gregation would turn (or be turned) against him, would refuse
even to hear his case, would not even observe the Lord's Supper
during the controversy, would vote in 1750 by a ten-to-one
margin to dismiss him. But if he lost the battle he won the
war for "when Edwards had been fifty years in his grave, the
system [of Stoddard] had been generally set aside by the Con-
gregational churches." [11]

During the seventeen years between preaching "A Divine and
Supernatural Light" and being dismissed, Edwards developed
the implications of that sermon for church membership and for
visible sainthood. His shift from registering saints by their verbal
profession to testing them by their sensible affections and discernible living is recorded in a stunning burst of writings that
are by turns historical, analytical, psychological, biographical,
autobiographical, hortatory, disputative, polemical. In writing
these pieces he pondered his personal experience of saving grace,
his knowledge of saintly persons who were his intimates, his
observations of souls touched by the revivals of 1734–35 and
the awakenings of 1740–42, his interpretation of religious
experience as responses to God's Spirit exhibited in the affections,
his study of the effects of baptism and communion on patent
hypocrites and visible saints and the offspring of both, his understanding of Stoddard's (and other divines') theories and practices
in identifying saints and admitting church members, and Scripture — always Scripture, Scripture, Scripture.

Following the 1733 sermon there came a reportorial letter
to Benjamin Colman in Boston describing the revivals in and
around Northampton in the mid-30s, published in London as
*A Faithful Narrative of the Surprizing Work of God in the Conversion
of many Hundred Souls.* Edwards knew about many harvests of
souls during Stoddard's long ministry. His surprise sprang less
from the fact than from the manner of the new outpourings
of religiousness under his own preaching. They arose among
lax youth. They produced a vast variety of influences on all sorts
of people. They spread northward up the valley to Northfield

and southward to and along the Connecticut coast. At Northampton the already large congregation swelled to embrace "almost all our adult persons" in its 620 communicants, more than one-fourth of whom became members during the revival by making "an open and explicit profession of Christianity," even though "it is not the custom here . . . to make a credible relation of their inward experience the ground of admission to the Lord's Supper" (WY, 4:157).

Edwards discerned, underlying the great variety of evidences of these conversions, some common tendencies, a kind of pattern: initial concern over sin, great anguish and longing of soul, a sense of God's mercy and Christ's sufficiency, apprehension of influences from without rather than from within the soul, calmness, delight in grace, charitable living. But these emotions or moods were not yet sharply defined by him as religious affections. They followed no set timetable, no regular intensities, not even a standard order. Edwards heard converts testify to their experiences. He told them whether their declarations signified true conversion or not. But he refrained from judging persons and advised that the real certificate of saving grace would be the fruit of good living and not "words alone" (WY, 4:175–77). As mysteriously as these revivals had begun, they ceased.

The minister wondered why some conversions "took" and others did not. All the questions about the experience of conversion that Edwards was formulating during the early revivals became the basis for his systematic observation of the more intense, more far-flung, more varied awakenings of the early 1740s. In discoursing on them at Yale's commencement in September 1741, published as *The Distinguishing Marks of a Work of the Spirit of God* (Boston, 1741), he mainly defended the awakenings. He also began to identify certain kinds of religious experiences that seemed to signal the work of God's Spirit and the kinds that indicated other influences.

God, man, or Satan, he argued, could induce extraordinary

spiritual exercise, bodily agitations, widespread talk about religion, vivid impressions on persons' imaginations, and the preaching of hell's terrors. To reject these features of the awakenings, or to condemn the revivals because some of its participants acted imprudently, would be to throw out the baby with the bathwater.

But Satan could not oppose Satan's own interests, could not induce in a person the love of Christ, could not increase true regard for scriptural truth, could not elicit love toward God and neighbor. If these phenomena endured they could not be mere pretenses. Enduringly, they signaled a work of the divine Spirit, although not necessarily in a saving (as distinct from a common) way.

This last distinction, old hat in Puritan theology, nagged at Edwards' mind. Some persons confessed to having been saved, others only to having been more deeply convinced of gospel truth. So far he spoke of *degrees* of the Spirit's influences, pleading for open-minded, hopeful estimates of the rare awakenings. But observing the revivals while they flourished sobered his judgment: "I once did not imagine that the heart of man had been so unsearchable as I find it is. I am less charitable, and less uncharitable than once I was. I find more things in wicked men that may counterfeit . . . piety, and more ways that the remaining corruption of the godly may make them appear like carnal men, formalists and dead hypocrites, than once I knew of" (*WY*, 4:285). Only God could search the hearts of men and women. But Edwards could not help wondering!

Weeding

The nagging question persisted. The revivals had hardly cooled before Edwards published, much in the spirit of the commencement address, a longer defense. But in *Some Thoughts Concerning the Present Revival of Religion in New-England* (Boston, 1742) he also analyzed many spiritual aberrations that people were mistaking for true religion. For criteria by which to identify such aberrations he appealed to the Bible instead of to philosophy or "history, or former observation" (*WY*, 4:306). At the same time he gloried in the movement's novelty, its "uncommon degree, extent, and swiftness, and other extraordinary circumstances," and he proved by precedent that the awakenings were "the work of God" and "a very great and wonderful, and exceeding glorious work . . . such as never has been seen in New England, and scarce ever has been heard of in any land" (*WY*, 4:307, 343–44). Edwards wanted both to write a new chapter in the history of experienced salvation and to fit it into the book of God's revealed plan of redemption.

His editorial device, as it were, was to test revivals by their effects on lives lived, not by hearsay or by prejudice against affectional religion. However mixed in result, the revivals produced many good fruits. Therefore, he pleaded, everybody should support the awakening. Yet he also found many harmful effects, such as censorious attacks on professed Christians who were untouched by the awakeners, lay usurpation of ministerial prerogatives, and the arrogance of pronouncing some souls saved and others damned. Although Edwards acknowledged these flaws, Charles Chauncy, the Boston bombast, refuted the book as giving blanket approval to religious enthusiasm. But more important than the famous controversy with Chauncy is the fact that Edwards offered one particular, lengthy case history to illustrate the glorious work of God at its best, the anonymous record of sanctifying experiences in the life of a person whose name Northamptonites could supply: Sarah Pierrepont Edwards.

Now, knowing this person's lasting delight in God's holiness and her life of constant charity; now, having a record of her unusually lively and sensible affections; now, reviewing his own pilgrimage through several stages of religiousness to a perseverant, palpable holiness — now Edwards could set forth the positive marks of saving operations by God's Spirit. No doubt his pastoral work with parishioners enlarged his empirical knowledge of saintliness. By fitting empirical data about religious experience into clues drawn from Scripture, Edwards devised a nosology of holiness and a set of diagnostic criteria by which to distinguish genuinely visible saints from persons who, from whatever influence, mimicked sanctity. The heavenly Good Shepherd alone, he always taught, would separate eternally saved sheep from eternally damned goats. But now the churchly gardener could tell wheat from tares, flowers from weeds.

One of the last (and presumably latest) entries in Edwards' notebook of analogies says, "The time for WEEDING A GARDEN is when it has newly rained upon it. Otherwise, if you go to pull up the weeds, you will pull up the good herbs and plants with them. So the time for purging the church of God is a time of revival of religion. It can't be so well done at another time" (*ISDT*, p. 132). Before Edwards knew for sure how to identify the good plants in his congregation, saving grace had stopped raining on Northampton. He never proposed to test church members already in good standing for heightened affections of conversion. Far short of weeding the garden, he only resolved to plant in it no more weeds. For that, the congregation fired him.

With the revivals still in full force, Edwards began purging the church according to his standards of saintliness. In March 1742 he led the adults (above fourteen years in age) of his congregation to promise honesty and justice and uprightness in all their dealings, to pledge restitution for wrongs committed against "any of our neighbours in their outward estate," to honor Christ in all business and public interest — in effect, to live by Christ's law and to test themselves by it when they prepared for communion (*WD*, 1:166). By summer the awakenings were subsiding even as Edwards began preaching the sermons that later became *Religious Affections*. These sermons exposed the pastor's position quietly but unmistakably. He would measure applicants' saintliness by his tests of religious experience. By 1744 he resolved to enforce Edwards' Trail to church membership.

He would wait four long years for the first applicant to scale the cliff. When the pastor would not smoothe the path, *this* candidate withdrew. Edwards had jeopardized his career.

The storm was still gathering when Edwards urged the congregation to extraordinary, united prayer for religious revivals. His plaintive plea in 1747 that they pray for the extension of Christ's earthly Kingdom seems to have been aimed at more than renewed awakenings. For the Northamptonites to pray, in concert with Christians in Scotland and throughout the world, for a revived church might mollify the controversy over church membership. Indeed, their prayers would exhibit their sensible concern for the cause of Christ, which the pastor counted a sign of visible sainthood. But whatever Edwards may have hoped for this scheme, it did not head off the collision. His flock might have reasoned that their pastor's too-rigid requirements had stanched the revival. The church could as well be replenished by his compromise as by their supplications. He had been tactless in publicly naming some youths whose snickering over a book on midwifery fell short of the town's and congregation's mores. And in 1748 death took his uncle, his most powerful advocate.

The inevitable dismissal came in 1750. The intrigues and ironies, already often told, need not be repeated here.[12] Nothing he wrote about the controversy improved the psychological profundity of *Affections* — indeed only when he had removed himself to the far west (Stockbridge) did his writing rise again in intellectual power to the height reached by that book.[13] The arguments he published in the heat of controversy for his narrow view of qualifications for communion are contentious, repetitious and rather woodenly erudite; there are a few charitable and fewer profound passages. In fact, all he would require of full church members was a trusting (not only an assenting) faith. But he seemed to be demanding perfect saintliness made visible in deed as well as word. In a farewell sermon that does not entirely lack the magnanimity for which it has been extolled, he referred the controversy for review to the time when minister and congregation would meet at the Last Judgment; he was confident the decision would go his way.

One more notable work on affectional religion came out of the controversy, an edition of the journals and diaries of the Reverend David Brainerd complete with Edwards' reflections showing the young man to have been a true visible saint possessing positive signs of conversion. Comments, summaries, and emphases by Edwards wove Brainerd's diaries into a classic case study illustrating the criteria of holiness that Edwards had adumbrated in his seminal work on religious affections. Once again in Brainerd's life — as in that of Edwards' daughter Jerusha (to whom the dying Brainerd was betrothed), as in Sarah Edwards' spirituality, as in the piety of many a parishioner, as also in his own experiences — Edwards' eyes had "seen the glory of the coming of the Lord." In *Religious Affections* he ground lenses through which everybody else with the same discernment could see "the saints go marching in."

The Signs of Sanctity

Unless we understand how Edwards conceived of human experience we likely will write him down as placing religion in the heart instead of the head.[14] That makes too little of his achievement. We can also make too much of it if we forget that, in his world, persons actually experienced Christian salvation, actually received forgiveness of their sins, actually possessed a new spiritual sense. Some did. Others did not. Still others thought they did but did not. The fourth logical possibility — those who did but thought they did not — is what Edwards nullified by his conception of human experience.

The conception (to whose subtlety a few sentences can hardly do justice) allowed no division of soul from body, head from heart, understanding from will, knowledge from thing known. Humans differed from both animals and angels by virtue of their embodied intelligence, their psychophysical indivisibility.

To be sure, either of the soul's faculties, the understanding or
the will, might take the lead when a situation called mostly
for knowledge or action. But neither could proceed in disregard
of the other any more than the soul could get out of the body.
By the understanding, a person was "capable of perception and
speculation"; by the will, he was "some way inclined with respect
to the things it views or considers; either is inclined to 'em,
or is disinclined, and averse from 'em" (*WY*, 2:96). The understanding, in this view, made one "an indifferent unaffected spectator"; the will or inclination made one a participant. But always
one was *both* spectator *and* participant, however at any time more
or less one than the other. The understanding could, for example,
apprehend the truth of Christian doctrine ("truth" meaning consistent relations among ideas) whether the person's will was
inclined to them or averse to them. But a person could participate
in these divine things only if the will was inclined to them,
pleased by them. Since the will *was* the inclination it could
not reincline or disincline *itself*. By the will, persons chose
the thing they liked more than another, even if they liked it
only a little. But they could not choose to like what they disliked.
Their liking could be changed only by some power working
on or reinclining the will. Acknowledging that some acts were
coerced rather than chosen, Edwards interpreted the freedom
of the will as the ability to choose what pleased one — not
whatever one pleased to choose. The notion that we could be
pleased in doing what displeased us was not freedom but nonsense. Certainly we could choose among our live options, but
we could not by choice enliven a different set of options.

As with the will, so with the understanding. Anybody could
understand divine things by learning about them. But, as William James would later teach, such *knowledge about* was not the
same thing as, and indeed could not change itself into, *acquaintance with* God. Only by a divine act could a person who was
averse to divine things be tilted toward loving them. Thus
whenever a person who did not love God came to love Him,

it was God who wrought the change. In its simplest meaning, salvation or sainthood was the effect of such a change.

Privacy

"True religion, in great part, consists in holy affections"; so Edwards laid down the doctrine of his *Affections* (*WY*, 2:95). The definition did not describe everything about religion but told its essential effect. Therefore "wherever true religion is, there are vigorous exercises of the inclination and will, towards divine objects: but . . . the vigorous, lively and sensible exercise of the will, are no other than the affections of the soul" (*WY*, 2:100). Edwards was describing religious salvation in concrete human experience. This second principle of his theory, though less complex than the relation of the understanding and the will, may be more difficult for moderns. For moderns tend to grant that General Washington's and King George's armies really fought, but want to admit only that Edwards and his contemporaries felt or hoped or imagined they were saved. In fact, the category "salvation" is needed to explain what entered and formed Edwards' human experience quite as much as "war" is needed to explain what the soldiers did. For Edwards salvation was as real as war. The religious question was not *whether* salvation was actual but *how* sainthood stamped itself on the soul and how its being stamped there could be accurately known. In the cases he (and Stoddard) observed, professing saving faith correlated very little with possessing saving faith. Therefore he emphatically rejected the notion that one received sainthood simply through the understanding alone. Therefore also he mistrusted persons' verbal claims to their own sainthood. True religion knew no mere spectators, nor did it stir the will as something detached from the understanding; rather it called forth the whole person's participation. The agency of this whole-person participation, being the agency of will accompanied and endorsed by mind, Edwards referred to as the affections or the heart or the new spiritual sense.

Thus Edwards taught that sainthood became visible in those lively, vigorous, and sensible exercises of the mind (not the body) that were the springs of religious action: the religious affections. Love was "the chief of the affections, and fountain of all other affections" (*WY*, 2:106). When the Spirit of God stirred in persons an intense, enduring, sensible, and unselfish love of God for His own moral excellence, they could be tested for sainthood by ascertaining whether certain general qualities ruled their affections. They would know, even though not with absolute certainty, that God's Spirit was acting savingly upon them if their religious experiences were (1) *ostensive*, or sensible; (2) *intensive*, or lively and vigorous in quality; (3) *extensive*, or durable and increasing through time; implying (4) that one would *love divine things* for themselves and not from personal interest, and (5) that visible salvation *known* by the person who had it would become *recognizable* to other saints.

This way of describing the qualities of sainthood becomes more concrete when we consider the actual experiences that Edwards classified. He distinguished *true* affections signaling the *saving* work of God's Spirit from *indifferent* affections that might spring from self-interest or delusion or Satan's power or the *common* working of God's Spirit. The twelve indifferent affections Edwards called "negative signs"; they "are no signs one way or the other, either that affections are such as true religion consists in, or that they are otherwise" (*WY*, 2:127). In each case Edwards took pains to show how these experiences, giving the appearance to some observers of a saving work of God's Spirit, *might* be just that, or might as well be a common or preparatory work of God or a self-deception or an inducement by a spiritual power other than God. None of these negative signs gave grounds for writing off an experience as *not* that of salvation, yet the simultaneous presence of all such signs would not attest conversion.

Cast in Edwards' own words, the twelve "negative signs" were: (1) "that religious affections are very great, or raised very high";

(2) "that they have great effects on the body"; (3) "that they cause those who have them, to be fluent, fervent and abundant, in talking of the things of religion"; (4) that the affections "are not purposely produced by those who are the subjects of them, or that they arise in their minds in a manner they can't account for"; (5) "that they come with texts of Scripture, remarkably brought to the mind"; (6) "that there is an appearance of love in them"; (7) that there are "religious affections of many kinds, accompanying one another"; (8) "that comforts and joys seem to follow awakenings and convictions of conscience, in a *certain order*"; (9) "that they dispose persons to spend much time in religion"; (10) "that they much dispose persons with their mouths to praise and glorify God"; (11) "that they make persons . . . exceeding confident that what they experience is divine, and that they are in a good estate"; (12) that their "outward manifestations . . . and the relation persons give of them, are very affecting and pleasing to the truly godly, and such as greatly gain their charity, and win their hearts" (*WY*, 2:127, 131, 135, 141, 142, 146, 147, 151, 163, 165, 167, 181).

The insight that certain religious affections indicated neither the presence nor the absence of saving grace had long served Edwards both when he was defending the revivals and when he was criticizing their excesses. Anti-revivalists to the right, he contended, should beware lest in opposing affectional religion they exclude actual cases of salvation. Enthusiasts to the left, he pleaded, should take care lest they mistake Satan's work for God's. Moreover, to say precisely which affections were indifferent ones clarified the significance of the other, decisive affections. The affections attesting the Spirit's saving work were those other specific religious experiences, the ones that Satan could not imitate and that men and women could not enduringly pretend to have. To identify and describe these experiences Edwards needed, of course, Scripture, but also a vast range of experiential data and the ability to assort them with uncanny sensitivity.

For although his modestly stated aim was to help persons know
whether they themselves were visible saints, his logic unswerv-
ingly drove him to say how to recognize visible sainthood in
others. Saving grace conferred a spirituality that showed itself
in practical life. What was truly sensible in one's own life would
in practice become visible to others. In effect, eleven of the
signs told the saints themselves of their own gracious affections,
then all of them combined into a grand summary of the way
sainthood exhibited itself publicly. This twelfth sign was that
all of the "Gracious and holy affections have their exercise and
fruit in Christian practice" (*WY*, 2:383).

Leaving to God alone to know who was ultimately saved,
a saint would know the Spirit was working savingly on his soul
in a dozen ways. First a saint would *possess a new spiritual sense.*
This "new inward perception or sensation of their minds" arose
not from the saint's human nature but flowed from a supernatural
source and redirected all the faculties (*WY*, 2:205). Second,
a saint would *love God* for the sake of God's loveliness and not
for the soul's benefit. "The first objective ground of gracious
affections, is the transcendently excellent and amiable nature
of divine things, as they are in themselves; and not any conceived
relation they bear to self, or self-interest" (*WY*, 2:240). Third,
a saint would *sense the moral excellency of divine things*, would primarily love God for His loveliness as faithful, true, righteous, and
good, and only secondarily for the attributes of infiniteness,
omniscience, omnipotence, omnipresence. In a word, the holiness rather than the grandeur of God preoccupied the saint
because men and women could be converted to holiness but not
to majesty. Fourth, a saint would *receive an enlightened understanding* and thus know in a new manner the excellence of divine
things. The mind or understanding (not the imagination)
worked by a new light quite as much as the heart worked by
a new love. Fifth, a saint would *experience the gospel's truth*. A
special operation of the Spirit implanted "a solid, full, thorough
and effectual conviction of the truth of the great things of the

gospel" (*WY*, 2:291). No arguments could produce this "sense
and taste of the divine, supreme and holy excellency and beauty
of those things" (*WY*, 2:297).

Sixth, a saint would *continue in humility*. This "evangelical
humiliation" brought a sense of unworthiness after conversion,
something quite distinct from the "legal" humiliation that prepared one for conversion. Because of it, saints would not prize
themselves over others in matters of religion and would eschew
that acme of self-conceit, pride in their own humility. Seventh,
a saint's soul would *be changed in nature* so that a spiritual light
shone not only upon but also from within the soul. Eighth, a
saint would *receive a Christlike spirit* and would live meekly, lov-
ingly, forgivingly, mercifully. Converted persons became, in the
phrase of an ancient philosopher, "little christs." (This eighth
sign implies identification by others.) Ninth, a saint would *know
softness of heart or tenderness of spirit*, spiritually becoming a little
child. "As he has more holy boldness, so he has less of self-
confidence and a forward assuming boldness, and more modesty"
(*WY*, 2:364). Tenth, a saint's holy affections would *appear with
symmetry and proportion*. Holy joy balanced holy fear; comfort balanced sorrow; the proportion showed itself in constancy through
time. (Edwards explicitly distinguished the private from the public affections of holiness, and insisted that one kind balance the
other, thus again making sainthood visible to discerning
observers.) Eleventh, a saint would *yearn for increased spirituality*.
Conversion began a lasting process of sanctification, of growth
in likeness to Christ.

Twelfth and finally, a saint would *live a Christian practice*.
All of this person's behavior would be "directed by Christian
rules"; one would "make this practice of religion eminently his
work and business . . . to the end of his life" (*WY*, 2:383).
Every preceding sign pointed to this one. Each private indication
of holiness here became public in its fruit and effect. Saints
themselves knew whether they were saintly. If they were, and
knew it well, other saints could tell.

Publicity

Had Edwards' signs of sainthood been *only* autobiographical we
should fault him for arrogance. But had they been *not* autobiographical we would call him entirely presumptuous. In *Affections*
he was explicitly neither writing about himself nor describing
the lives of other personal exemplars, yet implicitly he was doing
both things. Soon after his treatise was published he found a
model saint in Brainerd, whose life manifested all the gracious
affections with the lone flaw of a disproportion of melancholy
over joy. Edwards first met Brainerd briefly at New Haven in
September 1743, after *Affections* had already taken shape in sermons. The fledgling minister after 1742 missionized Indians
on Long Island, in western Massachusetts, and at the forks of
the Susquehanna River. Later, in spring 1747, desperately ill
of consumption, he went to live in Edwards' household under
the care of daughter Jerusha, to whom he became engaged. That
autumn he died at the Edwards home; Jerusha soon followed
him. His diaries and journals, skillfully edited by Edwards and
published in 1749, had a wide reading. (Both piety and Indians
were popular topics.)

Edwards' sermon at Brainerd's funeral, especially his reflections
on Brainerd's life, show the preacher's unusual equanimity amid
troubles in the parish. Even more they attest his ingenuity as
a student of religious behavior. The 1746 treatise had accurately
analyzed the kind of religiousness Brainerd was even then recording in his private journals, which Edwards did not read until
after he buried Brainerd. When he did read them, Brainerd's
piety struck him so forcibly that he called the journal "probably
the best manual of Christian experience, ever yet published"
and the man's life "a clear transparent mirror, [in which] the
reader if he is not voluntarily blind, will discover the true character of his own heart" — not Edwards' neatest metaphor, but
the meaning is clear (*WD*, 10:vii–viii). Edwards actually discovered a *thirteenth* sign of grace in Brainerd's having taken "all

opportunities to discourse on the peculiar nature, and distinguishing characteristics of true, spiritual, and vital religion; and to bear his testimony against the various false appearances of it" (WD, 10:393, 390–99). The final sign of visible sainthood was indeed to be concerned for accurately distinguishing visible saints from hypocrites. Edwards' other, far less serene book of 1749 on qualifications for full communion with the visible church emphatically insisted that sensible sainthood would show itself publicly to the eye of Christian charity.

Visible sanctity, then, resulted from holy affections that made one sensibly aware of the condition and produced a life-style recognizable by other visible saints. The logic by which this sensed holiness became public can be traced along at least three strands of Edwards' thought. First, as we have seen, in his view of human experience inward realities issued in and were tested by outward actualities. Actually, the spatial metaphors of inwardness and outwardness are more ours than his. For Edwards, having the idea or awareness of a thing, so far as one escaped ignorance and delusion, was the same as having the thing itself in one's mind and life. Whatever inhered truly in experience would surely surface objectively. Edwards turned the equation around. By discriminating between what *appeared* enduringly in practice and what a person, possibly ignorant or deluded, merely *said* about his own faith, Edwards distinguished the signs of true holiness from the signs of indifferent religiousness.

The second, much more complicated logical strand, leading from sensible to public sainthood, runs along Edwards' interpretation of life as social and developmental. Persons became saints through a process that their communities noticed, encouraged, and registered. This man's own religious history, of course, began with a baptism whose pledges first came into his consciousness as a religious busyness in the prepuberal boy, encouraged by his parents. Later the college student searched the church's repository of truth for some token of salvation. The young adult among theological students and parishioners came to delight in the beauty of holiness. The professional minister instructed parents in their responsibility for their baptized offspring; he catechized children about the wonders of religion; he prayed and talked with adolescents about the application of faith to their lives; he exhorted adults (especially young adults) to beware of hell and rejoice in the sweetness of Christ. Moreover, in his accounts of the revivals he chose case histories of different-aged females: Phebe Bartlet, the four-year-old girl; Abigail Hutchinson, the young woman; Sarah Edwards, the mature adult.[15] In the memoirs of Brainerd the earliest remarkable spiritual experiences came at about seven or eight years of age; at thirteen he "was roused out of this carnal security"; at twenty he adopted a religious regimen that included avoidance of young company; by twenty-four he had experienced first a false and then a true conversion (*WD*, 10:34). Out of the ages and circumstances of extraordinary religious experiences in these and other case histories, Edwards built a scheme of spiritual development and nurture that ran as follows.

Baptized infants generally stood fair to be regenerate (those who died in infancy were saved) but invisibly so because they could neither be aware of holiness nor apply to themselves the means appointed by God to sustain it. Therefore God appointed their parents to devote them to Him and to carry on their spiritual strife vicariously. As they came into childhood their pastors and the church joined the struggle, and "God has his eye partly on them and partly on parents" and ministers and church, gradually looking more and more to the growing persons themselves to use the means of grace on their own lives. While appropriate means were being used simultaneously by parents, ministers, the church, and themselves, "if they ha'n't been brought into a state of salvation before they stand fairer for it then than ever afterwards and if, when they first come to adult age and come to be fully capable of acting for them[selves], they are equally thorough in the use of proper means for themselves, they stand fairer for being brought into a state of salvation

than afterwards" (Misc. #849). To postpone such serious business made it ever more difficult.

This scheme of religious nurture rested on the ability of a
visible saint to discern visible sanctity in others, particularly
by seeing into their private lives. Although the clearest signs
of gracious affections were likely to come to them in their solitude, the practical life of the saints showed their holiness to
other saints. Parents and pastors would see more of young
people's than of independent adults' private lives. (Indeed, saints
in heaven, Edwards thought, were yearning for and examining
sainthood in the earthly church; he thought God had pledged
Himself to regard as visible saints anybody so recognized by
the church, and as excommunicate anybody expelled by the
church.) Always careful to reserve to God alone the knowledge
of the secret state of each person's heart, Edwards held that
one would know one's status as a saint and other saints would
recognize it with reasonable clarity. "Though undoubtedly, if
others could see so much of what belongs to men's practice,
as their own consciences may see of it, it might be an infallible
evidence of their state" (WY, 2:420). The observing community
logically implied public sanctity.

The third strand of Edwards' logic running toward the outward
publication of inward spiritual states has to do with his valuation
of evidence. He mistrusted persons' verbal professions of conversion. How else could hypocrites or deluded persons so easily
and impressively misrepresent their own salvation (and to their
own peril)? Spiritual claims, especially to humility, smacked
always of spiritual pride. From the very nature of being Christian
sprang this strong prompting to mistrust persons who made
much noise about their holiness, as well as a corollary impulse
to avoid claiming for oneself the identity of Christian. Who
one was under God came clear in what one did toward God
and neighbor. Intention made itself most reliably manifest in
action, "as long as soul and body are united" (WY, 2:425).
Therefore, when Edwards had described eleven signs by which

a person could know holiness in himself, all these signs logically
indicated his holiness to other saints. In this psychology of
religion, self-responding subjects deserved less credence than
eyewitness observers who, by definition as visible saints, were
trained observers. Saint was as saint did, and it took one to
know one.

Beauty

Three strands of Edwards' thought, then, forced private holiness
into public sainthood. By similar logic, his desire to keep
theology coherent with experience led him to translate religion
into another idiom. Given the fixity of theological landmarks
in his world of thought and experience, the most surprising
thing about this interpreter of surprising conversions is his
attempt, late in life, to translate his religious thought from
theological idioms into the language of true virtue. In doing
so, Edwards transposed both theology and morality into esthetics. He does not tell us explicitly why he made this move,
stark as it is, why he did not rest his case on *Affections* with
its categories deduced from Scripture and illustrated by excerpts
from Puritan masters, with its compass boxed by Christ and
Trinity, creation and fall, sin and redemption, church and Last
Judgment. These orientations characterize the rest of Edwards'
literary output from Northampton as well as the 1752 book
closing the controversy there. Then in Stockbridge his mind
turned to freedom of will, God's end in creating the world,
the nature of true virtue, original sin, and the history of redemption.

With the dissertation on "The Nature of True Virtue"
Edwards became so confident of a universe characterized by
mutual exchange between God and creation, between spirituality
and its sensibility, that he could restate the essence of his thought
nontheologically. The treatise contains only one quite incidental
appeal to Scripture and only three very casual references to Chris-

tianity. God became "being in general, simply considered."
Sainthood became true virtue. The leading category of religious
experience became not salvation but beauty.

Perhaps the absence of urgent exhortation and of explicit
theology in this book is what has led some interpreters to find
the work without passion, cold, weary, unpolemical.[16] Nicely
chiseled and intellectually empyreal, yes, but also passionate
enough to be downright playful. Two games go on at once,
the game of translating without loss from the language of religion
to what seems to be the language of morality but is really that
of esthetics, and the game of trapping utilitarian moralists in
snares of their own making. Whatever we may think of the
translation, the ploy is neat. For this once, Edwards piles burdens
of proof on his adversaries' back. Let them build on self-love
storey after storey of justice, familial love, approval of virtues,
disapproval of vice; Edwards plucks away the foundation and
gleefully watches the walls come tumbling down. Let them make
their life ever so dutiful; it remains equidistant from their goal
of a beautiful soul. Even the title plays with the book's central
argument: the nature of true virtue is such that natural virtue,
to the extent it is truly natural, is no true virtue, which, by
its nature, is a supernatural gift.

Edwards even concedes what other pleaders for original sin
fought to the last ditch; the instructed natural conscience
"concurs with the law of God, is of equal extent with it, and
joins its voice with it in every article" (*NTV*, p. 68). He grants
this conscience to all mankind, assigning it not only to self-love
but chiefly to "a sense of desert, or the natural agreement between
sin and misery" or virtue and happiness (*NTV*, p. 92). The
law requiring man to love God agrees, that is, with the justice
perceived by the conscience: God *deserves* to be loved. The law
that one love his neighbor as himself generates natural uneasiness
in neglecting to do to others what "he would be displeased with
them for neglecting to do to him" (*NTV*, p. 61). Self-love
approves love to others; sense of desert approves love to God;
both approvals arise in the natural man!

Good is done and evil is avoided by natural man if he is unprejudiced and if he responds to conscience, self-love, natural instincts, moral sense, pity, gratitude, justice, and familial love. This goodness possesses real moral worth. But it looks like true virtue only when tested simply for its morality, and that is the wrong test. True virtue, far from being moral approval of good and moral disapproval of evil, means having a heart in consent to and union with being in general, considered simply for itself. Of course true virtue immediately *issues* in the exercise of a general good will (and in acts looking much like those of natural man) but it *consists* in the beauty of union between a being and general being. Like natural virtue, true virtue loves particular objects, but natural virtue loves them out of private interest as partial or private systems, while true virtue loves them for the sake of universal existence out of general benevolence.

In *Affections*, to be sure, Edwards had not asked which were pious and which impious affections, rather which were imitable and which were inimitable works of grace — a far subtler matter. Translated into the language of virtue construed as beauty, the subtlety of the distinction increased immeasurably. The natural moral sense, so-called (or self-love and conscience), could approve all the noble deeds that true virtue would benevolently perform. Indeed, a natural conscience would even see fairness in true virtue's opposing the enemies of its beloved object, being in general. Edwards is granting and proving that no *ethic* as such could transcend the morality of self-love and natural conscience.

Self-love and the sense of desert arose from a person's private interest and made the objects of his regard instrumental to his own happiness and well-being. The good person lived true to his own integrity. By contrast, true virtue sprang from the beauty and excellence of being in general, considered for its own sake, and it exercised benevolence for the happiness of those it loved. The genuinely virtuous person lived true to the beauty of the universe. The difference lay neither in the deed done nor even in the psychological motive behind it, but rather in the frame of mind — whether one was in or out of tune with the universe.

Edwards granted natural man a natural religion along with a
natural morality, provided natural man was restrained from his
worst proclivity to evil and self-destruction. Natural man
lacked only the crucial capacity to taste the sweetness of God
and the universe. The duty of such persons differed little or
none from those of truly virtuous ones. But the loveliness of the
universe sensed by the two kinds of men and women, and
therefore the beauty of their duties, differed enormously.
Natural man could approve what he had no power to enjoy or
delight in, no power to attain. Therefore natural virtue knew
a limited, private, secondary, derivative, instrumental beauty
of proportion among parts, not the full beauty of the whole
universe. Natural virtue approved benevolence in order to receive
benefits, not complacent, harmonious benevolence, purely for
the sake of others. His natural virtue, debasable and distortable
into evil, lacked enduring attraction by positive goodness.
Natural virtue produced apparent instead of genuine gratitude,
justice, patriotism, familial devotion, sexual love. The difference,
in a nutshell, was "the frame of our minds" — "a certain
spiritual sense given them of God" (*NTV*, p. 99). Logically
enough, then, persons would recognize true virtue in themselves
if they had it. They would be able to identify it in others and
would manifest it recognizably to others who had it. The naturally virtuous person looking for good or evil in human deeds
would see no important difference between himself and his truly
happy companions.

Perhaps we can appreciate the revolutionary nature of Edwards'
achievement in translating Puritan religion from the language
of ethics into the language of esthetics if we *re*translate his
concept of living a beautiful life back into the idiom of moralistic
Christianity. There the virtuous person enjoys God and uses the
world; the corrupt person uses God and enjoys the world.
Edwards recoiled from the notion that we might use God, just
as he recoiled from the doctrine that we should not enjoy the
world. The beauty of God and the beauty of all created beings

impressed itself on him as a single, indivisible beauty. Truly virtuous men and women, sensing that they had been given a new frame of mind, both enjoyed God and enjoyed God's world. Lacking that frame of mind, men and women at worst would destroy themselves and at best would ascribe to being in general an abstract loveliness that they themselves could not actively love. To the person of true virtue, given a new frame of mind, the divine beauty of true holiness became reciprocal with the human holiness of true beauty.

"And it pleases God to observe analogy in his works, as is manifest in fact in innumerable instances," Edwards wrote, "and especially to establish inferior things with analogy to superior" (NTV, p. 30). Man was the chief instance, inferior yet analogous to his Maker, just as lesser beings were sometimes images and shadows of man. Edwards would allow no middling kind of people standing halfway between natural conscience and true virtue; nevertheless the truly virtuous person stood on middle ground halfway between Creator and the rest of creation. His proper relation with God allowed no bad relations with the world. The old divines believed God would bring home to heaven those He loved. Edwards came to be at home with God as a way of being also at home in the stark world of Massachusetts' western frontier. He was really neither a mystic nor a pantheist; rather he knew and taught a holiness of enjoying God and the world, both because the world was from God and because God was in the world. Visible sainthood and visible virtue were one and the same matter: letting one's existence be made beautiful and enjoying the beauty of existence.

The Holiness of Beauty

The Puritanism whose tradition Edwards summarized and transformed had long operated on oscillating impulses. The theological urge to credit God alone with all the work of saving men and women alternated with the moral impulse to identify the

steps persons took toward, into, and through conversion. Reciprocally, to ponder conversion evoked again the impulse to credit
God. For most preachers it was enough to follow one impulse
and then the other, depending on the circumstance and hoping
to balance the two. No theologian ever outstripped Edwards
in guarding the worthiness and majesty of God, even if that
meant affirming the worminess of humans. Nor did any student
of religion ever surpass him in distinguishing those affections
involved in preparing for conversion from those sensible signs
accompanying conversion itself. And what preacher more consistently glorified God with tropes designed to arouse thirst for
conversion, for holiness, for sainthood, for a sense of the beauty
of divine things?

The revivals provided the opportunity and Edwards provided
the intellectual power for making these alternating impulses into
a single, steady force. Few had so much of that power. Less
clever folk could hardly understand the need for such precision
in making the theology and the religion of revivalism coherent.
Revivalism produced emotional excesses, Edwards readily conceded. The religious process of conversion involved walking up
to the door of sainthood, on any common-sense reading, even
though God alone could carry one across the threshold. Theological orthodoxy, Edwards insisted, required that the precise point
of change in transit be called the beginning of conversion. Thus
he solved in principle the predicament of evangelical religion
in America: to combine the majesty of God with the preacher's
desire for effect so converts could at once give themselves to
God and thank God for doing the giving. Or, in Edwards' own
translation, the activity of trying to beautify the human soul
succeeds when it fails — precisely as one is given a sense of the
true beauty of the human spirit and its universe.

Edwards' discussion of true virtue shifted the effects of religion
from duty to beauty, from ethics to esthetics, where inherited
categories were less muddied by controversy and language less
hackneyed by homilies. We strive, as Edwards had it, for the

beauty we desire as our own self-fulfillment, and some of us
attain much genuine secondary virtue bearing the appearance
of true beauty. But true virtue consists in being dedicated to
being in general and therefore requires the erasure of personal
interest; the harder we seek the benefit of disinterest the more
we extend our self-interest; the more we seek the benefit of being
loved the more we intensify our self-love. True beauty at once
opposes and fulfills this quest. True beauty comes as a gift,
known to be unattained but received; to speak of it requires
the passive voice.

If translating theology and religious psychology into the language of esthetics forced Edwards to forfeit anything, it was
the idea of an institutional church, not that of sensible salvation
or that of visible sainthood. The rhetoric of beauty had no precise
synonym for each part of Edwards' theology but it conveyed
the sum of his spirituality: true religion is not to achieve moral
goodness but to receive holy beauty.

Thus to share today the legacy of Edwards is, in a word,
to let one's life become an act of beauty. For by that formulation
Edwards thrust the Puritan tradition forward into what Miller
calls (in the nonsectarian sense) "a magnificent *humanism*."[17] (The
ironies of the achievement include historical comedy as well as
personal tragedy. The irony is that Edwards' parishioners dismissed him for dragging them backward behind old Stoddard's
Way to what looked like the rigidities of the Founding Fathers of
New England; he thrust forward. The irony is that his theological
protégés (Joseph Bellamy, Samuel Hopkins, Jonathan Edwards,
Jr.) faced backward to an orthodoxy that allowed no goodness
in man apart from divine grace; Edwards faced forward. The
irony is that after these strict Calvinists had taken the real property, as it were, from the estate of Edwards' religious thought,
they conveyed it to so unlikely a successor as the modern fundamentalists. The irony is that the personalty of this bequest
fell to the emotional, sensational revivalists, to the Charles Grandison Finneys and Dwight Lyman Moodys and Norman Vincent

Peales, who enshrined religious feeling as a substitute for thinking. To be sure, Edwards honored the Founding Fathers of New England, cultivated religion of the heart, defended Calvinism. But no such part of his work constitutes the central legacy: to be grasped by God, not to grasp God, is spiritual beauty. The religious life equals the good life equals the beautiful life — a life made proportionate and proper and harmonious by the divine artist, a life lived at home in the universe.

If late-twentieth-century Americans cannot be as sure as Edwards was that such a divine artist is at work high in the heavens, maybe divine things somewhere else can still be to us lovely for their own sake. If so, we can still, on Edwards' terms, yield a visible sanctity, a sanctity of practical living that is harmonious, proportionate, virtuous, beautiful.

3   *Interlude*   *From Edwards to Emerson*

Pious Puritans in America had sought godliness for the sake of goodness. Jonathan Edwards' saint dared rejoice in deity and creation and to live harmoniously. Their ethical quest for human virtue became his esthetic enjoyment of divine beauty. They hoped for covenanted betterment; he received a new spiritual sense. The human physicality that made them tremble for their souls became for him the image and shadow of participation in the divine life. Fear of God gave way to joy in divine things. Edwards was tasting Puritanism's forbidden fruit, plucked not from the tree of the knowledge of good and evil but from the bush of rejoicing in the world and its Creator. To the old query, What in man does God find worthy of redemption?, the Puritan theology gave the answer, Nothing save what God imputes. Edwards was asking, How can a person come to enjoy divine things for their own sake? He answered, Through a new spiritual sense that God implants.

Edwards' saint received this new sense, not as a sixth one added to Locke's standard five but as a new way of exercising those five, a new disposition or frame of mind and body, a divinely illumined understanding as well as a divinely inclined will, a new head and a new heart.[18] This saint let his daily life become a work of divine artistry. Rather than asking God to improve his goodness he let himself be enabled to find divine things, both on earth and in heaven, things eminently sweet and sensibly delightful.

But to say that Edwards changed an ethical into an esthetic spirituality is not to say he tried to cultivate the sense of beauty by which men and women found pleasure in works of art. Rather holiness consisted for him in the consent, the propriety, and the proportionateness with which one went about doing the things one daily did, practicing a new sense of God's beauty. Holiness made one's life a work of art. Of course, this esthetic strand of American piety can be — in fact it has been — debased into mere respectability. With a little push it falls over into the hypocrisy of paying respect to, or into the priggishness of desiring respect from, others. That is only to say bad religiousness can drive out good.

For Edwards the new spiritual sense gave men and women a new respect for themselves and for others because they felt truly at home with their God and the universe. To be sure, some received this new sense and others did not. But even the difference, between saints pointed toward bliss and unregenerate persons destined for perdition, revealed to Edwards the balance and proportion between divine mercy and divine justice. Double predestination illustrated the beauty of the universe. The saved were enabled to enjoy God. The damned, after all, got what everybody deserved.

Edwards' religious thought emphasized persons approving beautiful deity where the Puritans had emphasized God improving wicked man. However, his theology guarded the precious doctrines of divine sovereignty and human depravity. His genius was to make the old teachings foster a new spirituality, to build a new ethos under the old world-view.

For opposite reasons, to be sure, religious thinkers in America who were Edwards' contemporaries were downgrading God's role and upgrading man's role in the transaction of salvation. Strangely enough, the rationalists and the revivalists agreed on these key matters, although the former tended toward Unitarianism and the latter toward Trinitarianism — or at least Christism.

The enemies of revivals, arguing on the old moral grounds,

claimed that conscience enabled one to know and do the good
God required. If it pleased God to be obeyed and served by
His creatures, the rationalists reckoned, surely God would endow
creatures with the ability to serve and obey Him. In Boston
there was Edwards' formidable disputant over the validity of
the awakenings, Charles Chauncy of First Church, and also
Jonathan Mayhew of West Church. Both turned the same argument first against original sin, then against particular election
or predestination, then against Episcopalianism, and finally — perhaps of more symbolic than substantive force — against
the conception of God as Trinity. When Bostonians about 1800
"after four decades of continual concern with American constitu-
tional problems," Sydney Ahlstrom writes, paused to take their
theological temperature, they found themselves accused "of having become Unitarian," and "after a brief show of outrage" made
the charge a matter of pride (Ahlstrom, p. 38).

Outside Boston, rationalism took another turn. Samuel
Johnson, tutor at Yale during Edwards' student days, invited
people into the Church of England as a refuge from enthusiasm
and enthusiasts. He stressed the innate human ability to please
God and thus to find happiness. Moreover, he argued cleverly
so as to challenge neither the Calvinistic catechism nor the
Augustinian liturgy of his adopted church. Johnson, who
founded both the first Anglican congregation in Connecticut and
the college in New York that became Columbia University,
argued that God's sovereignty was proved by His distinguishing
and judging free men and women according to their virtue or
vice, praise or blame, just rewards or punishments. Johnson set
forth exactly those "modern prevailing notions" of free will
against which Edwards wrote his great treatise. Johnson's
heavenly ruler resembled the earthly monarch to whom he
remained loyal: sovereign God and sovereign George justly
rewarded subjects who lived dutifully and obediently in their
allotted stations. As author of the first philosophical textbook
written and published (by Benjamin Franklin, no less) in

America, Johnson helped spread the idealistic metaphysics of George Berkeley. His moralism, in which every man who wanted to please God could do so, prevailed among American Episcopalians for a long generation after his death, at least until the 1810s when new leaders adapted revivalism and made their church one of the American denominations.

Avid revivalists of the late colonial and early national epochs practiced an emotional piety that rationalists like Chauncy, Mayhew, and Johnson openly scoffed at. But they too enlarged the role of men and women in producing their own conversion. Insistent enthusiasts from Gilbert Tennent of the Great Awakening onward — onward through the so-called Second Awakenings at Yale and the southern frontiers, onward through the revivals of Peter Cartwright and Charles Grandison Finney, onward through the nationwide religious excitement accompanying the economic depression of 1857 and 1858, onward through the revivals among soldiers in Union and Confederate camps, onward through the citified preaching campaigns of Dwight L. Moody and Billy Sunday, onward even down to the televised crusades of Billy Graham — these enthusiasts held every adult person responsible and capable of generating within himself worthy religious feelings. They all made men and women less-than-depraved partners with a less-than-sovereign God in producing less-than-surprising conversions.

Why? First, common sense. When preachers and penitents strove to prepare for conversion, conversion usually followed. What went before seemed to cause what followed. Moreover, while Edwards' preaching had been the *occasion* for the surprising work of converting souls, his successors preached with the aim of *inducing* conversions.

Second, a veritable cult of revivalistic success, best illustrated by the Methodists. Because John Wesley had edited and published Edwards' *Faithful Narrative*, his successor in American Methodism studied the book. To Bishop Francis Asbury, God wanted more and more Methodists in America; ultimately, God

wanted only Methodists in America. So Asbury recruited and
commanded an army of circuit-riders willing to do God's bidding
(hardly different from Asbury's) or else be read out of church.
To Asbury conversion consisted in forsaking loose living for the
love of Jesus. Sanctification became the stairsteps of that love's
increase. Perfection in love was the goal of all piety. Because
perfection ruled his preaching, the experience of sanctification
could hardly be distinguished from the experience of conversion.
On its negative side religion meant, in Methodist parlance, having a sin-killing time. On the positive side it meant having
a soul-refreshing time. Both together meant having a melting
time, a time when human souls melted in the sweet love of
Jesus. (The sexual undercurrent of early Methodist piety is as
voluptuous as it is innocent!) Asbury made revivalism the normal
fare of popular religious nurture in America, made the surprise
of conversion into the ordinary content of piety. Asbury achieved
incredible success. He came to America in 1772 to serve a tiny,
localized sect within the Church of England. At his death in
1816 Methodism was a nationwide, mainstream denomination.
His personal presence undoubtedly touched more Americans in
a wider geographic spread than that of any contemporary. His
religious thought (if it can be so called) appealed to rude, rural
Americans. It was simple: love Jesus. It was successful: tens
of thousands were doing it. Asbury made enthusiasm both the
content and the form of religion.

A final reason that the new revivalist theology came into being
is simply that able people set about to create it. The only section
of America where Asbury's movement flagged was New England,
especially Connecticut. There sophisticated teachers were updat-
ing the old doctrines to bolster new revivalism. There common
sense and the revivals' success drove conservative Congregationalists to fashion an "alleviated Calvinism." Edwards' own grandson
and Asbury's contemporary, Timothy Dwight, president of Yale
College, styled himself the arch-foe of infidelity, meaning French
deism imported during and after the Revolution. When he heard

his understudies preaching a softened version of human depravity and divine sovereignty, something sounded vaguely out of tune. But Dwight tested preaching by revivalistic success. Common sense dictated a new theology.

Alleviated Calvinism was the stock in trade of Dwight's favorite disciples, Nathaniel William Taylor, formulator of the New Haven theology, and Lyman Beecher, director of campaigns employing that theology. Nobody states the difference between Edwards and these men more aptly than Sidney Mead: "Edwards," he writes, "preached sincerely and vividly of what he had experienced and apparently was genuinely surprised when the revival began. Dwight deliberately set out to start a revival . . . , and Beecher and Taylor perfected methods of fostering them. To Edwards the revival was a by-product of his shared experience; to the latter men revivals were the calculated means to an end." [19]

Moreover, the ends pursued by these revisers of Calvinism changed even as the revivalistic means remained the same. To save established Congregationalism in Connecticut from infidelity, Dwight had stirred up revivals. His understudies wanted to save this Standing Order from being disestablished; that battle lost, they took on the successive enemies of Episcopalianism, Unitarianism, and finally the orthodox doctrines of God's utter sovereignty and total human depravity — the very creed they had set out to recite. At each step they produced revivals and built voluntary organizations to reform society. Taylor designed a new "New Haven theology" in which "natural depravity" meant that everybody inevitably sinned by his own choice. To deliberate sinners, confronted with the truth of Christianity, fell the duty to change their own hearts and minds. This change did not compel God to redeem the sinner. Rather, they said, God limited Himself by His own merciful promise to do so. [20] In effect, people decided to be saved and were.

In theological policy and in ecclesiastical tactics the New Haven theologians opposed everything Edwards stood for. Yet

they too wanted men and women to achieve a new spiritual
sense of the universe as a welcome abode. They too backed away
from the rigid moral transaction between man and God that
permeated the old Puritanism. What Edwards had done by translation they did by compromise. In the nature of the case their
piety remained more moralistic than his.

Between Timothy Dwight and Lyman Beecher at one end
and their mutual namesake, Dwight Lyman Moody, at the other,
came the Civil War. Between them also came Finney, the master
strategist of new measures for inculcating enthusiasm, the religious carpenter who built the anxious bench and saved the shav-
ings to pave the sawdust trail. Just as Finney adapted revivalism
to the burgeoning town life of America, so Moody would later
conform revivals to life in the new industrial cities. The
techniques used by both these revivalists were minutely planned.
Every sound and every move they made was designed to stir
religious passions. Having instilled in masses of people a personal
sentiment of sin and guilt, at the crucial moment they invited
men and women to choose between Christ and Satan. To such
a voluntary option they reduced the old notion of "election"
by God. But Finney and Moody, like Asbury and Dwight before
them, *believed* in revivalism, and they tested their theology by
its ability to produce conversions and reawakenings. Along with
the hundreds of American preachers who were their imitators,
they purveyed a wholly moralistic spirituality, quite remote from
that of Edwards' new spiritual sense.

Edwards had formed his religiousness within the Puritan
world-view, placing responsibility for sin on men and women
who could not choose *not* to sin. He had ascribed every move
in the making of saints to God, who alone could implant in
each saint the new sense from which sainthood arose. Only three
years before his untimely death Edwards wrote, but did not
live to publish, *The Nature of True Virtue*, showing how the
new piety flowed from the old doctrine. But his own protégés
who systematized his thought clung to a fundamentally moral

relation between sovereign God and depraved mankind. His chief avatars were Samuel Hopkins, Edwards' literary executor, and Joseph Bellamy, an evocative preacher on the model of the master. These Edwardeans wished to defend affectional religion against its fulsome friends, the revivalists. They self-consciously resolved to build a theology of unself-conscious conversion. They predicted that true revival of religion must come unpredictably and unpredicted. They became like the nervous host who vows he will act naturally when his august guest arrives. They published *True Virtue*, reading it not as the translation of old doctrine into new spirituality but rather as the doctrine that any conversion a person yearned and prepared for would yield false religion. They kept God sovereign by the exercise of His disinterested benevolence, stripped of the esthetic connotations Edwards had suffused the notion with. They kept man depraved by the exercise of his self-interest, stripped of the large capactiy for agreeing with the law of God that Edwards ascribed to the natural conscience. They made being in general into the general aggregate of beings, duty to whom God enabled saints to discharge. In a word, the disciples organized Edwards' religious thought into a theological system he had not espoused, by applying a test he would not admit — that of "Consistent Calvinism."[21]

In these several ways (rationalism, enthusiasm, strict and revised Calvinism) Edwards' new spirituality broke on the rock of revivalism, a movement he at first praised and then regarded as a mixed bag. He could not imagine God's Spirit working savingly in a person without touching that person's most appropriate resonators, the religious affections. Just as unimaginable was the notion that a person's own stirring of these affections could coerce God's Spirit into doing its saving work. Thus revivals as such indicated neither the presence nor the absence of God's saving operation. Revivals rather produced "negative signs" — not signs either way that God was or was not working savingly. Sainthood hinged entirely on a person's having a new spiritual sense, received and understood as a special gift of God and demonstrated by the practice of delighting in God and in the universe for God's sake.

Those Americans who asked, What in us does God find worthy of redemption?, and then looked for clear-cut answers in the revivals, inevitably belied both Edwards' theological interest in divine sovereignty and his religious interest in our finding God to be enjoyable. Those Americans who asked, How can we find God lovely?, and then looked for answers by examining our natural endowments, distorted things equally but oppositely. The school laboring under Edwards' name defended the great doctrine by neglecting the spirituality he had made it support. The rationalists, according the new spiritual sense to everybody, generalized sainthood into trying.to improve. Revivalists, preaching sin in order to produce conversions, tested sainthood by moral and sentimental improvements.

What American took seriously the esthetic quality of Edwards' spirituality? What American articulated it pertinently to his own time and enduringly for our own time? The search ranges beyond pious and earnest people to find a thinker who possessed, who could identify, especially who elicited "a sense and taste of the divine, supreme and holy excellency and beauty" of "the things exhibited in the gospel" (*WY*, 2:297).

A genealogy of Edwards' religious thought might be traced through his grandson, Dwight, then to Taylor as Dwight's chief disciple, thence to Horace Bushnell, who studied under Taylor at Yale. This tracing identifies the wrong transmitters and the wrong terminus. Dwight had more in common with Old Calvinists than with his grandfather, whose "school" warned against Dwight's own revivals. Taylor took theological steps that even Dwight disapproved — until he saw them fostering more revivals. And for Bushnell's taste Taylor relied too much on common sense. For Bushnell the rationalists and revivalists and Transcendentalists alike overemphasized reason. Bushnell, as we will see, referred religion entirely to the heart instead of the head.

A more direct genealogy than the one running to Bushnell

went from Edwards to his disciple, Hopkins, under whose ministrations arose "the theologian of the 'Revolutionary generation,' "
in Ahlstrom's phrase, and "a great religious liberator for the
'Romantic generation' that followed" (Ahlstrom, p. 195). That
was William Ellery Channing.

The first and last words of religion for Channing were the
perfectibility of man. Perfectible persons made up communities
they should form and reform according to the highest justice.
To them Christ revealed God's will, exemplifying human perfection and laying down just principles of social reform. Of course
Channing, like the rationalists and the revivalists, broadened
the scope of the will's freedom to include spiritual self-
determination. Yet he admired the intellectual subtlety of
Edwards' arguments for restricting freedom of the will, and (more
important) he studiously adopted and elaborated Edwards' cardinal teaching that God's immediate impartation of a supernatural
light to the soul was at once scriptural and rational.

Channing liked Edwards' concept of virtue, but he preferred
Hopkins' rendering of it as disinterested benevolence. For Channing true virtue consisted in hearty consent to universal being,
understood as the aggregate of all beings. Channing's saint
regarded all things benevolently because God created all things.
For Edwards, God's self-subsistent beauty put the saint at home
in an approving universe. Channing reasserted the moral content
of religion in a new way, emphasizing the God-given benevolence
by which the saint strove to improve the universe to a degree
of goodness that God would approve.

Now Channing saw the apex of spiritual joy to consist in
one mind's enjoyment of the moral excellencies of other minds.
He saw the highest human joy to consist in spiritual appreciation
of the perfect Spirit, the heavenly Father. He saw the cogency
of the argument that only human spirits sharing God's excellence
could somehow share in that excellence. He was agreeing with
Edwards — down to the "somehow." Edwards found no common ground between Creator and creature. Rather our sharing

in divine excellence depended on a special gift by a graceful donor to an unworthy donee. But for Channing we *potentially* share God's excellence because we all possess inherent perfectibility.

Channing's yardstick for remodeling society was divine justice — not a flourishing church, not a ruling elite, not a political ideology. Among his many young followers Theodore Parker chiefly applied this sense of justice to the affairs of a democratized, then a polarized, nation. The learned, eloquent, tenacious, unfulfilled Parker clung to his Unitarian ministry when his scruples about the distinctiveness of Christianity gave him every reason to defect. Parker needed the pulpit. The social reform that meant everything to him required religious sanctions and sacred criteria of justice. In 1860, failing in health, he retrospectively summarized the great causes he had espoused during his ministry: temperance (but not prohibition), distribution of wealth (but not communism), education of the whole person (but not psychologism), greater rights for women (but not feminism), industrial as well as political democracy (but not socialism), high regard for truly great men (but not romantic heroism), the avoidance of cruel and needless wars (but not pacifism), freedom for the African slaves (but not egalitarianism), and finally humane and natural religion as over against ecclesiastical theology.

By including the last cause Parker underscored the relativity to its historical setting of every religion known to him. Had he spent more of his prodigious intellectual energy on relativizing the particular claims of religions he might have shaped the thought of generations to come. Instead, he incarnated in his day his nation's liberal conscience, absolutizing the justice of particular social reforms undertaken by his own generation. In doing so he remained truer to the social ethics than to the religious thought of Channing.

Channing had another heir, for he was also the formative spiritual guide to the young Ralph Waldo Emerson. Thus through Hopkins and Channing did Emerson hold lineal succession from Edwards. However true the heir to the patriarch's spirituality, such a genealogy suggests how we fill the blanks between the appearance of one religious genius and the comparable appearance of a comparable genius.[22] In Edwards the new spiritual sense made the saint "a partaker of God's beauty and Christ's joy" (*WY*, 2:201). A comparable holiness, communicated through nature, making a person "part or parcel of God," was the holiness of Emerson (*W*, 1:10).

4

The Hospitable Universe of Ralph Waldo Emerson

The Man and the Message

Returning in 1833 from his first visit to Europe, Ralph Waldo Emerson wrote, five days out of Liverpool, "I like my book about nature & wish I knew where & how I ought to live. . . . I am glad to be on my way home yet not so glad as others . . ." (*JMN*, 4:237–38).[23] He had suffered the death of his beloved young wife, left the pulpit, earned through European travel the credentials of culture, and aimed himself toward becoming a lecturer and essayist. By liking the book Emerson meant he intuited a philosophy of life worth living and teaching. By wondering where to live he must have meant finding a spot in the neighborhood of Boston. There he had spent all his thirty years. There his forefathers had lived and died. There his friends and kin remained. By asking how he ought to live he meant something more poignant, more problematic. His resignation from the pulpit of Boston's Second Church (Unitarian) pointed him toward an exit from his calling and training, the ministry. If he must test whether he could earn a living by lecturing and writing, still, with controlled fervor, he was glad to be going home.

From the themes of the little book on nature, barely formed as it was in 1833, Emerson over the next decades would draw out and ramify a new American religious consciousness and articulate it across the land from lecture dais and printing press in addresses, essays, and poems. Nature, the metaphor of God and mankind, beckoned men and women to an intimacy ennobling every soul who answered. A retrospective age must alter its angle of vision and attend "new lands, new men, new thoughts" (W, 1:3). Solitude and sociability compensated one another alternately as needs of the spirit. This compensation schooled people in the polarity and correspondence of all their experiences. In nature this correspondence was harmonious. From it man learned a beauty both without and within himself. All the gifts of nature — language, beauty, commodity, discipline — came from God the source and end of all things, from God dwelling within as well as without the soul.

These and a hundred other gems of the religiousness that Emerson developed lie in the first little book, already mined but as yet roughly faceted, unrefined, isolated. During his early European travel he was discovering them in his heightened sense of the American experience. Glad to go home, indeed, he soberly faced a duty to show and tell Americans how to become new persons with new thoughts for a new age in their still new land.

Career

Emerson settled near Concord, seat of his forebears, scene of his youth's happiest months, to which he insisted in 1835 on bringing his second wife, Lydia Jackson. In his refusing to move to Lydia's favorite Plymouth, symbolic of the pilgrim fathers' first landing, there may lurk a parable of the man. His home would overlook fresher monuments on the revolutionary battle-ground between Concord Bridge and Lexington, would remind him of newer American hopes, would be nearer fields and woods and ponds, would give more ready escape into untamed nature. In America's out-of-doors and America's dream Emerson's spirit beheld a beautiful universe. His expanding land at Concord allowed him to plant and harvest, to raise chickens and hogs,

to do what his fellow Americans were doing as they discovered
the identity he yearned to understand and to help form by his
message.

Farming, however pleasant when not one's livelihood, became
a formality, almost a ritual, for this member and soon-to-be
leader of New England's intelligentsia, who inherited money (not
a lot) from the Yankee merchant-families that gave him two
wives. He also inherited piety (not a lot) from a long line of
Puritan and Unitarian preachers named Emerson. By birth and
tendency he was an elitist who noted with unconcealed disdain
the populism attained and symbolized by Jacksonian democracy.
Though he never descended from his intellectual loft to the world
of politics he did retract some of his antipopulism as he came
more and more to share aspirations with the mass of Americans.
Intellectually too he was snobbish, cultivating a select company
of Transcendentalists (he once called the movement "Realist")
and fellow travelers, and hardly minding, after the famous Divinity School Address, the snubs of Harvard folk (*JMN*, 5:504).
For Harvard's veneration he could wait until he had become
venerable.

At the Boston Latin School and then at Harvard College and
Divinity School Emerson had furnished an able mind, earned
decent marks easily, and indulged a nomadic intellectual
curiosity. The sickly adolescent became the healthy man and
donned the pulpit gown of his ancestors, winning instant success
as a parish minister. In his mid-twenties he held the pulpit
that had belonged to Increase and Cotton Mather, served as chaplain to the Massachusetts Senate, sat on the Boston School Com-
mittee, and married delicate, frail Ellen Tucker. At thirty,
already a widower, he resigned his pulpit and traveled in Europe
to become a popular philosopher. At thirty-five he had gained
a second wife and a first son, published *Nature* as a manifesto
of American spirituality, declared intellectual and artistic
independence from Europe on behalf of America's scholars, and
was about to challenge the whole tradition of institutional reli-

gion in the name of a new, self-critical religiousness. By the time
Emerson was fifty, English and Scottish as well as American
audiences were gathering to hear the spirit of America incarnate.

The free spirituality of this free man, who knew calamity
but refused to let it epitomize man's lot, took shape between
the early 1820s and the early 1850s, while Americans were
occupying and consolidating the Indians' space across the conti-
nent's temperate zone. They were also choosing the collision
course of slavery in the South, antislavery in the North. Emerson
almost became a social activist on behalf of Indian rights and
black freedom, but his forte was envisioning freedom, not
institutionalizing it. At the age of sixteen he had begun keeping
journals and notebooks, for five years headed "The Wide World"
or "Wide World" or "Wideworld," so early announcing his
teaching in a slogan he was unsure how to phrase. From this
beginning until the end of the old man, hazy in eyesight and
faltering in memory, he took "the universal question of modern
times," as a late lecture put it, to be "the question of Religion"
(W, 12:88).

Emerson was a visual man, always approaching truth through
sight rather than hearing or touching. Could he but help his
people see their wide world in all its literal width and spiritual
breadth, and could he but help them see their souls and the
divine Soul as twin images in the metaphoric mirror of nature,
they would come to possess and exhibit a humanity enlarged
enough to fill the vast reaches to their horizons — from ocean
to ocean, from earth to heaven, from individual person to mankind. Properly invited, they would see the world as friendly,
accepting it and themselves in a peculiar blend of personal,
moral, and religious insights.

He wanted to impart rather than to systematize his vision
of American religiousness. From the outset, in a sense, he made
the medium the message. He meditated, thought, wrote, and
spoke by way of asking others to meditate, think, speak, and

live anew for themselves. The object of his effort and theirs, he took it, was to set people at peace with nature — both physical nature itself and the nature of the universe. He invited his audiences to try on for size the experience of overcoming estrangement between themselves and their world. So he read eclectically, thought imaginatively, articulated himself originally and almost telegraphically. When he found words of spiritual insight and wisdom, whatever their source, he stored them in his notebooks. Drawing on these savings-banks (his phrase) he fashioned addresses lasting about an hour each, around literary, moral, and religious themes: sometimes a motif such as character, again a hero like Michelangelo, then a doctrine like the Over-Soul, once more a topic like English manners. His chiseled paragraphs and sentences, loosely touching one another in content, invited a certain experience more than they declaimed a doctrine or pressed a cause or laid bare a system. He rarely spoke extemporaneously. From the first lecture-course for Boston subscribers (not to mention the early sermons) to the old man's lionized but disconnected recitations, Emerson wrote to speak and spoke what he wrote.

"Lyceums," he noted late in 1835, "— so that people will let you say what *you* think — are as good a pulpit as any other" (*JMN*, 5:109). If preaching means exhorting and evoking religious experiences, he always preached. But the office of preacher had made such preaching impossible. "I have sometimes thought," he wrote in 1832, "that in order to be a good minister it was necessary to leave the ministry. The profession is antiquated. . . . Were not a Socratic paganism better than an effete superannuated Christianity?" (*JMN*, 4:27). He left the pulpit to preach a new religiousness from a new platform to what he thought was a new age of new men.

Combine Emerson's evocative intent with his desire to be heard rather than read, add his impatience with consistency and the miscellaneousness of some sixty volumes of his books and manuscripts, and it becomes bold to summarize his religious message in an essay, except for his remarkable single-mindedness. Emerson lived and taught a singularly coherent religiousness.

Sensibility

Emerson's own sensibility seems more esthetic than religious in any traditional sense. Nevertheless religion or religiousness is an effective theme by which to organize and interpret his message. He thought his generation faced a fork in the road of American spirituality. He urged the path that led to a new quality of spiritual consciousness on which every person could fearlessly work out his own salvation. Indeed, each person would become his own manifestation of God, if only he were inspired to be at home with nature, at one with his fellow man, and in tune with deity. Emerson espoused a theory of religion concerning just such a spirituality, not one that classified or graded various kinds of formal religion. Forms and institutions were the showy part. Inward convictions really made the difference. He liked the phrase, "God is in us, and when he stirs we become warm."[24] That indwelling deity, Emerson believed, transcended the gods of Stoic and Christian and other religions precisely because man was more profoundly identical with deity than these traditions had preached. To this identity persons must aspire if, in their best moments, they would attain it — would, in a chance Emersonism, "realize theology."[25] Seized of this new religiousness, man would find the universe wonderfully hospitable.

The universal soul that made Emerson and all people its fellows made them therefore fellows one to another. On account of this Over-Soul, as he called the force during his Transcendentalist period, every good deed contained its own reward and every evil act brought down its appropriate penalty. Compensation solved the problem of evil. The great soul present in human experience was always evening things out. The universe, thus

justified, became a universe one could rely upon. Because in
the nature of things one belonged to this reliable universe, one
was really relying upon the self by being at home in the world.

On either side of Emerson's religious innovation lay a trap
he avoided. On one side was blind optimism. However hopeful
Emerson's personal grasp on life may seem, he knew that men
and women going about their chores — reading the newspaper
and going to the bathroom, as a later poet put it — did not
always act out the noble divinity that was in them. However
insistent he was that God made Himself present to human life,
he knew people could not actualize that presence on every dreary
or sordid occasion. In Emerson's vision God retained, as it were,
self-respectful remoteness, and the world remained pocked and
bumpy.

The other trap Emerson avoided was that of pantheism, of
equating God with the universe or mankind. The universal soul,
he emphasized, "is not mine, or thine, or his, but we are its;
we are its property and men" (W, 1:27). In all kinds of circumstances, Emerson preached, man and God could meet. But he
masterminded no merger, built no way-station between heaven
and earth where God was a big person, people little gods, and
the two identical twins. To explore the boundary between them
as they did business with one another was the dare Emerson
laid down in the familiar lines, "Draw, if thou canst, the mystic
line/ Severing rightly his from thine,/ Which is human, which
divine" (W, 9:280). His religious thought is nothing but the
way he worked out this dare through his self-cultivated power
of observing life and his evocative means of thinking and talking
about it.

An astute critic writes of Emerson's way of living and thinking
and writing, "In nonsymbolic experience, organic experience,
life comes first and thought second. But in the realm of
imagination, 'life' turns out to be the creation of thought working through language" (Bishop, p. 64). This distinction of
approach or emphasis, taken just that way and not as a settled

epistemology, clarifies everything Emerson had to say about religion. Being religious could mean to have organic experience, to live first and think later. Again, being religious could mean to have imaginative experience, to evoke life by means of thought. Yet again, being religious could mean to blend or unify the two modes into one overarching kind of experience. Religious institutions, however, signified to Emerson neither organic nor imaginative experience; institutions were but derivative, secondary, artificial forms and beliefs that people produced in a futile effort to cast the organic and the imaginative aspects of religious experience into static molds. Of course, he believed that religious traditions and institutions could be reformed when the religious sentiment flashed blindingly, as in the life of a Jesus or a Gautama, a Confucius or a Martin Luther. Then the poetry of these men redefined and even redirected life. Although nobody can standardize Emerson's terminology without handing him over to his own proverbial hobgoblins of foolish consistency, he often referred the *moral sentiment* to organic experience and the *religious sentiment* to imaginative experience.

When Emerson discussed the three substantive doctrines of his new-found religiousness — Over-Soul, compensation, and self-reliance — he alternated between describing (organic truth) and evoking (imaginative truth), between reporting and eliciting the truth of these themes. But the imaginative task — to arouse the reader or hearer to experience truth personally — challenged Emerson as the higher and the harder of the two. For the religious force of truth reached beyond the realm of cognitive understanding in which one usefully distinguished the two modes of experience. When a perception of nature grew bright with divinity, or when the principle of compensation presented the correspondences of life as arcs about to form a full circle, or when an act of self-reliance joined a man to the deity — these rare moments effected something that our taking thought would never prepare us to expect. In such moments (said the same

critic) of "*first* discovery or illumination . . . the mind actively
experiences a double perception of reality and of the system by
which it is known" (Bishop, p. 56). In such moments, for
example, nature glowed with divine meaning even while knowledge of nature was being gained. Then intuition and intellect
formed one act. Then being and knowing were not two motions
but one. Then, by an incursion from beyond, experiencing subject and experienced object interpenetrated one another as the
content of experience.

Emerson thought of religiousness as being receptive to an
experience in the full range of its meaning. Religiousness combined spontaneity of origin with simultaneity of subject and
object (or intuition with intellect). In religious experience one
sensed that one was receiving a given universe whose hospitality
was everywhere self-evident and thereby one was realizing truest
selfhood. Such, for example, was the wonder with which Emerson
recorded on October 31, 1836, the birth of his first son, Waldo:
the infant "makes the Universe look friendly to me" (*JMN*,
5:234). In these moments "We are advertised that there is
nothing to which man is not related; that everything is convert-
ible into every other" (*W*, 8:23).

Institutional as against this personal religion required "religion
for its expositor"; Emerson proposed that a new kind of spirituality would improve on all institutional religion by looking more
to the poet than to the prophet or apostle, who "can only be
rightly understood by prophet or apostle"(*W*, 5:225). The poet
of Emerson's longing would reveal the meaning of existence as
powerful correspondences among nature, man, and God. Where
the theologian or systematic philosopher had to insist on one
symbol as capable of teaching everybody a single truth, the poet
of this new spirituality could personify nature even while he
naturalized or objectified the soul. The poet's imagination thus
created a kind of universe capable of arousing and rearranging
the religious sentiment of men and women. Its every object was
the deed of a will, and in it every human deed was no less

the expression of human will than nature expressed the Over-Soul. Emerson's ideal poet thus could do for religious man what Edwards reserved to the saving act of God's Spirit: present the universe as lovely, and enable a person to love the universe for its own beauty.

Of course Emerson looked in vain for the poet he dreamed of. He could only try to offer himself as such a wordsmith — even worldsmith — for America. How far he succeeded may be debated. Nobody can question that he proposed and described a new American religiousness. And he stated his message not nationalistically but universally, discussing the history of religious institutions, religious reforms, a new religiousness, the moral sentiment, the religious sentiment, and a threefold content of religious living.

Whatever topic Emerson addressed, he did so as a man who saw in the world a vision of beauty. In that sense he was a seer, an esthete, not a systematizer. As such, he sought to be comprehensive, not partial, reckoning every person's relation with humankind and deity as well as with nature. But for Emerson nature always issued the invitation for man to be at home in the universe; tucked into the same envelope came welcomes from God and from human society.

Two features of Emerson's religious vision make his thought tricky to convey.

First, he trusted intuition, activated by inspiration, as a source of knowledge and truth. Thought, he believed, derived from many individual beholdings of truth and not from steadily communicating with a revealer who was Himself something of a systematic theologian. Therefore Emerson's thought is diffuse and occasional, not architectonic, not finally cohesive. He wrote apothegms and sentences, sometimes paragraphs, rarely treatises or dissertations. The pieces can be fit together into something comprehensible, especially if the theme and experience of religiousness is employed as connective tissue, but the overall cogency awaits nowhere in an Emersonian summa.

Second, and rather paradoxically, Emerson believed truth, like beauty, was harmonious and reciprocal. "In learning one thing you learn all," he taught (*W*, 12:442). Since an infinite universe presented itself to him in each of its particles, nothing mattered except the whole even though one approached it piecemeal. So each notion he expressed became an arc that could be joined with all the other arcs of his thought into a circle. This image of the circle, a favorite with Emerson, is useful if we avoid making religion or the soul or fate or anything else the circle's *center*. For his whole point about truth was that our thought cannot find the center but life can build accurate, symmetrical arcs of our experience. The theme of religiousness runs through all Emerson's intellectual arcs (to be sure, less apparently in some cases than in others); the religious theme traces and closes the circle.

Emerson left us a vision of religion or spirituality, not a full philosophy of religion, not a developed theology. Literally he *theorized* — beheld, saw, visualized — religiousness in three ways. (1) He had a *diagnostic* theory of the formalism of institutional religion, of religious reforms, of critical religious consciousness. (2) He had an *analytic* theory of the moral sentiment and the religious sentiment. (3) And he had a *constructive* theory of true religious experience as at once universal, profitable, and exalting.

Religion and Religiousness

Preoccupied as he was with the infinite, Emerson cared little for definitions. Yet more than once he called religion something like "the emotion of reverence which the conscious presence and activity of the Universal Mind inspires" (*EL*, 2:181). An earlier and a later version of the same phrase said more simply that "the presence of the universal mind always" (or "ever") "excites" this emotion "in the individual" (*EL*, 2:84; *W*, 10:198). A person's character, holiness, and obedience to universal laws arose from the emotion of reverence, even though the person became conscious of the religious impulse only occasionally. Conscious or unconscious, however, reverence heightened personal individuality by joining one into the universal soul that indwelt all persons. Moreover, in all persons and societies the impulse became conscious on certain occasions that they then wanted to cherish, formalize, and repeat as religious routines or rituals.

Institutions

Formal religion, itself inevitable, also inevitably distorted the impulses of reverence it meant to express and elicit. To *express* the human sense of reverence, societies evolved religious forms. But when a society came to rely on such a form to *generate* reverence, the emotion was grossly distorted and people were estranged from the universal mind they aspired to serve. These forms replaced the love of God with fear of God. When that happened, religious impulses could renew themselves only as disbelief or moral protest against formal religion.

Expressions of the religious impulse pointing to universal human nature and universal laws of life had been "announced at different times and through many media"; taken together, these expressions constituted religious revelation. "The effort to embody these truths and laws in some outward form, for the sake of preserving to the seer himself the remembrance of his vision, and of provoking all men to efforts after this beatitude, makes the *Church*." Both the revelation and the church depended on the presence of their originating spirit to validate them, for even "The truest state of thought rested in, becomes false" (*EL*, 2:92, 93).

The grand rhetoric by which Emerson attacked religious forms in the famous Divinity School Address distracts attention from the true force of his argument. When he had talked informally with ministerial students at Harvard about giving this commencement address, he was reluctant because "I always find that my views chill or shock people at the first opening" (*JMN*,

5:471). The views themselves had been ripening for years. As
early as 1824 Emerson the theological student had regarded
creeds "as fine spun textures through which rebellious doubt
is impatient, sometimes desperate, to plunge" (*JMN*, 2:244).
And not only religion's formal*isms* but the very forms themselves
caused the trouble. Jesus Christ would be "better loved by not
being adored" (*YES*, p. 195). That idea had gathered momentum
between notebook and sermon, for the earlier entry had it "by
being less adored" (*JMN*, 4:92). The teaching by Jesus of the
principle "that God incarnates himself in man" fortified and
made demands on those who heard it, while adoration of Christ
"shows God out of me, makes me a wart and a wen" (*W*, 1:128,
132). The preachers who ascribed to Jesus a unique divinity
both denigrated his human work and profaned mankind by taking away its rightful divinity. Most living persons, fortunately,
ignored this false deity being hailed from pulpits. But unfor-
tunately the preachers continued to represent Him as the living
God and thereby led people to think they were atheists when
actually, in the spirit of true religiousness, they were only rejecting a false husk.

The theologues in Divinity Hall who heard the 1838 address,
professors and graduates alike, were Unitarians trained to ridicule
Calvinism for the emptiness of its forms. This commencement
speaker adopted their habit of criticism, then turned it against
present as well as past forms, against Unitarians as well as Calvinists. He fervently believed that every religious error had begun
as spiritual truth and had soured in the process of exaggeration.
The Unitarians were exaggerating their distinctive insights quite
as much as the Calvinists had done. Nor would the speaker
let his hearers off the hook by proposing new Unitarian forms
to replace old ones. Rather they must "let the breath of new
life be breathed by you through the forms already existing";
when (and only when) religious persons vibrated with true religious emotion would these or any other forms become "plastic
and new" (*W*, 1:150).

Even these revitalized forms, full of new life, would wrench the religious impulse out of its connection with truth: "The very fact of worship declares that God is not at one with himself, that there are two gods" — a message that sounded "like high treason" but that in fact only "threatens our forms but does not touch injuriously Religion" (*JMN*, 4:313). If the Divinity School Address stung the audience, the real point of Emerson's developing religiousness would have drawn their blue blood: "As men's prayers are a disease of the will, so are their creeds a disease of the intellect" (*W*, 2:79).

Should people therefore avoid worship, stop praying, reject all belief? If to many the young Emerson whispered a guarded "No" on this question, he countered with an audible "Yes" to a few. For the sake of morality religious forms were both inevitable and necessary; for the sake of the profoundest religiousness all traditional forms, being dead, should be buried. Emerson would not sound their death-rattle in Divinity Hall, out of respect for persons (like his Aunt Mary Moody Emerson) whom the forms still habitually inspired. But he was already honing a sharper attack.

It was one thing to goad the church by pleading the need for vital faith among its tombs. It was quite another for Emerson to sense himself to be living in a moment of radical shift in the nature of man's capacity to be religious. For both purposes he explored the nature of reform in the history of Christianity and other religions. For the second purpose he meditated on a reform that might *un*form all religion and replace it with a new kind of spirituality. The emotion of reverence always required some formal expression. But a new age was dawning, in which the entire inheritance of specifically religious expressions, however reformed and revitalized, would fail to evoke real reverence. In that age persons must look elsewhere than to religion for ways to awaken and articulate their religious sentiment.

Acknowledging that reshaped religious institutions would be adequate to express conventional religious impulses, Emerson designed his own life's work so as neither to attack nor to reform these institutions. To be sure, he disliked the controversy that the Divinity School Address aroused. But his determination to found a new spirituality instead of refashioning the old religion sprang more from his venturesomeness than from his aversion to conflict. His first meeting with Thomas Carlyle had impressed on him the difference between the Scotsman's grudging "the poor peasant his Calvinism" and Emerson's own believing "in the wholesomeness of Calvinism for thousands & thousands." He saw no profit to him or to others in his winning them away from "their scrupulous religious observances. I dare not speak lightly of usages which I omit" (*JMN*, 4:80–81). Even in 1833, freshly resigned from the Boston pulpit, Emerson was resolving to explore a new religious consciousness. But to understand how the religious sentiment created reforms he needed to know the work of previous reformers.

Reformers

For examples of religious reform Emerson searched the history of Christianity and stretched himself to learn something of Islam, Buddhism, Hinduism, Confucianism, neo-Platonism, and the mythologies of ancient Greece and Egypt. As a teen-ager he called his first publication "Thoughts on the Religion of the Middle Ages," signing pseudonymously as "H.O.N." — the last letters of his three names. "He often spoke of a wish to write the story of Calvinism in New England," reported his son.[26] Biographical studies of religious heroes garnered more than incidental knowledge of reformers like Luther, George Fox, John Milton, Jacob Boehme, Augustine of Hippo, and Emanuel Swedenborg. Personal associations gave him insight into the spirits of Samuel Taylor Coleridge, William Ellery Channing, Theodore Parker, Carlyle, and the leading Transcendentalists.

In the life and work of Fox he found the religious impulse

to have overwhelmed all others, earning Fox a place alongside religious geniuses like Zoroaster, Confucius, Orpheus, Mahomet, Numa Pompilius (revered by the Romans as the founder of their religion), Manco Capac (the legendary first Inca of Peru), Moses, and Jesus. All these persons had used the religious sentiment to realize their intimate unity with "the Cause of all beings" and to regard all people as their brothers (*EL*, 1:166, 167). The religious sentiment had liberated their minds and made them determined reformers.

In Fox the reforming force became in part a power to elicit reverence and its effects in plain people, without resort to dogmas or cultic practices as his transmitting — and distorting — vehicles. To be sure, the Quakers, like all religious people, had in time channeled this spontaneous impulse into certain external practices. But to Fox and his immediate disciples the inner light ripened the real fruits of religion — renunciation of self, peaceful and nonviolent relations with all persons, reform of institutions, religious liberty and toleration. Life centered on "the conviction that his [each human's] soul is a temple in which the Divine Being resides — that astounding paradox which is always lurking in the heart of every church and is at intervals announced anew with more or less clearness and fulness but whose limitations have never yet been written down in any book. . . . He who deals truly with himself and[,] renouncing all wilfulness, acts after his clearest sight, can never repent his action, and has the assurance of the author of his constitution that it is for him the best action" (*EL*, 1:181). In a word, the religious impulse to rely on God produced self-reliance and a sense of good and evil as compensating one another in all experience.

In another early lecture Emerson developed the themes of self-reliance and the religious impulse by attributing these virtues peculiarly to Luther. Emerson's second-hand knowledge of Luther's religiousness was at least unclouded by personal sympathy for the reformer! Luther "adhered to the lowest form of the popular theology, — I had almost said, — mythology," according to Emerson (*EL*, 1:134). Luther constantly sensed his own soul to be the prize in a contest between God and the Devil. It was Luther the poet, for whom there was "no crack, no schism between the man's act and his conviction," who commanded admiration (*EL*, 1:142). His deeds rather than his letters were his poem. On this reading, Emerson wrote of Luther, "No man in history ever assumed a more commanding attitude or expressed a more perfect self-reliance." Emerson explained this view of Luther, who was self-reliant precisely because he "deemed himself the conspicuous object of hatred to Satan and his kingdom, and to be sustained against their malice by special interpositions of God. This is the secret of his indomitable will" (*EL*, 1:136).

The religious sentiment put such a person at close quarters with God, assured him that his daemon or creative genius was guiding him, endowed his actions with determination and courage, made him self-reliant and therefore reliable. For their reforming religiousness, Emerson, the self-appointed modern Plutarch, canonized preachers as well as poets, obeying the dictum of his friend George Ripley: "Let the study of theology commence with the study of human consciousness."[27] Emerson's new "divinity" began with humanity.

Every human society known to Emerson had organized its spiritual energy in creeds, in liturgies, "in temples, in pictures, in sculpture, in hymns"; by attempting to transmit reverence through these forms, societies more and more objectified the goal of reverence "until finally flat idolatry appears" (*EL*, 2:96).[28] The great ages of belief invented forms that then ossified until true religious devotion could only protest against the regnant devoutness. In Christian nations these periods of faith arose and fell with increasing rapidity, evoking ever newer reforms that appeared to be unfaith: "the Protestants reformed the Catholic Church; the Presbyterians, the Protestant; the Independents, the Presbyterian; the Quakers, the Independent" — then Methodists and Swedenborgians and Unitarians took their turns (*EL*, 1:174;

2:94). An even more sweeping genealogy of reform reached back
to Stoic philosophy as protesting against Roman government
and to early Christianity as unmasking superstition, then came
forward similarly through Protestants, Puritans, Quakers,
Unitarians, down to the Transcendentalists' protest against
Unitarian idolatry (W, 1:339). But Emerson believed this last
protest, his own, differed in degree and in kind from preceding
ones.

Spiritual inspiration lifted the leaders of all these reforms to
human greatness: "The religions of the world are the ejaculations
of a few imaginative men" (W, 3:34). Again, "All church reforms
must begin by putting an emphasis on sentiment" (UL, p. 45).
At the same time, however, each religious movement had sprung
from an inward core or genius that the reformer recaptured and
reemphasized. Each religious reform produced its distinctive
institutions. The chief cumulative benefits of Christianity, for
example, were the Sabbath and preaching. In the custody of
earnestly spiritual reformers, preaching and the Sabbath had
repeatedly revitalized Christianity; to the extent that this religion
remained reformable in Emerson's own day, these true expressions of its genius needed fresh embodiment. The Sabbath invited
regular repose and spiritual stocktaking. Preaching lifted reason
out of the trite realm of understanding and, at best, confronted
the spirit with the imagination of the poet, changing organic
experience into imaginative experience. What held for Christianity in particular applied also to other religions in principle.
Indeed, over the years Emerson increasingly discerned a common
core among all religions, saw an abiding faith as "a central doctrine which Judaism, Stoicism, Mahometism, Buddhism, Christianity, all teach."[29] And "the charm of the study is in finding
the agreements and identities in all the religions of men" (W,
10:226–27; 11:490).

This study taught Emerson that "The progress of religion is
steadily to its identity with morals" (W, 10:208). Even so, he
clung lifelong to the conviction, arrived at in 1827 when he

was in South Carolina recuperating from pulmonary disease, that the morality of man was constant and only the science of morality showed progress. The cumulative development of insight into good and evil was pointing his age to the doctrine of compensation. "Instead of denouncing a future contingent vengeance I see that vengeance to be contemporary with the crime," he concluded (*JMN*, 3:62). Add that doing the good is its own reward, and Emerson will have brought the science of morality close to the essence of religion. In that sense religion and morality were trending toward an identity, but neither would displace the other.

The reformers' sense of morality, justice, and proportion gave religious reformations a comic rather than a tragic character. Emerson looked on comedy as "a non-performance of what is pretended to be performed, at the same time that one is giving loud pledges of performance"; because "the religious sentiment is the most vital and sublime of all our sentiments, and capable of the most prodigious effects," its false performances had drifted hilariously far from its pledges, and "the oldest gibe of literature is the ridicule of false religion" (*W*, 8:157, 164). When religion yields to superstition, science to pedantry, wisdom to sophistry, truth to mendacity, lest the falsification cover us with grief, we laugh. In Emerson's own day such substitution of falsehood for truth in religion came in the garb of appeals to ecclesiastical or scriptural authority. One always falsified truth by finding an authority for it. The truth is true because it is self-evident. The disproportion was funny.

Every grand conception of religion stood proportionate to its own age, and a neat symmetry between belief and other modes of dealing with the world signaled what Emerson called ages of belief. So "Calvinism suited Ptolemaism" because when heaven was up and earth was down it took a mediator to put them in touch, but "The irresistible effect of Copernican Astronomy has been to make the great scheme for the salvation of man absolutely incredible" (*JMN*, 4:26).

Religiousness

As an eighteen-year-old Harvard senior, Emerson confided to his "College Theme Book" that things now stood differently between God and mankind. The ancients believed that the person who met deity face-to-face would die; for this reason their angels and devils wore disguises. But the moderns had "formed a philosophic, a godlike serenity," banishing their fear of spirits and emboldening them "to meet the Deity" daringly (*JMN*, 1:191). If not a boy's daydreams, then the proposal of a radical mode of being religious! Developed over the years into a full-blown conception of deity welcoming us into his presence and of our returning the hospitality, the thought is surely more than a musing.

Aging humbled Emerson's confidence in this radical spiritual stance and disturbed his earlier serenity, yet the conviction of youth endured: men and women occupied the full dimension of their humanity only when their inspirations dismissed all interlocutors between themselves and the universal soul. To all persons came moments — "sometimes a religious impulse, sometimes an intellectual insight" — of immediate inspiration, lifting them to a preternatural awareness that they belonged to and with all aspects of their experience (*W*, 8:272). Then their deeds rose beyond normal intensity to heroism, even beyond heroism to holiness. Then spiritual power inhered so profoundly "We might say of these memorable moments that we were in them, not they in us" (*W*, 8:279). Then we sensed that even time embraced us in welcoming arms.

These times could be relied upon to come, although moderate persons, knowing that constant inspiration would burn out the soul, sought them as punctuations in the syntax of living. Concentrating one's attention, being alone with nature, reading poetry undulled by prior familiarity with its words, working in a place just suited to one's genius, writing letters to friends — such acts and many more occasioned inspiration. But by

no sluice gate could it be controlled. Thus the aging Emerson
on "Inspiration" (W, 8:279–97). The fire of youth, banked, to
be sure, still smoldered.

The American who, inflamed by a sense of novel religiousness,
developed a new religious sense — now resigned from pulpit,
sure of his power as lecturer and writer, inspirer of the Transcendentalists, in full possession of physical and intellectual powers
— was the Emerson of the period from the early 1830s to
the late 1840s. Then a certain critical mode of consciousness
made his whole being "a transparent eyeball" perceiving the
entire spheroid universe and belonging to it (W, 1:10). To be
hailed as a long-lost friend by nature, mankind, and God
required a spirituality that conventional religionists liked to call
unbelief. But to take Emerson as pleading for naturalism against
supernaturalism, or even as wanting to renaturalize "a spiritual
outlook which was denatured" is to distort him.[30] Emerson
wanted just as much to respiritualize a natural outlook that had
been despirited. His new religiousness stood face-to-face with
nature and God simultaneously, without flinching or turning
aside, seeing God through the pictures of nature by seeing nature
with the eyes of God, a feat that became possible only to persons
who were aware of their unity with all humanity.

This religiousness at once utilized and transcended intellectual
understanding. In Emerson's sense of the term, to understand
how people went about understanding things involved nothing
more than externalizing the steps by which we externalize our
sensations. He did not so much belittle this epistemological
enterprise as he found it belittling him. Thinkers had played
this game since Plato and Aristotle. But to become aware of
the way we are aware of ourselves and of the world around us
involved our developing a critical self-consciousness (and in the
realm of action a critical conscience). In such awareness, to aspire
for unity with God meant to realize the presence of God within
us. To Emerson the time was ripe for Americans to make such
a leap forward, a leap that would leave behind all traditional

modes of being religious and therefore give the appearance of superstition or irreligion.

Emerson borrowed his vocabulary of self-consciousness from Coleridge and Victor Cousin and Carlyle — and through them from Friedrich Wilhelm Joseph von Schelling. It was straightforwardly romantic.[31] One characteristic Emersonism states it simply: "the raw material of knowledge . . . was sensation; when memory came, it was experience; when mind acted, it was knowledge; when mind acted on it as knowledge, it was thought" (W, 8:24). This view finessed the problem of whether objects existed independently of their beholders. The objective world presented itself in appearances; the observer could deal with it superficially as *seeming* to be or take it seriously as *being.* To do the latter it was enough to know that God made the human mind "the receiver of a certain number of congruent sensations" (W, 1:47). The senses instinctively took nature as simply being and took themselves as being simply in touch with nature. The understanding perceived this relation as merely apparent, but the reason reestablished the reality of each party to the relation (and the relation itself). In the second step reason "tends to relax this despotism of the senses . . . and shows us nature aloof, and, as it were, afloat" (W, 1:49). Reason saw nature as an emblem of the soul and as a metaphor of deity; nature and the soul became real and really participated in one another. Because the understanding took the world to be merely apparent, Emerson called it the "downlooking brother" of the reason (JMN, 4:365). But the nobler "brother" was rushing forward in the modern American consciousness and ennobling everything that persons would allow him to touch.

The critical self-consciousness aroused by this reason set a person into a new relation with mankind, nature, and God; all three became hospitable. The romantic in Emerson led him to emphasize the new relation with nature. Reason presents nature as real; at the same time, nature is the metaphor or the language or the emblem both of the human soul and of the universal soul. In nature as both symbolic and real the human soul meets the universal soul, becoming conscious that they are one soul. In nature this consciousness discovers the divine, the touching of which makes a person "in some degree, himself divine." Then "We become immortal, for we learn that time and space are relations of matter; that with a perception of truth or a virtuous will they have no affinity" (*W*, 1:57). As another early (1837) statement of the new religious self-consciousness puts it, "the moment we look at ourselves in the light of thought, we discover that our life is embosomed in beauty. . . . Not only things familiar and stale, but even the tragic and terrible are comely, as they take their place in the pictures of memory. Even the corpse that has lain in the chambers has added a solemn ornament to the house" (*EL*, 2:144).[32] Softened somewhat over the years, the main outlines of the doctrine might be drawn as well from lectures given late in Emerson's life.

Early or late, this new religiousness enabled Emerson to become "the vehicle of that divine principle that lurks within," allowed him to accept life as *being* instead of holding life at the arm's length of merely *seeming* to be; it prompted him "to make the exchange evermore of a reality for a name," helped him to realize "that beyond the energy of his [the person's] possessed and conscious intellect he is capable of a new energy (as of an intellect doubled on itself), by abandonment to the nature of things" (*JMN*, 4:28; 5:504; *W*, 3:26). What Emerson called the "dramatic or allegorical style" by which Christianity had sought salvation through a transaction between the soul and God with Jesus as the saving mediator, gave way to an experience of "The soul of God . . . poured into the world through the thoughts [i.e. the awareness] of men" (*JMN*, 4:91; *W*, 10:88).

To drive home this distinction, Emerson remarked how Jesus' message to his own age began, "I"; were Jesus to return and address this new religious consciousness "he would say — You, YOU!" (*JMN*, 5:362). The change of personal pronouns radically transformed "historical Christianity." The preaching of a God who *was* instead of a God who *is* meant the preaching of God *seeming* instead of God *being*. The new religiousness of Emerson carried him beyond urging the present tense on preachers. It added an immediate apprehension of the presence of Him of whom Emerson spoke in the passive voice. "As children in their play run behind each other, and seize one by the ears and make him walk before them, so is the spirit our unseen pilot" — close behind, in real touch, guiding (*W*, 1:209). For the new sense consisted of a momentary coinherence of the Over-Soul in the experience of life harmonized by compensations and therefore evoking self-reliance.

If this consciousness liberated the human spirit, it also blew the umbrella of traditional religion into a convex parody of itself. In certain moods Emerson left it right there: if the new stance was religious, then the old belief was irreligion. In other frames of mind he thought the new religiousness fulfilled the very Christianity, even back to the founder's intent, that prepared its way. Either way, as Martin Marty puts it, the preachers' "belief was his unbelief; their revised ethic was to his mind the final immorality."[33] Explicitly from Emerson himself, "The Belief in Christianity that now prevails is the Unbelief of men. They will have Christ for a lord & not for a brother. Christ preaches the greatness of Man but we hear only the greatness of Christ" (*JMN*, 5:459). That stark assertion dates from 1838, less than a year before Emerson left off preaching and, then rather more dramatically than in 1850 when he took his name off the Concord Unitarian lists, broke from the church. In the history of religion today's faith must become tomorrow's dogma, renewable by a new faith that appears as unfaith. But to Emerson this succession no longer prevailed after the critical religious consciousness asserted itself — or would not prevail unless people foolishly took a predecessor's new religious act as pattern or surrogate for doing it themselves.

The problem of terminology — what is religion, what is irreligion — will not come clean, not because Emerson cul-

tivated inconsistency but because he switched back and forth
between the old language of grace or salvation and a new language of humanistic spirituality (Bishop, p. 235 n. 5). In a
typical early statement, "When we have broken our god of tradition and ceased from our god of rhetoric, then may God fire
the heart with his presence" (W, 2:292). The old Emerson
retracted by qualification, arguing that the trivializing understanding bloated the church's errors into an erroneous church
or hated veneration because it found a single case of idolatry:
"We laugh and hiss, pleased with our power in making heaven
and earth a howling wilderness" (W, 10:221). But the young
Emerson in 1832 had Christianity aiming all along "to form
in a man a critical conscience" leading into the new religiousness
(JMN, 4:40). Emerson, speaking freshly of his own spiritual
discovery, had the religious sentiment overflowing and washing
downstream the ecclesiastical vessel, needing unrestrained modes
of expression and requiring all literature for its rhetoric. Then
"the Religion of this Day . . . repudiates the unnecessary traditions & says What have I to do with them, Give me truth.
The unbelief of the day proceeds out of the deepest Belief" (JMN,
5:203). (The ambiguous "unnecessary" seems to describe all,
not to specify some, religious traditions.) Whatever the relation
of the new spirit to the old, Emerson cherished its novelty from
his first bold discovery down to the last wistful comment on
its partial realization: "I see movement, I hear aspirations, but
I see not how the great God prepares to satisfy the heart in
the new order of things" (W, 10:218).

Granted, Emerson's "doctrine of divine immanence" opened
"a new era in the history of religious thinking in this country";
closer to the mark, he will not permit "The inactivity of permanence . . . . He will not accept repose against the activity
of truth." Charles Ives' present tense is accurate, for Emerson's
religious like his poetic genius consisted in being not a "preacher
of a myth about the Soul" but "a prophet of the Soul itself."[34]
The only hedge that really applies to Emerson's religiousness

is Luther's hedge, written in italics: Nobody can believe for *me*. Emerson taught that to every person would come the opportunity to possess one's soul and the universe, to attain "his self-union and freedom." But to "give account of his faith, to represent to another" the meaning of it or to make words or deeds that would prompt another to attain *his* own freedom, *his* self-union, "requires rare gifts" (*EL*, 2:145).

Of course, Emerson had given precisely such an account of his faith. The alloy of symbolic and autobiographical rhetoric that is the little book, *Nature*, issued anonymously in 1836, invites the American religious spirit to enter upon its own proper era. Here is no threatening wilderness daring human wit and energy to tame it into a garden. Rather nature speaks her welcome to man: "he shall be glad with me." As proclaimed through stars and woods ("these plantations of God") the welcome seems a romantic voice to an elated human soul. But the word is just as eloquent, the greeting just as hospitable, when coming from "a bare common, in snow puddles, at twilight, under a clouded sky, without having in my thoughts any occurrence of special good fortune," and the invitation in this form is accepted by one who is "glad to the brink of fear." Make whatever one will of the author's becoming "a transparent eyeball," the response to nature's welcome both sees and is seen by "the Universal Being" and he who responds becomes "part or parcel of God." This nature that greets man does not personify divine power; the person who accepts nature's invitation to live in harmony with it personifies deity in himself. Nor is a mood of delight required. One may enter the hospitable house of God and nature and mankind "laboring under calamity" (*W*, 1:9, 10, 11).

Calamity, indeed! Emerson's beloved brother, Charles, the brother whose melancholy notebooks Emerson was just then reading, died only a month before Emerson prepared *Nature* for the printer. Being glad, indeed! Soon after publication, his son Waldo was born, "a lovely wonder to me, and which makes the Universe look friendly to me" (*JMN*, 5:234, 152).

Sentiments

Although Emerson posited no special religious faculty in man, no particular agent for doing spiritual business, he consistently referred to the sentiment of reverence or veneration or virtue as the means by which people responded to the stirrings of the divine soul within them. In later writings "the religious sentiment" and "the moral sentiment" became almost indistinguishable and sometimes interchangeable. In the essay on "Character" (1864), for example, "moral" stands for "religious" elsewhere (*W*, 10:89–122).[35] But during the formative period, Emerson discerned two distinct sentiments — distinct in the ways they occurred, in the intensities with which they struck, in the modes of their availability, in the attitudes they engendered, and in the effects they left. Each distinction needs brief comment.

The religious and the moral sentiments arose from a single source. Every person who took life seriously and the world as really being, according to Emerson, would hear the voice of the universal soul speaking within. Indeed, being human meant primarily being attuned to "the Author of Nature" (this is a late statement) who "has not left himself without a witness in any sane mind" and who is the "force always at work to make the best better and the worst good" (*W*, 11:486). The same Author, voice, or force that improved our deeds also inspired our respect, regard, reverence, trust. One might add awe, wonder, and adoration, could one forbid the inference of fear, which Emerson cast out of the soul's repertoire. These religious qualities for the young Emerson corresponded to the moral qualities of virtue, duty, obedience, and allegiance.

Literally anything might stir this deepest impulse in human experience. Nature, the steam engine, art, fate, trade, sky, calamity — all arose from the world in which persons and the universal soul were present with and to one another. In its ethical dimension, as it prompted good deeds, the sentiment remained everybody's constant companion. Sane persons could not escape their consciences, which heard and spoke the deity's commands every waking moment. (Indeed, Emerson believed the conscience functioned even during dreams.) Moreover, God and nature constantly reinforced the sense of moral duty. Morality suffused the universe. The reason could comprehend it and the understanding could explain it.

Emerson sensed, of course, the difference between knowing the good and doing it. He thought his public utterances would be more helpful if they praised good lives rather than condemning evil ones. Indeed, he believed the moral sentiment constantly urged righteousness even if we frequently failed to achieve it. In contrast to that steady urging, the religious sentiment came in bursts, as inspiration, bringing "that shudder of awe and delight with which the individual soul always mingles with the Universal Soul" (*EL*, 2:92).[36] The steady routine of the moral sentiment and the occasional occurrence of the religious sentiment made the former constant and reliable, the latter momentary and mutable, even fleeting.

Yet the two sentiments were not nicely divisible, for when moral impulses attained very great intensity they became religious and when religious impulses cooled to a steady operation they became moral. The keenest impulses, however, that "elude our persevering thought" even though "we read them hourly in each other's faces," touched the sentiment that "is the essence of all religion" (*W*, 1:121–22). Back to these spontaneous occurrences in his own life (for example, "I become a transparent eyeball"?) Emerson's memory no doubt carried him, so that, as Stephen Whicher writes, "He *had* to ascribe more reality to his brief moments of 'religious sentiment' than to the rest of life, or he could not live."[37] Because in such moments the consciousness sensed its encompassment by deity they were something like "more real" to Emerson, but ascribing this or that degree of reality to them could neither intensify nor multiply them.

The moral sentiment, real enough in itself, sustained rather than engulfed one. A person could profit by discussing morality, could learn from another what deeds were good and what evil, even if one could not learn to do good and avoid evil. On the religious side "The sentiment is instantly vitiated, if it is not primary, — if it is not my own, but, instead, is imported into me from another [human] soul" (*EL*, 2:355). Thus the two sentiments differed as to their accessibility. A person could beckon the sense of morality but must wait to be beckoned by the sense of reverence. "For the prevision is allied/ Unto the thing so signified;/ Or say, the foresight that awaits/ Is the same Genius that creates" (*W*, 9:197). Therefore one "can never go behind" the religious sentiment, move it, turn it on, get it going, for "it is an intuition. It cannot be received at second hand" (*W*, 1:125, 127). Not even by the initiative of one's own hand!

Just that receptive posture in relation to the universal soul — or as a late lecture put it, the "Perpetual Forces" of the spirit — most clearly marked the religious sentiment off from the moral. These forces in their religious form were "angels that take us by the hand, these our immortal, invulnerable guardians. By their strength we are strong, and . . . [made] willing to obey" (*W*, 10:78). Indeed, to try to possess them rather than be possessed by them was to Emerson what others called sin or pride, and "this perversion is punished with instant loss of true wisdom and real power" (*W*, 10:85). By contrast the moral impulse, arising from the same source, made people Promethean and immediately aggressive. The religious spirit was derivatively, secondarily moral; in itself it was "glad and conspiring reception . . . that becomes giving in its turn, as the receiver is only the All-Giver in part and in infancy" (*W*, 1:194). The traditional theological category, of course, is "grace." God's grace writ large was our grace, wit, strength, tendency, or art writ small: "To him who by God's grace has seen that by being a mere tunnel or pipe through which the divine Will flows, he becomes great, & becomes a Man . . . . I am willing also to be as passive to the great forces I acknowledge as is the ther-

mometer or the clock & quite part with all will as superfluous"
(*JMN*, 5:96).

When the will was made superfluous by the religious sentiment, the result was holiness. When the will was stimulated
under the moral sentiment, the product was heroism. Holy persons claimed greatness not for themselves through assertive activity but rather for God, humbling the self. Emerson recognized
that holiness in his day was a suspect virtue because traditionally
it involved locating God in past persons and events — a superstition impelling moderns toward atheism. More profoundly, holiness arose when persons ascribed thoughts and events to the
highest origin, recognizing that this origin "is as present to
every other creature, as to me." Therefore at its simplest functioning the source of inspiration made persons distinguish right
from wrong; in its highest working, "The self-surrender to this
moral sentiment, the acceptance of its dominion throughout our
constitution as the beatitude of man, is Holiness" (*EL*, 2:345,
346). The religious sentiment suffused its recipient with humility instead of a sense of accomplishment and produced holiness
instead of heroism.

In supreme manifestations of holiness a person knew God and
simultaneously knew that God "hides himself in the simplicity
of the common consciousness" as One who cannot be named
or contained, One who "refuses to be deified or personified"
(*EL*, 2:352, 353). Whenever people named this wind they indeed
reaped the whirlwind of idolatry. The true apprehender would
see God face to face but leave Him unnamed. For that very
reason Emerson refused to ascribe personality to God, even
avoided the term "God," not to make God less than personal
but because the impersonal remained nameless where the person
required a name (*JMN*, 5:467).[38]

Holiness as the gift of the unnamed God consisted of "our
highest happiness," made us "divine and deifying," was "an
inlet into the deeps of reason" (*W*, 1:124, 125). On Emerson's
reading, Fox became holy; Luther, heroic. Both were men of

religion. Both were religious men. Fox responded to the religious sentiment; Luther, to the moral. One Spirit gave both impulses. The recipient of the moral sentiment perceived God as other. The religious sentiment discovered and disclosed God within. To make sure that this distinction would not become a systematic separation of morality and religion, Emerson sometimes interchanged the terms.

The Welcoming Universe

Proud of everything his orchard in Concord produced, Emerson preferred his pears over his apples and his apples over his plums. All these were hybrid, whereas "Religion must always be a crab fruit; it cannot be grafted and keep its wild beauty" (W, 6:214). The religious sentiment, planted wild in the modern, critical consciousness, yielded the fruits of universality (being at home with mankind), self-reliance (being at home with deity), and compensation (being at home with nature). Thus listed, the three fruits show the order of increasing attention Emerson paid them and thus their importance to him. In the structure of his religious thought, *universality* — a kind of flexible theme shaping itself to the more fundamental ideas of compensation and self-reliance — translated into life as a sense of the presence of God in all human souls. *Compensation* meant that rewards and penalties inhered immediately in all actions and also in the relations of man and nature to one another and to God. *Self-reliance* meant the universe was already atoned if only a person would attune himself to it as atoned. Together these three fruits made up the content of Emerson's religiousness.

He briefly elucidated this triple content of the religious sentiment's activity for moderns in the 1837 lecture on "Religion," calling the three features by the names of universality, profitability, and the power to exalt. As to *universality*, the sentiment "acquaints us with the Unity of the human soul in all the individuals." By *profitability* Emerson meant simply that "All right actions are useful. All wrong actions are injurious"; of this truth the sentiment was explicitly "the sign or badge; never the motive." Again, "A man must not speak the truth because it is profitable to all but because it is the truth." The sentiment's *power to exalt* was its "most excellent property" because "an influx of the Divine Mind into our mind" enabled persons to rely upon themselves since in doing so they were relying on God. "No man, no power can harm me, for I rest on the soul of the soul" (*EL*, 2:86, 87, 89). Woe to the interpreter of Emerson who sees self-reliance as the soul curved in on itself; the soul's exaltation sprang from the fact that self-reliance was the obverse side of God-reliance. Were the self reliable and God unreliable, or God reliable and the self unreliable, then God and the self would be separate entities and neither of them universal, reliable, or exalting.

Each of the three fruits of religiousness — universality, compensation, and self-reliance — calls for comment.

Universality

The presence everywhere of the universal soul linked very closely in Emerson's thought with the idea that each person existed in spiritual union with mankind. To be sure, he once found "Much," even "All" of the divine in "a load of bricks . . . [or] a barber's shop or a privy" (*JMN*, 4:307). Yet he never rejected his early dictum that "Pantheism leads to Atheism" (*JMN*, 3:76). After all, bricks and barbershops and privies were human artifacts, and for Emerson the same divine soul inhered in everything humans could do or make or think or be, so far as they fixed their profoundest attention on such things (see Bishop, pp. 32–33). The doctrine of the Over-Soul meant fundamentally that even the most wretched person remained a god in ruin, even the most exalted mystic remained a person in god, and thus they retained their identities with mankind. Persons' benevolence toward one another hung on this inescapable brotherhood, inescapable despite the mystic's mistake (Emerson's

pun) "of an accidental and individual symbol for an universal
one" or the wretch's attempt to drop out of the human scene
(W, 3:34).

Every experience pointed to its origin in a source transcending
the human will. Thus the divisions that appeared in actual living
— divisions either among persons or particles of their experience — were only apparent because all life really flowed
from a unity shared among mankind and nature and God. Each
person was an organ of the Over-Soul (how could anybody who
understands Emerson's personalism accuse him of
individualism?). The Over-Soul breathed genius through a person's intellect, virtue through will, love through affection (W,
2:271). If we relied on our own intellect and will and affection
the results would be distorted into mere talent, reward-seeking,
and self-importance. To be sure, only by surrendering our souls
could we enter our true oneness with every common and uncommon human. Not to surrender meant to cling to "Individuality" — an "amabilis insania" or fond illusion (JMN,
5:484). Our greatness as persons arose neither from our endowments nor from our sensibilities but from our being in touch
through the universal soul with all other persons, from our taking
their personhoods as far as possible into our own. Thereby personality received spiritual power by having its distinctiveness
heightened instead of diminished. So Emerson's vaunted monistic
idealism embraced a dash of pluralism. "There is a crack in
every thing God has made" (JMN, 5:304; 4:362; W, 2:107).
"See two sincere men conversing together. They deport themselves as if self-existent. Are they not for the time two Gods?
For every true man is as if he should say, I speak for the Universe;
I am here to maintain the truth against all comers[;] I am in
this place to testify" (JMN, 4:309). Thus when "I am born
into the great, the universal mind" it happens that "I become
public and human in my regards and actions" (W, 2:296).

Emerson's fame as a philosopher of the soul may have come
to rest too singly on his having made nature a revealer of God
to the soul and of the soul to itself, detached from the corollary

theme of human solidarity. Perhaps the latter has been slighted by interpreters because Emerson posed a direct access to the past, unmediated by the reconstruction of events in which human experience was embodied. However, he thought that a person's soul participated in mankind quite as significantly as in nature and in God, even though his view of history led him to assert this principle rather abstractly instead of digging it out of historical details. In learning the past, according to Emerson, people came to know themselves and indeed also to evoke their own identities. Thus his own piety explained to him the piety of Jesus, his own yearning interpreted the yearning of Tantalus, not vice versa (W, 2:30–35). The entire range of human experience lay latently in each soul, which could take these previous illustrations of experience into itself.

Facile as appropriation of the past became in this view of history, it does not erase from Emerson's thinking the principle that all persons belonged ineluctably to and within humanity, sharing more than membership in a biological species. They partook of a common nature that transcended the personal and social character of humanity. They learned their divinity by sharing their humanity, seen from one point of view (W, 2:277). But religiously, that lesson came hind part before. "The one miracle God works forevermore is imparting himself to the mind" (UL, p. 45). A chief effect of such impartation was "peopling the lonely places" (W, 2:292). The miracle of mankind's unity was wondrous not in itself, certainly not in some organic entity called humanity, but in its emplacing each of us in the hospitable company of all our fellows. The first quality of religiousness was universality. The presence of God set all in the whole human family.

Compensation

Translating the presence or omnipresence of God into the solidarity of mankind was one exchange made possible by Emerson's critical religious consciousness. Its chief yield, however, was the discovery of every experience's principal significance in the experience itself and not in the judgment of some moral referee meting out favors and penalties after the fact. Life's meanings presented themselves within the lived life itself — immediately in the primary sense of "unmediated" (of course not always simultaneous with the experience). To accuse Emerson of easy optimism because he taught that each deed implied its own compensation, as many interpreters have done, requires their overlooking the fact that he presumed evil acts to contain penalties quite as proportionately as good actions yielded their own rewards. Far from cultivating an optimism at once blind and bland, Emerson hurled a challenge against the payoff ethics with which the religious revivals of the nineteenth century were suffusing America.[39]

In fact, Emerson's doctrine of compensation expressed an ingenious psychological insight, anticipating the psychological theory that emotions are caused by, rather than causes of, behavior. Radically he placed the meaning of an experience within itself. In William James's aphoristic formulation of the James-Lange theory, "we feel sorry because we cry, angry because we strike, afraid because we tremble" (*PP*, 2:450). For Emerson "retribution is the universal necessity by which the whole appears wherever a part appears." Again, "Every act rewards itself, or in other words integrates itself . . . first in the thing, or in real nature; and secondly in the circumstance, or in apparent nature. . . . The specific stripes may follow late after the offence, but they follow because they accompany it" (*W*, 2:102–3). The doctrine did not hinge on the promptness of one's awareness that the experience signified itself. The point was that the cause contained the effect so that reason must meld the two together rather than separate them in thinking of human activity. In more traditional terms, God did not interpose grace or wrath between deed and judgment. Moreover, the doctrine ran to a coordination of opposites, not just from act to desert.

Bitter bought sweet, pain paid for joy, and neither meant much if cut off from its correlate. There was therefore an "absolute balance of Give and Take" (W, 2:115).

The notion of compensation or balance in Emerson's thought had a universally esthetic and not a narrowly ethical implication. By this insight persons could internalize beauty and truth along with the accompanying ugliness and falsity, or salvation along with damnation, quite as well as good along with evil. "Thefts never enrich, alms never impoverish, and murder will speak out of stone walls." So far, moral compensation. But also "Giving is receiving. The lover is loved" (EL, 2:153). Ever "God makes us the answerers of our own prayers & so fulfils the cycle & perfection of things" (JMN, 3:268).

Shortly after his first wife's death, Emerson was observing that the rule of compensation "holds as far as we can see," whereas earlier he had believed extraordinary grief over losing a loved one required reference to future, mediated events for its meaning (JMN, 3:265–66; 3:5). Emerson was affirming the presentness of God and nature and society in *every* human experience, regardless of joy or sadness, good or evil. By the intensity of our being aware of this presentness some experiences surely loomed more important than others. Humdrum living barely glimpsed the inner meaning of its episodes. But moderns instinctively found the whole universe involved in, and thus more or less present to, their every deed. Here (and really nowhere else) is there clear warrant to write "optimist" beside Emerson's name: he held that God was somewhat present always and everywhere, never wholly absent (W, 2:122). He tested that conviction in sore bereavement. It worked. Then he could find compensation in all of life. The adolescent Emerson's effort at internalizing the Christian doctrine of providence became a way of being at home in the universe.

Orthodox Christians had been balancing payments for vice and rewards for virtue over a time-span running from Adam's sin to Christ's second coming. By both enhancing and attenuat-

ing the force of evil, they emphasized, perhaps exaggerated, the
power of good to be victorious. Emerson first shortened the time-
span to that of a person's life, then to the duration of each
experience. So those who blame him for attacking the preoccupation with sin that his Christian forebears enjoyed should, to
be consistent, also deplore his rethinking the old notion of good
as eventual payoff.

Much later, James would remark that Western thinkers made
a problem of evil but not of good. To Emerson, good was quite
as problematic as evil; the two reciprocated in every experience
and both were implicit within every act that either characterized. With regard to good and evil, then, Emerson was on
balance neither optimistic nor pessimistic. By his special religious consciousness he was only serene in the face of both good
and evil, because both were present to him in everything he
did.

The world Emerson occupied was less an ethical than an esthetic universe. Evil and good compensated or balanced one another
as did, to be sure, organic experience and imaginative experience,
prose and poetry, descriptive rhetoric and evocative (one wants
to say "invocative") rhetoric, even ugliness and beauty themselves. All these correspondences became available to the new
religious sense in every experience of being at home with nature,
humanity, and deity. Therefore, it is wrong to say one layer
of compensatory living, such as the esthetic layer, satisfied him
more than another, such as the moral layer. Nevertheless, the
correspondences in themselves exhibited an abiding proportion
in the universe. Emerson's evil did not become good, nor did
he assimilate ugliness to beauty. Rather the relation of evil to
good and of ugliness to beauty was a harmonious, balanced
relation, one that enhanced the general, final beauty of the universe.

The harmony of compensatory and compensating experience
became a retreat where Emerson found beauty in whatever happened. Life was a succession of alternations, swayings, ambiva-

lences, pendulum-swings. Human experience was split — but reciprocally so. "History is . . . two boys pushing each other on the curbstone of the pavement. Everything is pusher or pushed; and matter and mind are in perpetual tilt and balance, so" (*W*, 6:43). Or, "If I strike, I am struck; if I chase, I am pursued" (*W*, 10:8). Again, "Polarity is the law of all being" (*JMN*, 5:304). Emerson recognized and analyzed and emphasized the split. He refused to accept it as final or to lament it. Instead he turned his religious sense to appreciating it.[40]

In experience everything appeared split. True religiousness meant knowing and living (by faith, to be sure) the alternation and compensation and reciprocation of the seeming splits as actual parts of a true whole, a yin-yang. Or better, each experience partook of a piece of the nature of things and each piece was an arc that joined with the other pieces into a circle of faith. "Religion . . . is the attitude of those . . . who see that against all appearances the nature of things works for truth and right forever" (*W*, 6:219). This was indeed for Americans and moderns a new religiousness, for "When an ardent mind once gets a glimpse of that perfect beauty [of the great law of compensation] & sees how it envelopes him & determines all his being, will he easily slide back to a periodic shouting about 'atoning blood'?" (*JMN*, 4:314). The religiousness of compensation meant to be at home with the nature of things, to internalize the meanings of experience, to discover, beyond how things *seem*, what they *are*.

Self-Reliance

Emerson's spirituality united us as individuals with mankind and revealed to us the meaning of our experiences as we lived them. The soul exercising this religiousness also came to possess itself. Emerson called such self-possession by the now hackneyed term "self-reliance." Psychologically this meant that we, simply by doing our best in everything we undertook, could be at peace with the restless strivings and aspirings of our selfhood. Religiously it meant that atonement or redemption or salvation, already made available, awaited appropriation by our stern adherence to our own individual genius and calling. We needed no mediator to achieve or inaugurate our blessing. We needed only to accept the benediction of our intimacy with the universe. "Getting right with God" and "being your own person" and "doing your own thing" became one and the same act of self-reliance. What Puritan and Unitarian divines had urged people to yearn for, Emerson asked them to accept and celebrate.

Self-reliance was the state of the soul that responded to compensation in the nature of things. Since in every experience cause contained its effect, event contained its meaning, sign contained its significance, "Why should we fret at particular events? For everything you have missed, you have gained something else; and for everything you gain, you lose something" (EL, 2:145–46). Whatever had happened or would yet happen formed only a general context for what a person thought or did. Each present act provided its own meaningful content. Therefore what had seemed imprudent folly was really prudent wisdom, namely, to trust oneself — independent (but not ignorant) of traditional sanctions and unafraid (but not unaware) of future blacklash. Self-reliance, Emerson thought, came naturally to boys at their best but was hard won by adults, who liked to mortgage their souls to the notion that they must think and do what would indirectly be to their own advantage and play into their own hands.

With a major qualification the contrast between "inner-directedness" and "other-directedness," later made popular by David Riesman in *The Lonely Crowd* (1950), paralleled Emerson's distinction between self-reliance and other-reliance. "Whoso would be a man," Emerson wrote, "must be nonconformist" (*W*, 2:50). For Riesman inner-directedness was more conventional than intuitive. For Emerson inner-direction sprang not from habit but from intuition and inspiration. Such self-reliance freed persons from slavish consistency, which was an individualized and traditionalized form of reliance upon others. Emerson's self-reliant soul found ever new inner directions by virtue of its fidelity to itself and to God, and that was a single fidelity.

That is, self-reliant souls relied on the God with and in whom they were and who was with and in them. Thus a "true man belongs to no other time or place, but is the centre of things" (*W*, 2:60). The true person's intuition consisted of receiving ever-fresh wisdom from the universal intelligence. It drew upon "relations of the soul to the divine spirit . . . so pure that it is profane to seek to interpose helps" (*W*, 2:65). Emerson was denying any willful self, independent of God, in order to affirm an inspired self that was as reliable as God because it was indivisible from Him.

But that indivisibility neither deified the soul nor ensouled God so completely that no distinctions remained. The explicit vow made by Emerson in 1832 — never to "lose sight of his [God's] real eternal Being[,] of my own dependence, my nothingness, whilst yet I dare hail the present deity at my heart" — became implicit five years later in the aphorism: "The pure in heart shall see God. The pure in heart shall be God. Only God can see God" (*JMN*, 4:40; 5:298). In the meantime the idea of self-reliance first explicitly crossed Emerson's mind. He resolved to think this problem through, asking about self-reliance "what it is, what it is not, what it requires, how it teaches us to regard our friends." Already an answer glimmered: self-reliance meant to set one's own course; for another "to dictate to me the course I should take . . . were to unman, to un-god myself" (*JMN*, 4:269). In the famous essay "Self-Reliance," God is God and people are people, and the self-reliant person is enough at home with God to be relying upon God in the very act of relying upon himself. Or, in 1836: "As long as the soul seeks an external God, it never can have peace, it always must be uncertain what may be done & what may become of it. But when it sees the Great God far within its own nature, then

it sees that always itself is a party to all that can be, that always
it will be informed of that which will happen and therefore
it is pervaded with a great Peace" (*JMN*, 5:223). Emerson meant
to *magnify* God by conceiving of deity as both impersonal and
immanent, even though the orthodox of that day (and ours?)
took his ideas as minifying God.

At any rate, Emerson opposed *self*-reliance to *other*-reliance
and not to *God*-reliance.[41] The very point, put positively or
negatively, became Emerson's "highest truth on this subject":
the intuition came from neither man nor society nor tradition
nor church but arose "wholly strange and new" in the sense of
being from the "Great God far within" and custom-made for the
individual person; the soul then "perceives the self-existence of
Truth and Right, and calms itself with knowing that all things
go well" (*W*, 2:68, 69). Emerson's self-reliant person, domiciled
with deity, has appeared lawless or antinomian to critics of various theological persuasion. But in reality this person is at once
autonomous and theonomous, under a single law of self and
of God, a law delivered by God to the self and received by
the self from the God within the self.

Thus self-reliance was a radically new quality of religiousness
for the individual person who dared accept an intimacy of his
own soul with deity. Emerson believed that persons exercising
this new spirituality would bring about radical revolutions in
religion, education, and society. To be at home with God was
possible only as one was also at home with mankind and nature.
Self-reliant prayer would seek no private ends but contemplate
"the spirit of God pronouncing his works good. . . . As soon
as the man is at one with God, he will not beg. He will then
see prayer in all action" (*W*, 2:77). This person would seek
no escape from the self in traveling, in imitating others' art,
or in drawing authority from government, or in basing power
on property. Religion and education and art and society would
thrive as the products and processes of men and women who
took themselves for what Emerson taught them to become — by
nature friends to deity, to the world, and to humanity.

A Proffered Hand

Like the Over-Soul and compensation, Emerson's theme of self-reliance described a quality of living that persons could enter through the door of self-critical religious consciousness. Taken together, these three themes also formed the content of a new life-style, definitely centering on people without making God peripheral or even eccentric. Newly religious moderns received this life-style even while they continued to live according to their acquisitiveness (upon which the old forms of religion and the new forms of irreligion alike played). Thus the posture of Emerson's self-reliant soul, in touch with the Over-Soul and living the compensated life, was at once receptive (or passive) and donative (or assertive). To accept our souls as inhabiting a hospitable universe empowered us to be fully ourselves and thereby to give ourselves to God and to our fellows and to nature, from all of which we received ourselves.

Emerson's task of stating this religiousness was of course conceptual, verbal, even poetic — but remained more demonstrative than descriptive. That is, he spoke and wrote about it less to relate its parts or to contrast its doctrine with the old religion than to demonstrate and (where possible) to invoke its actuality in human experience. This is why the little glimmers of modern spirituality he detected in the lives of a Jesus and a Luther and a Milton made these men not so much the objects of narrative biography as exemplars of a life-style they barely knew they possessed. So the poets about whom Emerson lectured come through as illustrating a certain grasp of life rather than as the masters of literature that they were. Many of his own poems are prayers aspiring to and realizing this religiousness. And his thematic essays and lectures lead us into a new apprehension of reality rather than set forth Emerson's analysis of reality.

Emerson put the distinction between description and demonstration simply, if a bit tritely. Cleave to your own intuition, he counseled, for anybody else's can be to you only a tuition.

Following that advice I have cast the quality and intensity as well as the character and the effects of Emerson's religious intuition for the most part in the past tense. Not that his way of taking life is closed to us. Rather, I believe, the kind of religiousness Emerson was presenting remains practicable for critically self-conscious moderns. In any case, he was presenting it as an offer to his own contemporaries. And that, precisely and emphatically, we are not.

To regard the universe as hospitable was the essence of Emerson's offer — and dare. The offer may yet stand. To accept it may remain a dare. But in mid-nineteenth-century America the alienness of the world, such as it was, had for a long time been blamed on the world, on nature and mankind and God. Copernican thought had made the world ominous and foreign, and theology since the Renaissance had conceded the point. But in late-twentieth-century America the spokesmen of alienation seem to be declaring something about themselves rather than about their world. They take their relation to the universe to be unfriendly because *they feel inimical* to the world and God and mankind. So the terms of enmity, also the terms of any possible atonement, are unlike those of Emerson's diction. The awaited greeting of welcome today may be our word to the world, not the world's word to us that Emerson eloquently spoke. So the unheard greeting of hospitality may require today the language of feeling more than the language of thought and reality — although we must think as well as feel our way toward it. This much, at least, of Emerson's message persists into our time: there was once, so there still may be, a preferred handshake, even possibly an embrace, waiting out there in nature, in God, in mankind. To test whether the invitation still stands, one can only accept it.

5 Interlude From Emerson to James

During Jonathan Edwards' career, awakenings fell like sudden showers on the parched desert of conventional American religion. The America of young Ralph Waldo Emerson was a religious rain forest. By 1840 evangelical zeal dominated the main denominations and the new sects; indeed, such a zeal animated the Transcendentalists. Exploding immigrant populations involved Catholics in the equivalent of a vast revival. New revelations fell on Shakers, Latter-Day Saints, Adventists, and Perfectionists. The very decade of Emerson's *Nature* (1836) brought forth a flash-flood of religious publications, only sampled by mentioning Joseph Smith's *Book of Mormon* (1830), Episcopalian Bishop Charles P. McIlvaine's *Address to the Young Men of the United States on Temperance* (1833), Charles G. Finney's *Lectures on Revivals of Religion* and Lyman Beecher's *Plea for the West* (1835), the pseudonymous Maria Monk's *Awful Disclosures of the Hotel Dieu Nunnery in Montreal* (1836), Theodore Dwight Weld's *The Bible Against Slavery* (1837), William Miller's *Evidence from Scripture and History of the Second Coming of Christ, About the Year 1843* (1838), and Lutheran Samuel S. Schmucker's *Fraternal Appeal* (1838) to the nation's evangelical Protestants to form one American Apostolic Protestant Church.

This profusion of American religion seems in long retrospect to typify the American spirit. In the 1830s evangelicalism and religious pluralism were new and, to traditionalists, disturbing.

Indeed, at that time Americans were deriving from abroad
impulses to reappropriate forgotten traditions, to affirm man's
developmental progress, and to reform social institutions. Emerson helped introduce Americans to the traditionalist Thomas
Carlyle as William James would the psychoanalyst Sigmund
Freud; the generation between got to know the evolutionist
Charles Darwin and at least the main ideas of the socialist Karl
Marx. Although these interests in tradition, progress, and reform
seem quite disparate, actually they all merged into American
romanticism, if by romanticism we mean an attitude and not
a specific artistic movement.

These influences from abroad entered the American imagination through various interpreters and popularizers who had at
least this much in common. They stood on a watershed dividing
two native religious impulses: revivalism, running back to Edwards, and pragmatism, running forth from James. Religious
thinkers on both sides of the watershed thought carefully about
the significance of the feelings for religious experience. The
earlier students of revivalism, following Edwards, tied the feelings specifically to the experience of conversion. The romantics
generalized the same fascination with feelings into all aspects of
experience. The pragmatists took this generalized notion of religious experience and made it relative to human achievement,
asking what kinds of feelings arose from each kind of religious experience, paying attention more to the parts than to the whole
of experience, more to the fruits than to the source of religion.

The pragmatists likewise discounted institutional religion,
which in the romantic period busied itself with deriving symbols
of certainty from the Christian past. Catholics and Episcopalians
and Methodists and Presbyterians alike were erecting neo-Gothic
piles or, more poignantly, making pointed windows in wooden
meetinghouses. Presbyterians were rallying to biblical confessionalism, set forth as traditional at Princeton Seminary by the
conservative theological dynasty running from Archibald
Alexander through Charles Hodge down to Benjamin Warfield

and J. Gresham Machen. Liturgical as well as confessional en-
richment came to Lutheran and German Reformed congregations
partly in the valises of new immigrants and partly from the
romantic theologians at Mercersburg and Gettysburg. The very
people who were helping denominations relish their traditions
— Philip Schaff, John Williamson Nevin, Schmucker, and
William Augustus Muhlenberg — were also trying to unite
American churches around a common task of evangelizing the
nation.

Her secure tradition and well-defined authority were attracting
native converts to the Catholic church, notably two one-time
Brook Farmers, Orestes A. Brownson and Isaac Thomas Hecker.
Hecker then established theoretical grounds for the practical
efforts of three liberal prelates, Archbishop John Ireland of St.
Paul, James Cardinal Gibbons of Baltimore, and Bishop John
J. Keane of Dubuque, to fit Catholicism into the live-and-let-live
pluralism of the American denominations. While they were
hardly Darwinists or Marxists and certainly not spokesmen for
all their fellow Catholics in America, this trio sang the current
songs of the middle-class denominations: progress, social reform,
and shared religious traditions. The typical refrain of such songs
ran, "Thy Kingdom come, in America, *now*."

The religious thinker who was most responsive to the interest
in tradition, progress, and reform through these years was Horace
Bushnell, eponym of romantic religion. Bushnell was, writes
Sydney Ahlstrom, "As disaffected by revivalism as Nevin, as
romantic as Emerson, and as dedicated to the memory of his
New England forebears as [Lyman] Beecher" (Ahlstrom, p. 62).
The later social gospelers, almost to a man, paid him a homage
due as well from later social Darwinists like John Fiske. In
Bushnell's religious thought are all the impulses typical of
his time (tradition, progress, social reform, feeling as the
basis of religion) and, furthermore, he typifies the broad transition from evangelicalism to pragmatism in that he never quite
freed himself from the former and never quite arrived at the

latter. Yet he broke with the New Haven theology and founded
theological liberalism.

A Connecticut farm-boy trained at Yale (the College, then
the Law and Divinity Schools), Bushnell stepped ambitiously
into his first and only pastorate (North Church at Hartford) in
1833, the year after Emerson stepped respectably out of his
(Second Church at Boston). Late in starting his career, Bushnell
retired early, in 1859. His spirituality, while romantic, was
thoroughly sentimental and centered on the self's feelings more
than on its relations to the universe.

Bushnell shared his era's interest in history, progress, and
improvement. Indeed, the related themes of growth and wholeness pervaded his religious thought, whether he turned attention
to language and knowledge, to God and man, or to society
and history.[42] He preached to the interests of his parishioners
on the virtues of capitalism, on revivals, on the religious nurture
of children by pious parents, on metaphor and symbolism as
the religious sentiment's idioms, on slavery, on science and
religion, on the West, on education, on Unitarianism, on
nationalism, on the Civil War — always tendentious enough
to be timely, never quite timeserving enough to be sycophantic
(Cross, chaps. 5–8).

As a young man Bushnell embraced Christianity with his
heart, and ever afterward he believed the head unfit to comprehend religion. Thus with Blaise Pascal, and indeed with
Edwards and Emerson and James, Bushnell's heart had reasons
the head knew not of. The others took the dictum to mean
the head should try to figure out those reasons — for Edwards
by an enlightened soul, for Emerson by means of the reason
instead of the understanding, for James by means of sensation
and action looped together with thought. Bushnell read Samuel
Taylor Coleridge more avidly than did Emerson, and exaggeration if not plain misinterpretation increased proportionately. "To
the reviled Understanding," according to a recent biographer,
"Bushnell consistently opposed not the Reason but the heart"

(Cross, p. 28). His religious thought, stressing growth and wholeness, was organic; the heart was the organ of his religion. Thus Bushnell exemplifies better than Edwards or Emerson or James what Morton White, attributing it not to him but to them, has called American philosophical anti-intellectualism: "the espousal of the view that raw emotion, passion, or sentiment can *by itself* establish reliable belief" (White, p. 302).

Language, about which Bushnell theorized (with help from F. W. J. Schelling and Coleridge) was really a matter of the heart. Out of feeling and sentiment he clung to the religious vocabulary of Puritanism while radically altering its theology, clinging to the form of old doctrines after their content had evaporated for him. In his theory of language, Bushnell made both expression and signification matters of affective experience. To be sure, he conceded determinate significance to certain necessary ideas like geometric axioms, and he granted a certain precision to names referring to physical objects. But beyond this narrow range of thinking lay the spiritual and intellectual (which is to say the distinctively human) arenas, where words could at best approximate the experiences they were intended to express. The person to whom these words were addressed would feel their meaning, would find experiences, analogous to those the speaker referred to, evoked in his own feeling. "Bitterness" to Bushnell, for example, named no universal sensation; it only suggested a whole class of experiences entered into somewhat differently by each person who spoke or heard this word. Speaker thus strove to help hearer feel something close to what speaker felt. Explicitly, according to Bushnell, one would need a report of each and every person's religious experience before one could confidently build a general theory of religious experience. Even then the theory could evoke only a resemblance of what it sought to describe. To assume any neater correspondence between words and spiritual-intellectual experiences, according to Bushnell, was to overemphasize mankind's real but only very partial physicality, and to mistake a high level of experience for the mere naming of physical things.

On Bushnell's view, spirituality could be conveyed inexactly by allusion and evocation and example; it could not be transmitted. Words were necessary human forms because they alluded to and elicited feelings. This capacity for intelligent feeling was precisely what linked man to the supernatural order over which God ruled. Only the spiritual beings that belonged to this order were capable of purposeful, directed growth. Beings belonging to the realm of nature grew passively, because spirits so directed. The nature of man, meaning both his physicality and the corporate character of mankind, would grow just as man and God directed. Man was part supernatural and part natural and to separate these parts or, worse, to mistake the realm of one for the realm of the other, was to dehumanize or "unnature" personhood.

Bushnell translated "to sin" as "to unnature." To explain man by his partial physicality, to bind his freedom in the chains of cause and effect, would both impede and deflect man from attaining his spiritual destiny. Of course, everybody tended to do just that. It was not that God imputed the sin of Adam to his posterity. Rather, children congenitally inclined toward the unnatured humanity of their parents. The cumulative force of this corporate human trend could be countervailed only by God. Christ had vicariously sacrificed Himself to redirect the trend of mankind away from sin and toward supernatural freedom. Men and women could hasten or retard the new thrust. Inheritance of acquired characteristics? Certainly, for "what gets power in any race, by a habit or a process of culture, tends by a fixed law of nature to become a propagated quality, and pass by descent as a property inbred in the stock."[43]

On Bushnell's reading, revivalists were foolish to ask that each person wallow in his unnature as a necessary condition to putting on his true nature. Instead, Christian parents should raise their children never knowing themselves to be other than Christian. The pious family, forerunner of the Kingdom of God, would spiritualize mankind. Just so, Bushnell proposed that Christians spiritualize humanity by religious upbreeding, and he believed that Christian piety was the dominant genetic trait. He thus fathered the evolutionary optimism on which flourished American liberal theology. His spiritual children made World War I a humanitarian crusade for democracy and religion; his theological grandchildren could make little sense of the great depression, Nazism, and World War II.

Bushnell caused these events no more than he caused his disciples to overlook human impotence and historical tragedy and his sense of their necessary function in the scheme of things. To restore the human spirit's true direction cost Christ's life and would cost man's suffering. Because the tendency to spoil or to realize the true nature of humanity was influenced by a kind of hereditary momentum, every person's religious choice entered into the balance and would affect the destiny of all. Language could only suggest or hint at or evoke the tendency toward redemption, because men and women belonged to both the natural and the supernatural realms. But God influenced both realms, exercising His justice and His love, inflicting or allowing tragedy yet providentially wresting good ends from evil means. Bushnell so thought because, he believed, his times so taught.

The times indeed were teaching new spiritual lessons. Not long after Edwards translated the Puritan quest for righteousness under a sovereign God into the truly virtuous person's rejoicing in the beauty of that sovereignty, the popular American analogue of sovereignty changed. No longer did "the sovereign" signify a just Creator ruling a harmonious, dependent creation; it referred to an unjust British ruler lording it over colonies obliged under God to establish their independence. In the age and spirit of the Revolution, traditional theologians struggled to show how the sovereign God could honorably forgive deliberately sinful man. At the same time revivalists and rationalists and Transcendentalists (to be sure in different ways) were asking how men and women could claim the mercy of a beneficent ruler of the universe. Americans were declaring that God's governance and

man's independence guaranteed life, liberty, and the pursuit of
happiness.

In the stream of American theologies flowing out of this political metaphor of sovereignty, Bushnell's religious thought during
the period of his Hartford pastorate stands out like an island.
The notion of sovereignty simply failed to tally with his own
religious experience. He studied Edwards and Nathaniel W.
Taylor, Charles Chauncy and W. E. Channing, Emerson and
Theodore Parker. The darker side of experience, not a specific
personal tragedy but an ominous, unfulfilled mood, required
another metaphor. Much as he favored life, liberty, and the pursuit of happiness, he had a feeling also for finitude, spiritual
bondage, and personal unfulfillment.

The opportunity to think and write in retirement coincided
opportunely for Bushnell with the Civil War — another occasion
for him to cast spirituality in terms of current concerns. In the
process of an aspiring but, he thought, misbegotten nation's
receiving its true nationhood through the sacrifice of its sons,
Bushnell perceived a paradigm.

In two big volumes, *The Vicarious Sacrifice, Grounded in Principles of Universal Obligation* (1866) and its sequel, *Forgiveness and
Law, Grounded in Principles Interpreted by Human Analogies* (1874),
Bushnell, still true to his theory of experience and language
as grounded in the heart, educed from the Civil War a fresh
theory of Christ's sacrificially bringing creation into atonement
and reconciliation with the Creator. Always given to searching
out what he called, in the title given to a collection of sermons,
Moral Uses of Dark Things, Bushnell now found the underside
of life reflecting divine love. Now the logic of heart-religion
came full force: men and women who felt toward but could
not reach God could be reached by a God who through Christ
felt for and identified with men and women. Sentiment, which
in Bushnell's spirituality opposed the understanding and sur-
passed reason, came to reign in God as well as in man. "The
ecstatic union with Being," according to Barbara Cross, "which

Edwards had experienced and Emerson had recaptured, was to Bushnell won through an inexplicable, infinite mercy. Only a love that took no account of rational preference, that spent itself on the ugly, the inimical, the repulsive, could have made an occasion fit for ecstasy in the world. Christ's life revealed the strange impetus and relentless exactions of this love and burdened man with the duty of a similar compassion" (Cross, p. 150).

Or, in short, when the divine Word spoke the language of the divine Heart, the human heart responded in kind. By looking at the spirituality developed during Bushnell's retirement, we find the most eloquent, the most timely (for his time), and the most heart-bound of American religious geniuses. His strength was eloquence rather than clarity, projection rather than invitation. He taught liberal Protestant thinkers how to tune their themes to the times, how to generate religious sentiment in and of and for each age. His sense of the family and of children's spiritual nurture gave him a popular model of the Kingdom of God on earth, a metaphor from which his successors developed the social gospel. His feeling for the organic solidarity of mankind as a growing organism earned him prominence among the evolutionary optimists. And his insistence upon man's obligation to respond reciprocally to Christ's suffering love provided a central theological rationale for religious activism. In all these varied interests and influences, like Goethe's Faust to Gretchen in the garden scene, Bushnell proclaimed on behalf of God and man, "Gefühl ist Alles." [44]

Faust went on: since feeling is everything, "Names are sound and smoke/ Befogging Heaven's flame." Bushnell, on his own grounds, could not have much cared that he came to be called the father of liberal theology in America. Feeling was everything, and liberalism based itself on Bushnell's profound feeling of human kinship with divinity, a kinship he based on the shared capacity for self-sacrificial love (or unselfish feeling). Christ as deity felt for humanity. Returning the compliment, men and women increased their feeling for God. From his own standpoint

Bushnell was transforming human love from self-seeking eros
into self-giving agape, but from the standpoint of the elder
Henry James he was only confusing selfless with selfish love
in a double effort "to swathe the immortal form of truth in
the grave-clothes of a perishing sectarian dogmatism" and to
bring about "the pacification of his somewhat distempered
ecclesiastical conscience."[45] Bushnell was bringing together
divine love and human love by sentimentalizing both. His God
loved without awe or majesty and his humans loved without self-
interest or malice. The common denominator was the love of a
mid-Victorian mother.

Bushnell's organic way of thinking made him a theological
liberal who freed people from the orthodox bondage to sin. The
same style of thought also issued in social and political conservatism. Society would change by inexorable laws of growth, and
an elite vanguard must lead the way. Culture, wealth, education,
and power would accrue to persons who rose to positions of
social control, itself an organic function; the masses would be
watered by philanthropic overflow.

Bushnell, according to the elder James, tried "to reconcile
Orthodox forms with Unitarian substance."[46] His combining
of social conservatism and theological liberalism by means of
a concept of sentimental love required a certain ingenuity. But
the sage of Hartford never rivaled the genius of the sage of
Concord. He cuddled the traditional while he coddled the novel.

While Bushnell sat in lonely retirement, his ideas reached
the great, rising middle class of the American cities and suburbs
through the popularizing talents of America's "first, self-
appointed national chaplain," Henry Ward Beecher. In fact,
Beecher dovetailed conservative social policy into liberal theology
more solidly than Bushnell had done, using the glue of social
evolutionism borrowed from Herbert Spencer. Beecher presented
science and religion as dual routes along which man progressed
according to a divine master plan. Nature became to the sensitive
soul "a perpetual letter from God, freshly written every day

and each hour" — a view Beecher traced back to Edwards. Locating "God's sovereignty . . . in His love," Beecher made the romantic love between pious men and pious women into "the foundation of the family" and the family into the foundation of society. He deplored the cities' obvious evils, urged the wealthy to be generous, condemned chattel slavery, and gave the North a share of blame for the Civil War. But in the process he decried the labor movement, barely admitted blacks into the human race, and, according to a recent biographer, made "America, with England's aid, . . . the big brother, the policeman, the schoolteacher to the world." [47]

Like Bushnell, Beecher sailed with the breezes of American opinion. By his magic rhetoric he fanned these breezes into tradewinds of middle-class social doctrine. Both these mid-Victorians urged bourgeois Americans to share the aspirations of the affluent, and they contrast starkly with their younger contemporaries who made middle-class Protestants religiously aware of the plight of the laboring classes in the sweatshops and slums. Beecher died in Brooklyn the year after the Haymarket Riot in Chicago. Across the river in Hell's Kitchen, on the west side of Manhattan, a congregation of German Baptist slum-dwelling laborers was installing a minister named Walter Rauschenbusch. He would become the leading ideologue of the social gospel (and to him our attention will return). Also in the year of Beecher's death Josiah Strong was infusing a meeting of the Evangelical Alliance with social-gospel ideas, then being formulated most prominently by Washington Gladden, a friend of Bushnell's. The younger men turned the liberal theology to liberal reform, urging persons of good will to redirect social institutions into courses of justice charted, they thought, by Jesus in the Sermon on the Mount. These social gospelers (whether explicitly or implicitly) demonstrated their theories of providence and progress by asking that voluntary human efforts design and erect God's Kingdom on earth.

Yet the leading religious thinkers of the mid-Victorian generation in America temporalized the absolutes of the old religion without really relativizing them. The social gospelers made divine justice on earth contingent upon human effort — at least the negative effort of not obstructing its reign. Bushnell and Beecher derived God's sovereignty from His love. The social gospelers applied the will of God to the newfound human capacity to direct nature and history to chosen ends.

From the liberal theologians who were his contemporaries Emerson thus remained at a large distance. While they reinterpreted the beliefs and redirected the goals of religious institutions that then claimed human loyalty and labor, he developed a critical religious consciousness that allowed man to find a spiritually welcome universe. Although relativism as such only flitted across Emerson's field of vision ("there is a crack in everything God has made"), he in effect relativized the orthodox world-view that Bushnell and Beecher only liberalized. Insofar as Christian socialists made religion the ordering principle of American society — the emphasis of the early Gladden and the dominant theme of Rauschenbusch — they stood in the liberal tradition. Insofar as they made religion one of several means of human mastery over nature and human nature — the emphasis of the later Strong and of Richard T. Ely — they became relativists.

There is no need for us to assign to each of these men a precise hue on the spectrum between liberalized and relativized religious thought. Nor is such precision the aim of mentioning again in this connection the Catholic leaders (Keane, Ireland, Gibbons) of the movement called Americanism. Their conscious loyalties to Catholicism are not impugned by suggesting their sometimes overriding devotion to religious and cultural pluralism, even their regard for Catholicism as a means of Americanizing immigrants. Similarly, Isaac M. Wise, the American patriarch of Reform Judaism, accommodated the traditional aspirations of Judaism to those of modern America. The great immigration after 1880 brought to America ten East European Jewish immigrants for each of the Ashkenazim already here

when Wise was founding Hebrew Union College in Cincinnati
(1875). The Reconstructionist movement led by Mordecai M.
Kaplan relativized the religion of Judaism into a civilization
of Jewishness.

But the American who would center his religious thought
on relativism, who would refine Emerson's new religious consciousness to the extent of making God essentially man's deity
and of making man at home with his humanity, was neither
Protestant, Catholic, nor Jew, neither liberal theologian nor
social gospeler. He was William James, who learned from his
father to believe that American institutions were no organs of
might and sanctity in themselves but "purely *social* institutions,
. . . [having] no proper life apart from the uses they promote
to the great society [of man] which maintains them" —
indeed, that religion and its deity existed for the sake of mankind.[48]

The Human Religiousness of William James

The Father's Humanism

In early March 1842 came a letter to Ralph W. Emerson, then lecturing in New York City, hailing him as "a man who in very truth was seeking the realities of things" and inviting him to the home of the hailer, Henry James.[49] Just that January Emerson's first son, Waldo, had died at the family home in Concord. According to family lore, James took Emerson upstairs in the Washington Square home to see James's first son, William, born the same January at the Astor House, New York's finest hotel. Emerson, then at the acme of his intellectual power, had heard nature's summons to a spirituality of self-reliance that mitigated grief for his dead son. Henry James, by eight years Emerson's junior, learned a peculiar spirituality of "self-uncreation" that mitigated his profound sense of evil by joining his soul to the society of mankind. And the infant James would climb onto the shoulders of both these elders to post the great American manifesto of religious pluralism in which every kind of religious experience was measured by its benefit to the soul and to mankind. The younger James's many-sided spirituality is best seen against his father's religious humanism.

Doctrine

In 1789 the first American William James arrived in the new-constitutioned nation, a penniless, eighteen-year-old Scotch-

Irishman. He settled in Albany, New York, and at his death
in 1832 left his third wife and many children the handsome
fortune of three million dollars. To the father's strict Presbyterianism Henry paid serious attention as a boy. After the
father's death he entered Princeton Seminary to study with
the conservatives Charles Hodge and Archibald Alexander,
whose Calvinist confessionalism proudly banished new ideas.
Taken one at a time, the doctrines of this faith gave content
to James's religion. But the whole scheme of Calvinistic salvation
seemed to him the worst enemy of truth. In that system God,
by creating the universe and mankind, glorified Himself; man,
by sin, placed between God and himself an enmity he could
never overcome; reconciliation required persons to obey Christ's
law; the redeemed in God's sight and their own stood apart
from unregenerate mankind; the morality of Christian life on
earth led to rewards after death in heaven.

These doctrines, James came to believe, rightly diagnosed the
human malady as subservience to the force of evil, but the cure
the system prescribed seemed to advance the disease. To demand
that men be concerned for their own personal salvation enlarged
the very selfishness from which they needed to be saved. To
require that men obey Christ's law absurdly asked that a person
change himself — "put me at internecine odds with my own
nature, or obliged me to maintain an ascetic instead of a spontaneous relation to it" (LR, p. 181).

If the Unitarian system was tasteless to the even-tempered
Emerson, the Presbyterian scheme made the impulsive, ebullient
James retch, even long after he had repudiated the church and
located the absolute incarnation of deity in the society of mankind. Any other deity, "superior to this radiant human form,"
struck him as "inexpressibly treasonable to my own manhood"
(LR, p. 111). When this "human" divinity had delivered the
mature James from a long, morbid depression, to its praise he
devoted his considerable literary talent in a spate of pamphlets,
lectures, articles, letters, and books. These writings paradoxically

cloak and reveal a true American religious genius, one who with
great struggle and marked success conformed his life to soaring
spiritual motifs and let their humanized meanings rule his sensibilities. He also tried to fit all the parts of his religion into
a comprehensive theology, based only in part on ideas borrowed
from the Swedish mystic, Emanuel Swedenborg; here the failure
is all the more poignant for James's dogged perseverance in his
task.

The route of James's spiritual pilgrimage ran not from evil
to good, not from darkness to light, not from guilt to forgiveness, but from selfhood to humanity, from an individual
or personal to a general or corporate embodiment of human
nature — in his phrase from moral to spiritual manhood.
"Moral" men accepted their creatureliness in the form of
individual selfhood, establishing objective enmity with the
Creator. That Creator demanded righteousness, which the self-
centered creature must seek selfishly or self-righteously. What
was demanded could never by its nature be attained. Human
institutions only aggravated the predicament by scaling the
demands of complete altruism down to an achievable degree.
This moral compromise enslaved people to their own selfhood.
Its goodness consisted in avoiding avoidable evils like murder,
adultery, and unneighborliness. The family and the state, and
most disastrously the church, excused men and women from
dying to their selfhood and arising to an identity with the whole
human society — for James, the redeemed form of humanity.

This redemption, which James found definitively proclaimed
in the teachings of Jesus Christ, became a livelier option in
America than anywhere else. Americans lived in voluntary
associations. In Europe and Asia social institutions were organic.
In America the family (and by implication also the state and
the church) was "only a transmitted prejudice, having no public
prestige . . . but what it derives from the private worth of its
members" (*LR*, p. 187). Thrown back on naked selfhood by
their individualism, Americans could realize that God's law

"spiritually justifies every man who sincerely disregards himself, and spiritually condemns every man who sincerely seeks himself" (LR, p. 234). America made it feasible for people to live in "intimate and indissoluble fellowship, equality, and universal brotherhood of man," to actualize their identity with humankind in which God was incarnate (LR, p. 83).

This new basis of redeemed life sprang up from the soul. It could never be imposed from without. It expressed itself in freedom instead of force, in spontaneity instead of regulation, in spirituality not morality, in altruism rather than egoism, in sociality instead of individuality. Like Edwards and Emerson, James substituted beauty for morality as the main object of the religious sense — not exactly the beauty of Edwards' divine things nor exactly that of Emerson's refulgent nature but rather the beauty of a united, harmonious, universal humanity. Like theirs, James's religion involved each person's receiving a new spiritual sense. But unlike them, James approached the beauty of holiness "through moral suicide, or inward death to self in all its forms, and a consequent spiritual new-birth" (LR, p. 216). This "suicide" occurred when the self, unaided by any specific deity, came to its senses and realized its oneness with mankind.

The elder James's religiousness, according to his first son, "flowed from two perceptions . . . . In the first place, he felt that the individual man, as such, is nothing, but owes all he is and has to the race nature he inherits, and to the society into which he is born. And secondly, he scorned to admit, even as a possibility, that the great and loving Creator, who has all the being and the power, and has brought us as far as *this*, should not bring us *through*, and *out*, into the most triumphant harmony" (LR, p. 15).

Both these perceptions took form as humane inversions and appropriations of the Calvinistic transactions between God and persons. To James, God by creating the universe did not glorify but denigrated Himself. Human nature spelled holiness, not sin. Men and women contained God's very being and not merely

His image. By a kind of upward "fall" Eve led Adam from brute physicality to the knowledge of good and evil, a necessary moral step toward the true, altruistic, self-abnegating spirituality she would then teach him. Human moral worth thus became a spiritual liability. Christ, a purely representative figure, demonstrated how to die to the self and to become one with mankind. God's true glory consisted in His exhaustive self-incarnation in humanity, the chief end of His creation. Conversion meant a person's "finding his object a *life* within him, and no longer a *law* without him" (*LR*, p. 391). The Kingdom of God on earth, or universal human brotherhood, progressed against the church, requiring neither ministers nor social institutions. "Heaven, remember, is simply the harvested spiritual product of our *natural* or *associated* life on earth, of our unitary or *race* consciousness [the whole human race, of course], as hell is its unharvested waste product" (*LR*, p. 364). Penitence was the soul's sickness instead of its cure. The religious person profoundly yearned not to be saved but (in William's phrase) to lose himself "in the sentiment of unity with his kind" (*LR*, p. 73). Here are present the chief themes of Christian salvation, but they are inverted, they take place within a member of humanity instead of between the individual self and deity. Every function of the old scheme is undercut, ironically ingested, digested, assimilated by the human spirit.

Uncreation

Just how and when this spirituality came upon Henry James is not entirely clear. Passages in the last book he published record how in May 1844, having moved his wife and young sons to England, he suddenly fell into a deep depression that lasted about two years. He could find no surcease until a friend put him onto some of Swedenborg's writings. These books lit up his life. "Up to this very period I had lived in the cheerful faith . . . that my being or substance lay absolutely in myself," but now he could lose himself and find his salvation (*LR*, p. 69).

This recorded conversion at age thirty-five may have been anticipated much earlier. A fragmentary autobiography, in manuscript at James's death, throws back into his seminary days both his captivity to and his knowledge of liberation from what he called professional religion. In the autobiography a fictional friend, Stephen Dewhurst, is James very thinly concealed. But in the preface they are two persons, or possibly one James in two distinct frames of mind. However, the man named James personifies bondage and the one named Dewhurst, liberty. James, the "I" of the preface, took divine providence to be "essentially critical or discriminative, as ordaining certain persons to honor and others to dishonor," while "my friend" (Dewhurst) had "an unconscious, or at all events unaffected, habit of spiritualizing secular things and secularizing sacred things," so that the antagonism between the church and the world "for *his* needs . . . had more than fulfilled its intellectual uses, whatever these may have been" (*LR*, 126, 127). Dewhurst could not "deem any man in himself vitally nearer to God than any other man" (*LR*, p. 125).

Whatever light this passage may throw on James's life, the literary device allowed him (for once) to *admire* his spiritual vision. When he projected it onto another person, he could praise it — unselfishly! The admiring tone gives welcome relief from James's usual tactic of polemically demolishing each of his religion's enemies while saying little of its friends. In all that Dewhurst did, he evinced "frank, cordial recognition . . . of that vital fellowship or equality between man universal and man individual which is the spiritual fulfilment or glorification of conscience, and ends by compelling angel and devil into its equal subservience" (*LR*, p. 129). To be sure, James admitted he might have been giving Dewhurst at seminary some credit for intellectual understandings of spiritual truth come by later but he said the point was negligible. Dewhurst makes an impassioned

confession of God's providence "as guarding and guiding the
freedom of man *ab intra*," and other students query him; James
listens attentively, but his "own intellect stands yet far from
any clear or comprehensive grasp of the truths which constituted
the manifest strength of his [Dewhurst's intellect]" (*LR*, pp.
132, 133). Dewhurst dismisses all thought of objective heaven
and hell to concentrate on "the interest of the divine kingdom,
of God's promised reign of righteousness or justice in the
earth, . . . from which . . . [heaven and hell] alike derive all
their human or philosophic consequence" (*LR*, pp. 136–37).
And when the dying fictional friend after the Civil War calls
James to Washington, James honors Dewhurst's piety by the
epitaph that, to him, "THE CROSS TYPIFIED NOTHING
BUT THE NORMAL, DISTINCTIVE FORM OF GOD'S LIFE
IN THE SOUL OF UNIVERSAL MAN" (*LR*, p. 143).

In 1846 (and afterward) James read Swedenborg, but if he
was a Swedenborgian he must have taken himself for the only
one. Perhaps his spiritual liberation began long before he read
the Swede's books. At any rate, the Church of the New
Jerusalem, the Swedenborgian denomination in America, fell
under James's calumny for professional religion. He called himself a Christian but scorned all ecclesiastical Christianity. All
organized religion, committed by definition to preserving itself
and to focusing attention on individual selves, was to James
a spiritual compromiser, a Grand Inquisitor. Far more drastically
than Emerson he pitted formal religion against true religiousness.
"The church spirit," he wrote, "is *par excellence* the evil-spirit
in humanity, source of all its profounder and irremediable woes"
(*LR*, p. 93 n.).

He did not mean that churches encouraged immorality. On
the contrary, they cultivated men's and women's sense of moral
worth and thereby nourished selfhood or "*proprium*," producing
spiritual pride, something far more malign than outward, "good
honest natural evils" (*LR*, p. 94 n.). Spiritual pride not only
fought against the good. Worse, "it is the actual and deadly

profanation of good," securing in persons the subjective sense
that they possessed their selfhood absolutely without reference
to mankind or society or "to any grander natural objectivity"
(*LR*, p. 94 n.). It immunized a man against redemption, against
considering his life a gift and not an achievement — as William
would put it for himself, literally, a datum and not a fact — that
"belongs to him in strict community with his neighbor" (*LR*,
p. 95 n.). True "Religion says death — *inward or spiritual death*
— to the selfhood in man. Professional religion says: 'Nay,
not death, above all not inward or spiritual — because this
would be *living* — death . . . but an outward or *quasi* death,
professionally or ritually enacted, and so operating a change of base
for the selfhood" (*LR*, pp. 98–99). Ritualism locked refined men
into self-righteousness. Revivalism blessed the pride of coarser
people.

Henry James called himself a Christian. While William James
allowed the claim, he could not find in his father's thought
"any radical and essential necessity for the mission of Christ";
the emphasis on the solidarity of mankind meant "we are *all*
redeemers of the total order so far as we open ourselves each
in his little measure to the spirit of God" (*LR*, pp. 106, 107).
But in Henry James's dying to self and rising to newness of life
in charity with mankind — that is, in his spiritual experience
rather than in his tortured theology — there are unmistakable
marks of a radical kind of Christian piety. In every experiential
aspect of his striking innocence, an innocence that nevertheless
wrestled mightily with the tragic, evil side of life, there
is a bold assimilating into human existence of the divine-human
transaction that James as a boy met in its most starched, Presbyterian dress. Yet, once he had thoroughly dismantled and
humanized this religion, he felt driven to put it back together
again in a grand theological system. More bolstered by the example of Swedenborg than dependent on his thought — late in
life he wrote of the Swede's books, "I have now not looked
into them for many years" — James brought more literary punch

than intellectual power to his goal of setting forth a definitive theological synthesis for modern Americans (*LR*, p. 237).

This intellectualism, nevertheless, was honestly come by. For James believed that "the sentiment which men have of their natural *otherness* to God arising from their birth in space and time, is a strictly *subjective* illusion of the mind with no particle of *objective* reality in it" (*LR*, p. 207). Arousing men and women to their true nature as part of humanity (and therefore of divinity) meant occupying the battleground of the mind. Social reforms based on the selfhood of persons hoping to obey the decrees of an alien deity only retarded mankind's true progress. People must be made to *understand* their real nature, must philosophically be *taught* properly to regard (which is to say to disregard) themselves, must *learn* to "unself" themselves to realize their union with divine mankind.

Few arose to do battle, for James's trumpet sounded uncertainly. Over his writings the best self-epitaph might have been, "if I were only able to do justice to the great theme as it exists to my own mind, my readers would not be slow to confess agreement with me" (*LR*, pp. 208–9). Instead he commanded his daughter, a week before he died, to instruct the minister presiding at his funeral "to say only this, 'here lies a man who has thought all his life, that the ceremonies attending birth, marriage and death were all damned nonsense,' don't let him say a word more."[50] The grand scheme was nothing more than the unity of every man with humanity as the incarnation of God — but to fit a piecemeal, humanized, experienced, inverted Calvinism into *that* principle . . . !

The instructions for his obsequies stated the case negatively. Had he been able to elaborate it positively as well, his spirituality might have "taken" in his contemporaries enough to make him the prophet of late-twentieth-century Americans' religious concern for a voluntary unity of mankind to which all men and women are equally and justly, yet distinctly related. James cried his social gospel in a wilderness of individualism and romantic naturalism. He needed a garden of humane socialism. Ingeniously he let take place within the human soul itself what had been preached as an elaborate business between an alien, objective God and the cringing, striving, self-based person. Each part of his piety achieved a holy beauty, but he could not make it theologically harmonious.

Nor, to the best of his knowledge, could anybody else. In Emerson the man, James espied the spirituality he advocated, but Emerson the thinker had it all wrong from gazing into the mirror of nature instead of the mirror of mankind. Notwithstanding, James believed Emerson transcended selfhood, having neither conscience — that is, consciousness of himself as being either good or evil — nor a discernible private personality. Emerson "unconsciously brought you face to face with the infinite in humanity"; Emerson "recognized no God outside of himself and his interlocutor, and recognized him there only as the *lia[i]son* between the two. . . . In short, the only holiness which Emerson recognized," James wrote, "and for which he consistently lived, was innocence . . . [which] attaches only to what is definitively universal or natural in our experience, and hence appropriates itself to individuals only in so far as they learn to denude themselves of personality or self-consciousness" (*LR*, pp. 301, 302).

The parts of a rich religiousness that Henry James could not fit into a closed system, William James, his father's leading (if highly critical) disciple, resolved to take one by one, testing each for its capacity to ennoble the human person and society.

The Son's Spiritual Crisis

By his own reckoning James took from his father "the humor, the good spirits, the humanity, the faith in the divine, and the sense of his right to have a say about the deepest reasons of the universe" (*L*, 1:221). William's portégé and first biographer, Ralph Barton Perry, said, "he took the content and rejected the form . . . — his father's piety, and not his father's ideas" (*TC*, 1:467). In a way the legacy was both experiential and intellectual. In another sense it was neither. For James could take from others only what he could make distinctively his own. He no less than Edwards and Emerson kept religious thought tied to religious experience; like them he tested his psychology and philosophy by his life.

Experience

Although James's own generation had "ceased to believe in the kind of God it argued for," a God whose unitary being enclosed all existence in a single, ideal system, they remained ingeniously innovative, god-seeking, god-serving creatures (*VR*, p. 74). Every experience invited men and women to enter the strenuous mood, to choose between options so momentous and lively and inescapable that to choose *not* to choose was a choice shaping reality. To ask only which path would be better for the chooser involved morality or ethics. But truly momentous options affected reality itself and involved religion. Such choices molded this "half-wild, half-saved universe [to which] our nature is adapted" (*WB*, p. 61). When an action involved making the universe wilder or more saved, the actor was allying himself with powers beyond himself — not absolute deities but consciousnesses beyond his own — and was exercising his capacity to seek and to serve "the more." As John Wild notes, James distinguished religion from morality in that "for one who thinks radically, ethics will lead to religion," and one must read James superficially or backwards to collapse his religion into ethics.[51]

Radical thinking led to religion, but religion varied according to persons and circumstances. Many kinds of religious experience validly opened dimensions of human existence and made life worth living. There existed for James many powers with whom men and women could establish conscious relations. But the religious act, which James always tested by its humane character and result, remained a human phenomenon. To be sure, he made a "heroic attempt to examine religion critically on the inside," and he insisted "that God is man's god in essence, not by accident."[52] More precisely, "man's gods," for James found the range of religious aspirations and fruits too diverse to refer to any single principle or object or deity.

The monist's guaranteed safe end for the human voyage struck James as dogma rather than real belief. Monistic faith implicitly excused people from working to make things come out well. The official, monotheistic religion compromised the moral nature of man. Thus all institutional religion sat remote from the true religious act. The phenomenal world became a universe (always an unfinished one) so far as men and women, cooperating with the higher powers, made their many worlds turn as one. Cosmic shipwreck would be averted only by the kind of believing that stirred people individually to make their beliefs come true and to cooperatively achieve safe arrival. Action "trued" belief, for the truth of a belief was a function of its working.

This quality of believing permeated James's thought and animated his life, as his voluminous letters and essays subtly indicate. In these writings the author's thought and character and indeed his own religion and spirituality are revealed without actually being described. Far from professing the presence of God, James denied having experienced it. Yet many passages in his books as well as his letters are profoundly and autobiographically religious. The father's failure to erect a theology adequate to his religion struck the son not as one man's foible; something was intrinsically wrong in describing one's own spirituality and thereby implicitly prescribing it for others. James theologized negatively by denying false ideas of God. He pleaded that people together could alter reality, even though he considered himself "intensely an individualist" who believed "that as a practical problem for the individual, the religion he stands by must be the one which he finds best for *him*, even though there were better individuals, and their religion better for them"

(*TC*, 2:339). Again, "You see that, although religion is the great interest of my life, I am rather hopelessly non-evangelical, and take the whole thing too impersonally" (*L*, 2:58).

But "impersonally" here has a special and narrow meaning, almost the same as that of "non-evangelical." James brooked no separation of the subject from the object of experience. Nor could either the subject or the object be separated from the relation between them. Real persons were really in a real world with other real persons. Thus James did not write newspaporially (his neologism) to report his own encounters or experiences, nor to recount what he experienced, nor even to record him*self* as the experiencer. Instead he brought himself and his experiences and their objects into his letters and lectures as means of helping his hearers and readers stretch the range of their own experience, selfhood, experienced objects, and reality. The famous quip to the effect that Henry James, Jr., wrote novels like a psychologist while William wrote psychology like a novelist points to William's ability to depict human experiences of a factually concrete kind in such a way that his readers recollect having had such experiences — indeed are actually led to have them.

James's radically empirical insistence that experiences reflexively contain their own significance is thus the clue to his religious life and thought: religiously we are saintly when we pray, saved when we yearn for salvation, free when we choose, just as psychologically we are angry when we strike, sorrowful when we weep, and so on. Approached by means of this clue, James's writings reveal an original but imitable spirituality that they never really describe, much less systematize.

The son's spontaneous engagement with the world and its inhabitants is just what Henry James the elder meant to cultivate in his children by an informal, disorganized, transatlantic, mobile education. By the time William entered Harvard at nineteen, he had crossed the ocean six times to live and study in England, France, Switzerland, and Germany as well as in New York City and Albany and Newport. "Home" to the boy had multiple meanings, referring less to the place one departed from and returned to than to how much "at home" one made oneself with people and places, wherever he found himself. Census-takers would have put the family in New York City during William's young years until 1863, then briefly in Boston, and after 1866 in Cambridge. William spent his nineteenth year in Newport, learning to be a painter, then turned to Harvard's scientific school to study chemistry, anatomy, and physiology. He assisted the great biologist Louis Agassiz on a collecting expedition to Brazil in 1865 and 1866 and went to Germany for 1867 and 1868. When he applied for his medical degree at Harvard in 1869, he reckoned that during the five years since he had begun medical studies he had actually pursued them for barely the required minimum of three years.

Acedia

In Germany James suffered a bleak, suicidal depression attended by insomnia, eye trouble, weakness of the back, and digestive disorders. Baths and medicinal waters brought no cure (although he would return to them later in life for other ailments). During four years (1868–72) as an invalid in his father's home, fighting an inward battle to continue living, he confided the depth of his malaise to letters and a secret diary. Idleness and lethargy as well as bodily illness preyed on James as his early manhood drifted past him. Long bouts of disdain for life were briefly punctuated — and aggravated — by a few flashes of euphoria that "woke up the spiritual monad within me" (L, 1:152). The diaries for early 1870 reveal a deep crisis of dire disgust with his own existence, culminating in a downhill plunge of vital energy, of the will to live. Panic fear checked by religious consolation stirred the will and reversed the plunge. James found a new direction, tentatively at first, through self-consciously deciding to believe in living (Allen, 162–70; TC, 1:322; 2:675; L, 1:147).

In the last days of 1869 James, exceedingly morbid in spirit, had clung to life, when mere habit failed him, by acts of sheer will. At the beginning of 1870 he was weakly hoping for improvement. On the first of February he "about touched bottom." Could he develop "the moral interest," could he find within his spirit the affirmation of its own ground? He had been trying to do so "as an aid in the accomplishing of certain utilitarian ends of attaining certain difficult but salutary habits. I tried to associate the feeling of moral degradation with failure, and add to it that of the loss of the wished for sensible good end — and the reverse of success. But in all this I was more or less humbugging myself. Now I must regard," he wrote, "these useful ends only as occasions for my moral life to become active." As Gay Wilson Allen reconstructs the events, "Then he experienced a great emotional shock: the death of Minny Temple," a very dear friend. "He felt as numb as the crude tombstone he drew in his diary" (Allen, pp. 164–65).

In the midst of severe depression (whose character he only later understood) "suddenly there fell upon me without any warning, just as if it came out of the darkness, a horrible fear of my own existence." To his imagination sprang a catatonic, epileptic patient he had once seen, "looking absolutely non-human. This image and my fear entered into a species of combination with each other. *That shape am I*, I felt, potentially. Nothing that I possess can defend me against that fate, if the hour for it should strike for me as it struck for him. There was such a horror of him, and such a perception of my own merely momentary discrepancy from him, that it was as if something hitherto solid within my breast gave way entirely, and I became a mass of quivering fear. After this the universe was changed for me altogether." There was "horrible dread at the pit of my stomach"; there was "a sense of the insecurity of life that I never knew before, and that I have never felt since." He wondered "how I myself had ever lived, so unconscious of that pit of insecurity beneath the surface of life." James later compared the episode with an experience of John Bunyan's and with his father's sudden onset of fear in 1844. He told his own story in *Varieties* as though from a French correspondent, whom James said he had asked what was meant by saying the experience "had a religious bearing." The "correspondent" answered, "I mean that the fear was so invasive and powerful that if I had not clung to scripture-texts like 'The eternal God is my refuge,' etc. . . . I think I should have grown really insane" (*VR*, pp. 160–61). The antidote to this misery?

> Not in maxims, not in *Anschauungen* [contemplative views], but in
> accumulated *acts* of thought lies salvation. . . . Hitherto, when I
> have felt like taking a free initiative, like daring to act originally,
> without carefully waiting for contemplation of the external world to
> determine all for me, suicide seemed the most manly form to put
> my daring into; now, I will go a step further with my will, not only act
> with it, but believe as well; believe in my individual reality and
> creative power. My belief, to be sure, *can't* be optimistic — but I
> will posit life (the real, the good) in the self-governing *resistance* of
> the ego to the world. Life shall be . . . doing and suffering and
> creating (*L*, 1:148).

The resolve, encouraged by reading Charles Renouvier on the will and poems by William Wordsworth, gradually dispelled James's urges to suicide. During the next month "mere brute power of resistance" was all he had "to depend on in this world . . . in the last resort," for unless he denied the good he could not "blink the evil out of sight. . . . It must be accepted and hated, and resisted while there's breath in our bodies" (*L*, 1:158).

Now suspended between the urge to die and the will to live, leaning no more toward one than the other, James merely endured for many months by resisting his own boredom. The first clear testimony of recovery comes from his father's letter of March 18, 1873, to Henry, Jr., in England. The father had seen the change somewhat earlier. Now William had described it to Henry, Sr., as "the difference between death and life," between hypochondria and sanity. Reading the above authors "had promoted the change," he had told his father, "but especially his having given up the notion that all mental disorder required to have a physical basis. . . . He saw that the mind did act irrespectively of material coercion, and could be dealt with therefore at first-hand, and this was health to his bones" (*TC*, 1:339–40).

The language of these assertions bears the father's brand. The experience rings true for the son. As religious comforts enabled him to cling to life, he consciously affirmed himself in a way that allowed him to take hold on himself. Then he could deal as a self with himself, could will to believe (certainly not make-believe) and to act on that belief. James experienced a sick soul, a morbid spirit, one who met the dark powers. By James's own definitions the cure was distinctly religious: "a kind of experience in which intellect, feeling, and will, all our consciousness and all our subconsciousness together melt in a kind of chemical fusion"; a "moment of life that brings the reality of spiritual things more 'home' to one"; the experience of "conversations with the unseen, voices and visions, responses to prayer, changes of heart, deliverances from fear, inflowings of help, assurances of support, whenever certain persons set their own internal attitude in certain appropriate ways" (*TC*, 2:329; *L*, 2:215; *ER*, p. 428).

In 1873, after his first half-year of teaching (he first held a job at the age of thirty), James resolved not to accept reappointment at Harvard teaching physiological psychology and anatomy but to devote himself professionally to philosophy. Briefly facing the implications of this decision, he abjured it. The professional philosopher's business was to "criticize afresh and call in question the grounds of his faith of the day before, [and] I fear the constant sense of instability generated by this attitude would be more than the voluntary faith I can keep going is sufficient to neutralize" (*TC*, 1:343). Keeping everything open and optional, brooding upon the uncertainties of life, had spiritually paralyzed him. Making everything theoretically possible left nothing actual.

In an earlier era this plight would have been recognized as acedia, or torpor. Catholic moralists wrongly combined this eighth deadly sin of the early monks with sloth, mistaking the inability to act for laziness. Acedia was rather an overscrupulous wondering about what one ought to do. It prevented one from doing anything. It tempted one to suicide as the only escape from the ennui and the guilt of inactivity. Victims of acedia could love nothing, could hate only themselves and could hate themselves only for their inability to love anything, including themselves.

In the history of Western spirituality acedia had been treated by placing its victims under the absolute spiritual authority of another. Martin Luther's confessor dealt with such scrupulosity in the young monk by ordering him to teach biblical theology in Wittenberg. But James had no Doctor John Staupitz. The sole authority he could find was his own ability to believe that he might command his own will. Having envisioned the only escapes from acedia as committing suicide or having a shriveled soul, James became his own spiritual director. Reciting verses of comfort in the crisis of fear had held James back from insanity and suicide, but God had not delivered him. He began saving himself from acedia, a feat traditionally held impossible. He became, as it were, at once the sick-souled patient and his own absolving confessor. Nor does it detract from the feat to point out that his indulgent father could afford to let this thirty-one-year-old son teach or rest, work or travel, as best pleased him. The fiscal ease that allowed for this cure must also have deepened the malady.

By summer 1873 James was considering a year of reduced activity in Italy before taking up his professional work full tilt an autumn later. At that juncture, "The only thing with me now is my health; my ideas, my plans of study, are all straightened out" (TC, 1:349). He took most of the year out.

"I *must* get well now or give up" (*TC*, 1:351). He got well, by April 1874 was back at laboratory work in Cambridge, and in September began a full (and lifelong) career on the Harvard faculty, entering social and professional life with zest. He would often be concerned over bodily health, but he had conquered the spiritual paralysis rendering him unable to hope and believe, think and act, feel and will. He aimed his career toward psychology and philosophy, studies he called liberal because they cultivated "the habit of always seeing an alternative, of not taking the usual for granted, of making conventionalities fluid again, of imagining foreign states of mind" (*L*, 1:190). After establishing the basis of his mature thought in a physiological psychology that joined subject and object in interaction with mutable reality, James would be ready to open new avenues of philosophical and religious experience. And from 1878 onward he drew nourishment from the love he shared with his wife, Alice Howe Gibbens.

The first and most seminal of his books, *Principles of Psychology*, was contracted the year James married, but was published only in 1890. By then his family, housed in the commodious home he built in Cambridge, included Henry (born 1879), William (1882), Margaret Mary (1887), and Alexander Robertson (1890). James's mother died and his son William was born before James left for a lonely sabbatical leave, 1882–83, in Italy, Germany, and England. When he returned his father was dead, and he interrupted work on the *Psychology* to edit and publish the *Literary Remains* (1884). On the next sabbatical, 1892–93, he dragged wife and children (aged thirteen years down to seven months) around Europe on a journey more meandering than those of his own childhood. By that time he had abridged the *Psychology* into a text, *Psychology: Briefer Course* (1892).

During the next decade he taught philosophy and studied religion. *The Will to Believe and Other Essays* (1897) established James as a major philosophical voice. He began collecting material for the *Varieties* and lectured across the country on psychology. In June 1899, overexerting himself and being overexposed during a hike in the Adirondack Mountains, he seriously strained his heart. Travel to Europe for baths at several spas brought relief, but permanent damage was manifest in limited energy, recurrent pain, weakened eyesight. Illness and recovery delayed the Gifford Lectures so that *Varieties* could be published only in 1902.

During the eight remaining years James rounded out his philosophy and religious thought. In 1905 he journeyed to Greece and Rome. In spring 1906 he taught at Stanford University until the great California earthquake in April cut short the school year. In 1907 he gave his last courses at Harvard and then repeated them at Columbia University. After publishing *Pragmatism* (1907), he undertook the Hibbert Lectures (*A Pluralistic Universe*, 1910) at the Unitarian seminary in Oxford, bringing together religious thought and philosophy into a piecemeal metaphysic. Important works, especially *Some Problems of Philosophy* and *Essays in Radical Empiricism*, were nearly ready for publication when in spring 1910, frail, broken, and suffering, he went with Mrs. James to baths in Germany. This time there was no relief. Henry and Alice brought him to the beloved summer home at Chocorua, New Hampshire, where on August 26, 1910, he died.

Cure

These details of time, place, and event reach only the outward James. He poured his inner life into his philosophy even more sensitively than into the voluminous letters. For example, the foundation of his religious thought stands in an essay first called "The Psychology of Belief" and revised as the chapter on "The Perception of Reality" in the big book on psychology.[53] This piece of lucid, scientific psychology, appealing both to common human experience and to technical scholarship, also narrated James's spiritual crisis and cure.

This door to his thought becomes a window to his spirituality. He has already struck the axiomatic equation of experience and reality; "Everything real could be experienced, and all experience was real" (Allen, p. 510). He has already joined sensation, thought, and action into an unbroken arc of experience. He has already called consciousness a stream in which attention could be focused without excluding the fringes of marginal or even transmarginal reality. In its stream a man could choose — among lively and ineluctable options — what he would attend, believe, and do, thereby shaping the realities of his life. Believing was essential to living because disbelieving was part of believing: "we never disbelieve anything except for the reason that we believe something else which contradicts the first thing" (*PP*, 2:284). Already in 1870 this religious discovery — that belief involved personal consent as well as intellectual agreement, that the opposite of belief was not disbelief but doubt and inquiry — had allowed James to affirm and realize his life by an elemental act of will. Now in 1890 he proclaimed what Perry called his "gospel of belief": the general, practical rule that acts of consent frame the reality that humans experience (*TC*, 1:324).

Now for James both belief (the sense of reality) and doubt (the sense of unreality) could be "pathologically exalted." The former happened in drunkenness, most extremely in intoxication by nitrous oxide (James had whiffed amyl nitrate in 1875). Doubt, according to the book on psychology, became pathologically exalted by "the questioning mania . . . [called] *Grübelsucht* by the Germans" (*PP*, 2:284). In his diary on April 30, 1870, James had resolved, "For the remainder of the year, I will abstain from the mere speculation and contemplative Grübelei in which my nature takes most delight, and voluntarily cultivate the feeling of moral freedom, by reading books favorable to it, as well as by acting."[54] There was still another pathological state worse than drunkenness and the questioning mania, "as far removed from doubt as from belief" and countervailing both. That was acedia, "the feeling that everything is hollow, unreal, dead"; in this state "nothing is believed in . . . as it used to be, and . . . all sense of reality is fled from life"; the sufferer is "sheathed in india-rubber; nothing penetrates to the quick or draws bloods, as it were" (*PP*, 2:285, 298). James had been afflicted by just such acedia when he was "in this state of philosophic pessimism and general depression of spirits," and the panic fear that cut through his sheath and drew blood "had a religious bearing" (*VR*, pp. 160, 161).

James's personal experiences certainly framed the chapter on the psychology of belief. Intoxication engendered a pathological emotion of consent and deepened the sense of reality without the attention's being focused on objects or ideas or relations; it made life a conceptual forest without perceived trees (*WB*, pp. 294–98). The questioning mania, the opposite malady, shifted attention from one thing to another without concentrating anywhere enough to realize anything; it made life a flux of perceived, discrete trees failing to constitute a forest. But the profoundest alienation of the self was acedia, the inability either to focus on experienced things or to generate any sense of reality; life was no forest and there were no trees — only stumps.

Although James did not use the term "acedia," his famous analysis of the sick soul in *Varieties* described the disease. Once again he distinguished it from the form of melancholy that pondered and questioned the world pathologically (*Grübelsucht*). James took for this total absence of faith the general term "anhedonia," or "the sense of incapacity for joyous feeling." Its extreme form was "positive and active anguish, a sort of psychical neuralgia wholly unknown to healthy life." But anhedonia did not always have a religious bearing, especially in the form of "Querulousness of mind" (not a bad rendering of *Grübelsucht*), which tended "towards irreligion" and "has played, so far as I know, no part whatever in the construction of religious systems" (*VR*, pp. 146, 147, 149). Only when some keen passion cut through the cover in which anhedonia sheathed the spirit could the religious impulse arise — precisely what happened to James in the episode of panic fear. This crucial passage in *Varieties* becomes nearly as autobiographical as the famous confession from the "French correspondent":

Conceive yourself, if possible, suddenly stripped of all the emotion
with which your world now inspires you, and try to imagine it *as it
exists*, purely by itself, without your favorable or unfavorable, hopeful
or apprehensive comment. It will be almost impossible for you to
realize such a condition of negativity and deadness. No one portion of
the universe would then have importance beyond another; and the
whole collection of its things and series of its events would be without
significance, character, expression, or perspective. Whatever of
value, interest, or meaning our respective worlds may appear endued
with are thus pure gifts of the spectator's mind. The passion of love
is the most familiar and extreme example of this fact. If it comes, it
comes; if it does not come, no process of reasoning can force it. . . .
So with fear, with indignation, jealousy, ambition, worship. If they
are there, life changes. And whether they shall be there or not depends
almost always upon non-logical, often on organic conditions. And
as the excited interest which these passions put into the world is our
gift to the world, just so are the passions themselves *gifts*, — gifts
to us, from sources sometimes low and sometimes high; but almost
always non-logical and beyond our control. . . . Gifts, either of the
flesh or of the spirit; and the spirit bloweth where it listeth; and the
world's materials lend their surface passively to all the gifts alike,
as the stage-setting receives indifferently whatever alternating colored
lights may be shed upon it from the optical apparatus in the gallery.

Meanwhile the practically real world for each one of us, the effective
world of the individual, is the compound world, the physical facts
and emotional values in indistinguishable combination. Withdraw
or pervert either factor of this complex resultant, and the kind of
experience we call pathological ensues (*VR*, pp. 150–51).

The gift, having a religious bearing, that shook James's own
acedia and enabled him to change his life by an act of will,
was not love but panic fear. Believing in some reality — any
reality that elicited action, even the negative action of simply
resisting evil without thinking it good — brought that reality
into James's experienced life and cured his pathological condition. The fundamental belief was belief in the spirit's ability
to believe. At the end of April 1870, James had resolved, "My
first act of free will shall be to believe in free will" (*L*, 1:147).
In the psychology book he presented the antidote to acedia in
the same saving formula: "The first act of free-will, in short,

would naturally be to believe in free-will"; more succinctly, "Freedom's first deed should be to affirm itself" (*PP*, 2:321, 573). Freedom became real so far as one exercised his spiritual consent to his own freedom, and freedom remained real (and reality remained free) so long as belief and affirmation were strivingly lived. Act, James exhorted, "in cold blood . . . as if the thing in question were real, and keep acting as if it were real, and it will infallibly end by growing into such a connection with our life that it will become real. . . . Those to whom 'God' and 'Duty' are now mere names can make them much more than that, if they make a little sacrifice to them every day" (*PP*, 2:321–22). That daily sacrifice to the god of human freedom and to the duty of improving the universe was the private ritual of James's spirituality and his religious summons to modern man. His religious experience and his "gospel of belief" coincided.

Believing and Religion

The gospel according to James assigned more reality to some human beliefs than to others. In the first place, he roundly affirmed the fixity of physical and historical fact. To fancy that fire is cold and that Abraham Lincoln never wore a beard was not belief but ineffectual make-believe. In the second place, he tested intellectual hypotheses by their workability and not by the intensity with which they were held. Monism answered to the human need for univocal commands and atomism accorded with the chaotic impression of raw sense-perceptions. But each view failed where the other worked, and no amount of "believing" one or the other could extend its narrow truth-value.

Belief shaped reality only when one had to decide between lively, forced (=unavoidable), and momentous options. Moreover, James's own personal experience and his work as a psychologist gave him a keen eye for hallucinations, delusions, misperceptions, errors, and lies. Of course, even these kinds of perceptions and testimonies had some status in reality. Validity, however, accrued to what was confirmed in a shared universe of human experience, a universe embracing many spheres. A perception or belief became real, provided nothing in its own sphere or world contradicted it, so far as it worked in other worlds.

James enumerated the most important worlds or subuniverses of common experience as: (1) "The world of sense, or of physical 'things' as we instinctively apprehend them"; (2) "The world of science, or of physical things as the learned conceive them"; (3) "The world of ideal relations, or abstract truths believed or believable by all, and expressed in logical, mathematical, metaphysical, ethical, or aesthetic propositions"; (4) "The world of 'idols of the tribe,' illusions or prejudices common to the race"; (5) "The various supernatural worlds" ("The various worlds of deliberate fable may be ranked with these worlds of faith"); (6) "The various worlds of individual opinion, as numerous as men are"; and (7) "The worlds of sheer madness and vagary, also indefinitely numerous" (*PP*, 2:292–93). Modern men and women lived in all these worlds (and possibly more) and their beliefs therefore underwent multiple tests of reliability — which is to say, reality.

Realization

Any thought, perception, or even illusion that functioned in any one of the many worlds had *some* sort of existence. But the more real experiences and objects were those commanding sustained interest and attention, and functioning in the worlds of sense and science in addition to some others. Universal fascination with a winged horse would not make it real until it worked toward desired results in the worlds of sense and thought and action. Interest and attention involved really caring, not mere whimsy. Persons who were serious-minded about reality were confronted with urgent options, options that were lively and not dead, forced and not avoidable, momentous and not trivial (*WB*, pp. 2–4). Thus an urgent belief involved risk because one staked his life on realizing it — on making it real, on "truing" it. (James liked the example of a mountain-climber who must leap a six-foot chasm or perish. He could not await more evidence about his ability to jump, could not experiment with practice jumps working up to the crucial one, could not take it in two leaps. Yet the more strongly he believed he could leap to the other side, the more likely he would be to make it.)

Moreover, the human community shared its reality and its experiences; cooperant beliefs and actions could change the universe. The healthy person would believe all he could believe to achieve his desired result. While his stream of consciousness would flow where he centered the current of his attention and interest, he would also hold in his consciousness the pools and eddies and backwaters at the fringes of the central current. Thus the *most* real reality embraced the broadest scope of human experiences of the most people in the "realest" of their worlds. For all his individualism, James occupied a republic of reality whose strenuously believing citizens shaped and reshaped their universe and, indeed, chose their deities.

Within these important limits, men and women by their believing and acting actually shaped reality. The believing, thinking, acting self, in James's experience as in his psychology, "is the hook from which the rest dangles, the absolute support. And as from a painted hook it has been said that one can only hang a painted chain, so conversely, from a real hook only a real chain can properly be hung. Whatever things have intimate and continuous connection with my life are things of whose reality I cannot doubt. Whatever things fail to establish this connection are things which are practically no better for me than if they existed not at all" (*PP*, 2:297–98). The philosopher's business was to ask in which world a believed reality functioned, how it stood up in other worlds, and how the various worlds fit together. Hypothetically he could design an ideal reality, but by adding coats of philosophical and theological paint he could not make a painted hook become a real hook. Reality came into being through belief and action by real selves living in the common world. "The perfect object of belief would be a God or 'Soul of the World,' represented both optimistically and moralistically (if such a combination could be), and withal so definitely conceived as to show us why our phenomenal experiences should be sent to us by Him in just the very way in which they come" (*PP*, 2:317).

But this ideal God remained hypothetical. Theoretically, this God would satisfy man's need to have his deeds count and his need to push against evil, for "the impulse to take life strivingly is indestructible in the race" (*PP*, 2:315). Theoretically, this God would satisfy man's need to believe in a universe richly inclusive of all the facts of sense, simply grounded and harmoniously organized by reference to the hypothetical God. But this God could not enter human consciousness as a prior reality ready-made and full-blown. Any such deus ex machina would render man a puppet, unable to take life strivingly. Toward an ideal object of belief men indeed strove in their changing universe, but actually they found that several gods were necessary to satisfy their large needs. "What is beyond the crude experiences is not an *alternative* to them," which this theoretic deity would be, "but something that *means* them for me here and now" (*PP*, 2:317). Man's freedom, arising in the context of his doubt, made belief *his* consent and reality *his* reality.

This man-made reality comprised the fundamental data of human existence, a "perceptual flux" bringing genuine novelty and change into the universe. Since "Biography is the concrete form in which all that is is immediately given," the activity of living and knowing had "no content save these experiences of process, obstruction, striving, strain, or release, ultimate *qualia* as they are of the life given us to be known" (*SP*, pp. 151, 212). In a word, for James reality grew.

How it changed depended on who was changing it. Particularly, its growth depended on religion, "on our not-resisting our faith-tendencies," which expressed "our good-will toward certain forms of result" and which were "constantly outstripping evidence" (*SP*, pp. 223–24). Men had to act on faith because they could not hedge their bets and distribute their risks. Acting fractionally — "if the probability is 1–2 that your partner is a villain, . . . treating him as a villain one day, and confiding your money and your secrets to him the next" — would be absurd (*SP*, p. 227).

In this unfinished universe, moreover, *not* to act on a given belief meant consenting to its opposite. Man fooled himself (or let himself be fooled by philosophers) into taking the Olympian spectator's seat from which to fancy a universe complete, closed, ideal. Actually, persons always encountered the universe from within. They were constantly called on to be participants instead of mere spectators. Participatory believing made new reality. Participatory believing was, in a word, being at home in the universe, was "the greeting of our whole nature to a kind of world conceived as well adapted to that nature" (*SP*, p. 221).

James modeled his melioristic or improvable universe on a social pattern that functioned rather like his father's social mankind. It was conceived "as a pluralism of independent powers" who could make the enterprise succeed or let it fail, depending upon "a lot of ifs" — "*If* we do *our* best, *and* the other powers do *their* best, the world will be perfected" (*SP*, pp. 229, 230). Persons "As individual members of a pluralistic universe" had to choose one of four courses: (1) await more evidence, meanwhile doing nothing; (2) mistrust the enterprise and *let* the universe fail; (3) trust the other powers and do one's best, in spite of the risk that the universe *may* fail; or (4) flounder by doing one thing one day and another the next (*SP*, pp. 229–30). The reality men and women established by their believing was the actual, shared reality of the universe they occupied and influenced.

James called his theory "no 'vicious circle' unless a circle
of poles holding themselves upright by leaning on one another,
or a circle of dancers revolving by holding each other's hands,
be 'vicious'" (*SP*, p. 231). To know the other dancers' religious
experiences promoted cooperation with other human (and transhuman) powers, at once enlarging and improving the reality
in which one participated. Therefore, James cultivated what he
called acquaintance with, not only knowledge about, the whole
range of religiousness open to the human spirit, for he wished
strivingly and seriously to try on for size, as it were, others'
relations with higher powers to see where and how those relations
would work for him. He did not simply ask *whether* these relations worked in *any* kind of world; he tried to discover in what
worlds and to what *results* they worked and for *whom*. However
little or much his own direct relations with God may seem to
figure in his big book on religion, he always exercised his religious sense by occupying the relations that others made real. He
refined the religious sense by tasting the fruit of those relations
and by inviting others to taste them.

Variety

In the *Varieties* James reached beyond simple curiosity about
unusual religious behavior, beyond classifying or even typing
spiritual phenomena. He charted human spirituality by the poles
of extreme or abnormal cases. Few case histories came out of
his own empirical observation. He needed the starkest examples
he could find in the literature, because by mapping the extremes
of their varied terrain he also was drawing the boundaries of
religiousness.

The next six paragraphs summarize, in the present tense, the
ingenious map set forth in this most famous of all American
treatises on religion.

1. Physical, societal, and psychic explanations of religious
phenomena, valid as far as they go, fail to reckon spiritual signifi-

cance, which carries its own validity. The task is to classify and appraise these phenomena by their fruits. The religious dimension of life consists in "the art of winning the favor of the gods," and this "relation . . . between man and his maker" reaches far beyond the emotions (love, fear, joy, and the rest) it engenders — especially in its personal if not also its institutional expressions (*VR*, p. 29). Unlike morality, which looks beyond itself and fixes values, religious experience finds its worth in the "divinity of the object and the solemnity of the reaction" (*VR*, p. 39). These objects are neither abstractly ideal and absolute (as Platonists believe) nor hallucinatory (as psychologists tend to think) but virtually or preternaturally real. The experience of them combines two impressions: something makes itself present, and this presence makes things intensely right. According to the believer's constitution and circumstance, the sense of divine presence can awaken joy or fear, gladness or sadness, expansiveness or constriction, submission or dread, peace or turmoil. The main types of religious experience are (1) emotional, (2) mystical or illuminational, and (3) intellectual; the first shows the most variety and richness.

2. The basic range of *emotional* religious experience is from the optimistic or *healthy-minded* to the pessimistic or *morbid*. The happier experiences revel in freedom, sensing no bondage or need for deliverance, and express themselves philosophically by conceiving things as good. This ingredient is necessary in every person's attitude. Taken to excess, it inures one to sensing evil or leads one to dismiss evil as ignorance or falsehood. Yet healthy-minded religion can cure many personal ills and enable persons to exercise passive relaxation, concentration, and meditation. The opposite extreme, the sick soul, does not flee from sin but groans and writhes over its commission, finding in evil the key to the world's meaning. Moments of evil, fear, woe, melancholy, or pain occur in most lives. Pessimistic religion takes these passions as gifts that generate "urgent wondering and questioning," gifts that lead the sufferer to salvation by being "swallowed up in

supernatural good" (*VR*, pp. 152, 157). Morbid-minded religion embraces more of human experience than healthy-minded. Therefore the religions of salvation are the more profound.

3. Most religious experiences contain some mixture of the two types, depending on the degree of harmony or heterogeneity in the person and his condition. Both types can undergo *conversion*, the religious reunifying of a discordant personality. Splits between the ideal self and the actual self, between the conscious and the unconscious, may be overcome swiftly or gradually in conversion, and the change may be from belief to disbelief or from moral scrupulousness to license, as well as vice versa. In any case, the result of conversion is "a firmness, stability, and equilibrium succeeding a period of storm and stress and inconsistency" (*VR*, p. 176). Such experiences involve some sense of a power, not necessarily divine, outside the self. In conversion religion becomes "*the habitual centre of* . . . [one's] *personal energy*" (*VR*, p. 196). That centering, although impossible for some persons, is common in adolescents. Many conversions are imitative or induced by suggestion, but original models stand. One's own effort may produce gradual conversion, in which one step is crucial to the process, or conversion may involve sudden, passive self-surrender. In both cases the deliverance is sensed as received rather than achieved. In sudden conversion, the classic type, "one's ordinary fields of consciousness are liable to incursions" from "ultra-marginal" regions of life (*VR*, p. 234). The experience is memorable and to some degree ineffable. But the value of conversion is tested by its fruits, not its origins. The sense of the presence of a higher agency can bring an assurance that all is ultimately well, a perception of new truth, and a new relation to the objective world. Spasms, visions, unconsciousness, luminosity, and other involuntary behavior often accompanying conversions make the experiences memorable but "have no essential spiritual significance" (*VR*, p. 251).[55]

4. Extraordinary acts flow from religious experience when a sovereign impulse overcomes usual inhibitions. This religious

heroism or *saintliness* means that the subject lives, habitually and with uninhibited emotional intensity, "in his religious centre of personal energy" (*VR*, p. 267). The saint in any religion feels himself to be participating in an ideal power, willing to surrender to that power, breaking beyond a confining selfhood into elation and freedom, and attaining "loving and harmonious affections" (*VR*, p. 273). The fruits of saintliness are (1) charity, flowing from the higher power toward one's fellows (even one's enemies); (2) purity, involving a desire to sacrifice for the higher power's sake; and (3) asceticism, eschewing one's natural habits or appetites. The value of saintliness, in all its variety, is tested by its effects and what they add to human life. Allegiance to certain deities brings certain additions, and since man's needs and demands change from time to time and from place to place, his deities will change accordingly. These changes are wrought by *founders* of religion more than by their organizers. But founders of religious trends can also illustrate *excesses* and imbalances that yield corrupt fruit. Too much devoutness produces fanaticism and intolerance and persecution. Purity unbalanced by social responsibility leads to selfish withdrawal from useful life. Excessive charity makes beggars and parasites. Extreme asceticism yields egotism and morbidity instead of the heroism that is "the moral equivalent of war" (*VR*, p. 367). In proportion, and in harmony with one another, these qualities of saintliness fructify in superior happiness and steadfastness of soul — in persons "adapted to the highest society conceivable" (*VR*, p. 375).

5. *Mystical* experiences tend paradoxically both to defy expression and to transmit special knowledge of divine things, such as a profound sense of the meaning of a maxim. Complex mystical experiences produce déjà vu, trances, anesthetic ecstasy, and moments of cosmic consciousness. Even when religions develop regular exercises for cultivating superconsciousness of the divine, mystical truth exists for the devotee alone and usually cannot be shared. Mystical rapture tends toward optimism, pantheism, unification, negative definitions of God, and replacement of the self by the deity.

6. *Feeling* is closer to the heart of religion than the doctrines
of theology that describe these feelings. Only the theology that
stirs or guides action has positive religious value. To think about
God's moral — not His metaphysical — attributes engenders
religious feelings (without proving the attributes). Thus theology
generalizes about religious experience but cannot offer universal
truth. Specific human needs, however, are fulfilled by the religious consciousness. The sense of beauty is exercised in esthet-
ically rich religions. The urge toward self-surrender finds scope in
sacrifice. The desire to be pure and honest is met by confession.
Man's yearning and aspiring and questing for divine communica-
tion are answered by prayer — the essence, indeed the necessary
and sufficient condition, of religion. Inspirations, revelations,
sensations, and motor automatisms increase conviction by opening human nature to "unusually close relations to the transmarginal or subliminal region" (*VR*, p. 483).

Such was James's map of religious experiences, drawn according to their fruits or effects. Reflecting on the subject raised
certain questions. What spiritual objects did these beliefs and
experiences realize? How did religious believing change the universe? On these grounds James trod cautiously. On his view
of reality, religious objects (whether divine or not) could not
be real quite independently of men's beliefs in and encounters
with them. There could be no single God with whom all religious
encounters took place. Deity therefore was contingent and plural
so far as it entered our "perceptual flux." But, for all that,
our gods were no less real.

Psychological investigation and reflection convinced James
that the human spirit participated in a conscious life broader
and deeper than a given person at a given time could focus
in perception, thought, and action. On the *"hither* side" this
" 'more' with which in religious experience we feel ourselves connected" was "the subconscious continuation of our conscious
life" — emphatically not less but *more*, and no less real than
other reality actualized by conscious life (*VR*, p. 512). This
"more" of religious experience was "a positive content . . .

literally and objectively true as far as it goes" (*VR*, p. 515). As to the *farther* side of the "more," James invoked not beliefs but overbeliefs. Among them he advanced his own "'piecemeal' supernaturalism," the explanation that higher or transmundane or transhuman powers and consciousnesses "produced immediate effects within the natural world to which the rest of our experience belongs" (*VR*, pp. 520, 524). Elaborate and especially monistic theologies strained at the gnat and swallowed the camel. "All that the facts require is that the power should be both other and larger than our conscious selves. Anything larger will do, if only it be large enough to trust for the next step" (*VR*, p. 525).

The Larger Powers

In James's emerging universe, whose reality depended on our believing, there could be no deity existing independently of men and women. At the same time his physiological psychology convinced him that theism best accorded with the reflex-action nature of human behavior. If the inner function of man the perceiver made deity contingent and plural, the outer function of acting man made theism necessary. In the reflex-action view of behavior, sensory impressions of the world furnished the only data on which thought could work, and thought functioned solely to link feeling and action. Thought was the loop of a rope both of whose ends were firmly fixed in the objective world. The chaotic impressions given by that world to the senses resisted monistic ordering. Moreover, they could issue no clear guidance to the will; thought ordered them so as to command action in the objective world for man's subjective purposes.

Theism

James rejected the canard that every object of a man's deep loyalty became his God. A God must also be *other* than ourselves, the profoundest power in the universe (and therefore capable of commanding *loyalty*), and He also must be *like* us enough to

be in commerce and communion with us (therefore capable of
commanding loyalty). He must be "A power not ourselves
. . . which not only makes for righteousness, but means
it, and which recognizes us." Or again, God and man must
differ enough for each to "hear the other's call," yet resemble
one another so far that each cares for purposes the other could
share (*FM*, p. 122).

In deciding whether the universe was made reasonable by
positing such a deity, the senses and the will cast equal votes
with that of the thinking faculty. Thought nominated three constructs of possible, consistent relations with the universe. Listening to the chaotic data perceived by the senses, it proposed
materialism or agnosticism; the will vetoed materialism for
allowing purposeful action no scope and vetoed agnosticism for
issuing no instructions on which to act. Listening to the will's
urge for moral clarity, thought then nominated gnosticism,
which the perceiving faculty vetoed for its swallowing up the
self and the world in a mystical monism.

In a word, the will demanded that the chief power of the
universe be *more than man*, while the senses required that it
be *not too much more*. If "God's being is sacred from ours" by
James's decree, so by his logic man's being must be sacred from
God's. Thus conceived, the theistic hypothesis "changes the dead
blank *it* of the world into a living *thou*, with whom the whole
man may have dealings" (*FM*, pp. 141, 127). Therefore, to
James, anything less than a personal God was irrational; anything
more, impossible. Or, "Between agnosticism and gnosticism,
theism stands midway, and holds to what is true in each. With
agnosticism, it goes so far as to confess that we cannot know
how Being made itself or us. With gnosticism, it goes so far
as to insist that we can know Being's character when made,
and how it asks us to behave" (*FM*, p. 142).

And all this positing of the theistic hypothesis by James
touched not a hair on the head of God's independent existence.
Such a being, *if* He existed, James insisted, would need to be
of this sort. On psychological, moral, esthetic, and religious

grounds, he posited deity. His refusal to affirm the existence of deity, which has led interpreters on many a merry chase, is wholly in character with his spirituality as well as his philosophy.

In 1904 James answered another psychologist's questionnaire about God and religious experience by saying that religion meant to him more a social reality than an emotional experience, that in God were combined ideality and efficacy, and that religious experience brought "home" spiritual reality. Did James, who had set prayer at the heart of religion, pray? "I can't possibly pray — I feel foolish and artificial." Had he ever experienced God's presence? "Never" (L, 2:214–15).

On these testimonies James's agnosticism would seem to arise from the personal honesty of one who would not profess a God he had not met. But, as usual with James, other testimonies countervail.

If panic fear in 1870 had a religious bearing on his life, surely his night in 1898 of nature-rapture on Mount Marcy in New Hampshire, when "the Gods of all the nature-mythologies were holding an indescribable meeting in my breast with the moral Gods of the inner life," had all the earmarks he ever named of a profound religious experience.

James wrote his wife of

The intense significance of some sort, of the whole scene, if one could only *tell* the significance; the intense inhuman remoteness of its inner life, and yet the intense *appeal* of it; its everlasting freshness and its immemorial antiquity and decay; its utter Americanism, and every sort of patriotic suggestiveness, and you, and my relation to you part and parcel of it all, and beaten up with it, so that memory and sensation all whirled inexplicably together; it was indeed worth coming for, and worth repeating year by year, if repetition could only procure what in its nature I suppose must be all unplanned for and unexpected. It was one of the happiest lonesome nights of my existence, and I understand now what a poet is. He is a person who can feel the immense complexity of influences that I felt, and make some partial tracks in them for verbal statement (L, 2:76–77).

James made a place in the pluralistic universe for religious
experiences "not deducible by analogy or psychological reasoning
from our other sorts of experience," pointing "to the continuity
of our consciousness with a wider spiritual environment from
which the ordinary prudential man . . . is shut off" (*PU*, pp.
299–300). And in reporting his "regular Walpurgis Nacht"
to Mrs. James, he wrote, "The two kinds of Gods" — of nature-
mythologies and of morality — "have nothing in common," one
arising in this experience from memory and the other from sensation, yet all whirled together (*L*, 2:76). Just after the experience on Mount Marcy, he could not "find a single word for
all that significance, and don't know what it was significant
of, so there it remains, a mere boulder of *impression*," but at
the same time he realized "things in the Edinburgh lectures
will be traceable to it" (*L*, 2:77). Sure enough, in *Varieties* James
distinguished the "two kinds of Gods" and related them to one
another as the environing and the indwelling Gods, or, more
profoundly, the God of mankind's cosmic consciousness and the
(same) God coming into a particular person's consciousness. One's
consciousness retained the significance of crucial religious experiences, and this sense of significance could be released from the
storehouse of memory when sensations lowered the threshold
of consciousness to allow an entry of "the great cosmic consciousness in which we live." [56]

James's insistence on testing religious experiences by their
fruits instead of their roots has tempted interpreters to collapse
his religion into ethics or psychotherapeutic self-help. He himself
underwent, as well as observed, experiences requiring judgment as to their roots. To his own question, "Is life worth
living?" James was known to pun, "It all depends upon the
liver!" — which has been Frenched, "*C'est une question de
foi(e)!*" [57] Similarly, if we insist on asking James, "Does God
exist?" he responds with something like, "Not while you are
seriously wondering," and might add, "nor while I am taking
your question seriously enough to argue that He does or does

not exist." God, like the worth of living and free will and all other urgent options, depended for *existence* on people's believing in Him, not on their making intellectual constructs about Him.

For James the kind of God who existed didn't insist on it. Propositional proofs made so serious-minded an option trivial; propositional refutations made it fatuous. James the philosopher denied both the proofs and the disproofs of free will, of the worth of living, and of God's existence, not because he was religiously agnostic, not because he reduced religion to morality, but to show that these options became urgent only in the realm of believing and living. He believed them. He lived them. He refused to sacrifice the risk and the joy of believing and living them on the altar of intellectual certainty.

"The More"

Quite as resolutely as Edwards and Emerson, James determined to show and to tell religious experience so as to open doors through which others might enter it. But James assigned being religious neither to special affections nor to a particular sentiment. He would not affirm either a religious faculty or distinctly religious objects existing in a world of their own. He resisted defining religion because to him it represented an intensity or dimension of human existence involving no special emotion or response or objects. Very mildly stated, "as there . . . seems to be no one elementary religious emotion, but only a common storehouse of emotions upon which religious objects may draw, so there might conceivably also prove to be no one specific and essential kind of religious object, and no one specific and essential kind of religious act" (*VR*, p. 28).

Of all the experiences flowing into the human stream of consciousness, the most constant for each person was the experience of his own life, whose reality, like that of other experienced things, hinged on believing and willing. To be sure, one "sensed" himself in the ordinary ways, seeing and touching his

own body, hearing its sounds and smelling its odors and tasting
its juices. Beyond these sensings, the self had an acquaintance
with its life by being aware of consciousness itself. Indeed, "our
own reality, that sense of our own life which we at every moment
possess, is the ultimate of ultimates for our belief" (*PP*, 2:297).
This sense of reality fastened on unseen things — life itself, of
course, but also space and the higher powers ("the more").
Because the higher entities had intimate and continuous connections with life and palpable effects upon it, because they stirred
active impulses of will and awakened emotional interests and
feelings of love, fear, admiration, dread, desire, and others, they
involved "ultimates of our belief" and were real. As with visible
so with unseen things, Perry writes, "There can, James insisted,
be no relations without terms, no transitives without substan-
tives" (*TC*, 2:78).

A person experienced "the more," then, just as he experienced
"the less" of the physical world and "the same" of himself as
the experiencing subject. James's radical empiricism needed no
transcendental ego or soul or mental stuff ("mind-dust," he liked
to say) independent of the phenomenal world. For James the
distinguishable functions of the mind — perceiving, thinking,
and willing — involved no divisible faculties. Thought ordered
experience by making relations, not by dealing with distinct
ideas. Because unified selves did all of mankind's business with
the universe (and, indeed, with one another as members of that
universe), they were radically at home.

There was no "other" universe, alien to these selves; the human
self was radically the ground of its own life and of God's reality.
James wrote: " 'Other world?' says Emerson, 'there is no other
world,' — than this one, namely, in which our several biographies are founded" (*SP*, p. 110). Encounters with "the more"
signified no *other* realm — save in a manner of speaking. Rather
they widened this world, opening a profounder dimension of
the universe to which one ordinarily belonged. James's
psychology made persons at home with physical nature and "the

more" because it made them radically at home with humanity, including their own piece of it.

By grounding the world, the self, and the higher powers (which is to say, in more formal terms, nature, man, and God — or, less formally, "the less," "the same," and "the more") in the humanness of mankind, James meant to enlarge and enrich the range of being human beyond the confining poverties of materialism and rationalism, atomism and monotheism. By conceiving the universe distributively, he made room both for infinite variety and for a high degree of unification, even while he denied the possibility of sheer diversity and of finished unity. By centering the experienced universe on the self, he was not rendering the objective world pliable to human wishes but rather emphasizing people's only agencies of relating to the hard world, namely, their perceiving, thinking, willing selves. By placing individual persons in a society of human selves, he was also setting them among the larger powers which, at once akin to and distinct from human powers, could relate to men and women only through the self's experience of them.

The only two ways one could escape from the reality of life were negative: either to trivialize or to terminate it. Otherwise everybody remained plugged into a reflex-action relation with the universe. The burden of James's message, then, was far from being that, if one chose, he might center reality in himself; it was that by every person's choosing he convoked around the self the only available reality. The famous theory of the emotions, although he stated it "we feel sorry because we cry, etc.," really had less to do with causation than with simultaneity. The link between feeling and acting was inescapable in life; truer to his thought he might have said, "we feel sorry *when* we cry, etc." As Wild tersely puts it, "The feeling cannot exist apart from its expression." [58]

In precisely that way James joined the sense of reality with the expression of reality in the religious dimension. We sense the higher powers' presence when we believe and serve them;

the sense cannot exist apart from its expression. We may neglect, oppose, or cooperate with "the more" but the choice is always momentous, lively, and inescapable, because it shapes reality for everybody now and to come. By believing and acting, thus qualified and understood, men and women choose, indeed *elect*, the gods of the universe.

Transplanted into a soil of attitudes less serious-minded and less strenuous-mooded than James's own, his insight nourished in some twentieth-century Americans a spirituality so superficial we may file it by title: having faith in having faith. According to this distortion, if the deities are ours, we choose the God most agreeable to our momentary whims. Thereby the message of Christainity became, in H. Richard Niebuhr's quip, "A God without wrath brought men without sin into a kingdom without judgment through the ministrations of a Christ without a cross" (*KGA*, p. 193). Even James's respected colleague, George Santayana, parodied him: if "All faiths were what they were experienced as being, in their capacity as faiths," then James "did not really believe; he merely believed in the right of believing that you might be right if you believed." [59] If the content of religion were believing in believing, what one believed in believing in could be anything that made one feel better. If God belonged to man's universe purely on man's terms, men and women could be as chummy with Him as they liked. To James all this is not belief but make-believe.

But a profile as sharp as that of his religious thought is easily caricatured. If nobody more rigorously gave men and women the responsibility for shaping their spirituality, it is also true that nobody exerted a wider influence on the palliative-peddlers of twentieth-century American popular religion. [60] Especially James's own more evangelical statements, which abound in the lectures on *The Will to Believe and Other Essays in Popular Philosophy* (1897), torn from the full context of his thought, were easily misinterpreted.

Although James kept his humor about him as well as his

wits, he was dead serious in treating the momentous options
of life and the higher powers with "a desire both to express
and to induce *conviction*" (*TC*, 2:208 n.). His personal struggle
had been against the inability to believe anything, not the more
common tendency to believe too much. "Having committed no
excesses of credulity in his youth," Perry remarks, "there was
nothing to repent in his maturity or old age" (*TC*, 2:210–11).
On matters evoking the serious mind and the strenuous mood,
he knew, mastery of many facts (or "knowledge about") could
interpose itself between the knower and the known. Thereby
Grübelsucht, the questioning mania, would thwart "acquaintance-
knowledge." To know about (*scire* or *wissen*) life and reality,
reduced fact to doctrine. To be acquainted with (*noscere* or *kennen*)
life and reality, involved respecting "the mystery of *fact*" by
realizing that "Fact forms a datum, gift, or *Vorgefundenes* [what
presents itself], which we cannot burrow under, explain or get
behind" (*SP*, pp. 44, 46).

Acquaintance-knowledge gained urgency from the view that
reality changed under pressures from man and the gods. The
stance of spectator had its uses, to be sure, but participation
and acquaintance required the more serious-minded, more
strenuous-willed stance. Healthy men and women would ver-
satilely adapt their stances to their situations and goals. The
scientific stance took the things of the world to be understood,
named, sorted, and classified, and in this stance a person learned
about the universe. This perspective extended and refined quan-
titative knowledge, remaining morally inert and religiously
neutral. The trivial-minded let facts speak for themselves as far
as they would speak, then asked no more questions. The theological stance seemed opposite to the scientific one, because it referred
the universe to a single divine principle, guaranteeing that in
the end all would be set to rights. But it achieved, in fact,
much the same result. Both engendered what James called "the
easy-going mood" in which "the shrinking from present ill is
our ruling consideration" (*FM*, p. 211). These stances and the

mood they induced met one genuine but partial need of man's spirit; they failed to exercise his fullest capacities and left him deeply yearning.

That the momentous facts of life were neither brute nor immutable was the refrain of James's thought as it ranged from physiological psychology to the study of religion. Facts became data, literally gifts, when one took the moral or the religious stance, and both perspectives commanded the strenuous mood. From these perspectives the primary datum or gift of experience is the self itself. Not only do I understand the self's existence as given, I also receive the self as a gift. Not only my body of which I am aware but also my awareness of it presents itself to me. The same holds for the physical world and the society of persons; they too, and my acquaintance with them, are data. Add to all this the higher powers and my relations with them, and the emphasis passes from the moral to the religious, altering the strenuous mood by radically intensifying its seriousness. "In religion the vital needs, the mystical overbeliefs . . . proceed from an ultra-rational region. They are *gifts*. It is a question of *life*, of living in these gifts or not living" (*TC*, 2:328).

Still, man's gods were gods and were man's gods by virtue of man's choosing. Reality accrued to what men and women chose in their lively, demanding, and momentous decisions. Men and women elected their deities. But the deities standing for election presented — nominated — themselves. Since all the nominees went unnoticed by scientific men and since the theological perspective produced its lone nomination, the "genial mood" that befit them actually prevented man from entering the religious dimension of life. The religious stance was most urgently serious-minded, even transmoral. Recall Wild's dictum that, for James, to think radically about ethics led beyond morality to religion.

Both morality and religion thrived in the strenuous mood, which "probably lies slumbering in every man" but "needs the wilder passions to arouse it, the big fears, loves, and indignations; or else the deeply penetrating appeal of some one of the higher fidelities, like justice, truth, or freedom" (*FM*, p. 211). Precisely when these passions and fidelities came as gifts, when the appeal presented itself from beyond and penetrated deeply, morality gave way to religion. The "infinite perspective opens out" when "we believe that a God is there, and that he is one of the claimants" (*FM*, p. 212).

But the givenness of God, or the presence of the higher powers as gifts, did not for James close the logical circle and turn back onto the theological perspective. Unlike the finished monism of that view, the religious stance required choices so momentous as to bring new reality into the universe. God became "but one helper, *primus inter pares*, in the midst of all the shapers of the great world's fate" (*PR*, p. 192). From James's metaphysical pluralism followed a theological polytheism that supported a religious henotheism — taking one higher power at a time for its appropriate function. But so momentous, so ominous were the consequences of the way we "add our *fiat* to the *fiat* of the creator" that the henotheism became radical (*PR*, p. 188). So radical, in fact, that it accorded in religious quality and ethical import not with any bland, self-seeking henotheism but with what Niebuhr called "radical monotheism" (*RM*, pp. 24–63).

The Atoning Self

Thus the higher powers or deities are elevated not lowered, our religious act becomes utterly serious not trivial, by virtue of James's insisting that the gods are our gods, existing so far forth as we use them and cooperate with them to make reality purposefully grow. The occasions for occupying the religious perspective, the times of seeking and serving the gods, are consummately those times in which life, the world, and deity present themselves profoundly to us as gifts. For James as for Emerson, moral heroes summoned their human energies to mold the universe to their principles, while saints opened themselves to gifts from higher

powers by which to improve reality. Edwards drew a similar
distinction between natural virtue and true virtue. Heroes threw
their power against evil in order to minify it. Saints joined harmoniously with the powers, human and divine, to magnify the
good and the beautiful, as James said in another connection,
"with that welcoming attitude of the will in which belief consists" (PP, 2:315–16).

To summarize, in this spirituality, we, by our believing and
willing and acting, reconcile ourselves with humanity. We sense
our embodiment of humanity. Centrally we live our consciousness of humanity. Ultimately we act with the gods to reshape
humanity's social reality. The philosophy in which James expressed this religiousness introduced polyphonies, falling dis-
agreeably on American (and European) ears used to monistic
idealism (until then the best philosophical note Western religion
had known how to sound). In his life and thought James practiced
an imitable but radically humanistic religiousness. It appealed
to and resonated with human experience because it opened
an older American ethos to new aspirations. Pluralism for James
countered both atomism and monism by cleaving to the gift-
character of experience, making those gifts congruous with the
universe but not forcing them into a precast, ideal unity. The
universe waited to be improved and unified by men's and
women's acts. Lacking these religious acts it could be ship-
wrecked. In those acts men and women cooperated with the
higher powers in making reality, conceived on a social analogy,
into a thing of beauty — the circle of dancers holding hands —
a beauty that, for all the divine influences on it, retained its
human character. Mankind and the universe shared potentiality.
"Ever not quite!" was James's slogan, not only for his philosophy
but for humanity and the universe (MS, p. 409).

For all James's vaunted and even self-professed individualism,
by which he meant starting with the parts and building toward
the whole, he made the chief concerns of religion the social
form of humanity and mankind's social reforms — for example,

inventing channels of strenuous activity that would become "the moral equivalent of war" (MS, pp. 265–96). Edwards had had to exclude from true virtue the causes and interests of human groups, even of mankind itself, because they undercut the beauty of absolutely divine things. His piety ended in each saint's letting his life be a work of God's artistry. Emerson erased self-interest from the human quest for the divine by making both man and God at home in nature and by placing human experience under the law of compensation in which energy balanced matter, in which effort equated with effect. Emersonian men and women could be works of art if each person would be his own sculptor. James made God's reality contingent upon our beliefs and actions and thus plurified deity. With the higher powers we could cooperate, adding human fiat to divine fiat, without blasphemy (as it would have been to Edwards) or self-divinization (as it would have been to Emerson).

James allows us to act in true virtue to the benefit of society, indeed for the improvement of reality. Thus he achieved what his father attempted, to make social responsibility spiritually significant. He tested the religious act by its immediate or mediate improvement of the universe. Reality, the world, the universe itself became the artifact of spiritual or religious persons, who welcomed the higher powers' cooperation in their art while being fully at home with their human creativity.

7   *Postlude*   *After James*

With progressive thoroughness and intensity Edwards, Emerson, and James considered our relations to God, nature, and humanity to be questions concerning the human experience of holiness. While all three thinkers insisted that they had found the right way of asking the religious question, none claimed finality for his own answers. In a certain sense James culminated the progression by making us spiritually at home even with our humanity. The choice of deities and the enlistment of their cooperation in shaping the nature of reality becomes the most serious and the most strenuous exercise of that humanity. In spite of Edwards' fealty to his inherited world-view, his attention had focused on human experience when he made the religious question to be, How do men and women and children find God lovable? And regardless of Emerson's idealistic monism, the same focus was implied by his discovery of a transcendent spirituality, shared between man and God, through beholding nature as a mirror of the soul. James drew out the implications of his forerunners' positions. In so doing he set the agenda for American religious thought, now fully distinct from theology, in the twentieth century.

Without hedge or qualification, James asked the perennial questions of our relation to God and nature and humanity in an irreversibly humanistic manner. It is as though he forfeited a certain primitive innocence or spiritual chastity by daring to

have men and women realize — make real — not only nature
but also the higher powers as their own realities, yet still as
noumenous and mysterious ones. Successors who took seriously
that daring move, whatever else they may have considered,
looked radically at people and their history instead of at God
and His providence as the subjects of religious activity and the
objects of religious thought.

On James's reading, no answers to the questions he framed
about religion could be final. Indeed, the very unfinality of every
conceivable answer lent an inherent permanence to his question.
As religion was made a matter of human experience, traditional
doctrines more and more were assigned to compartments of
thought and activity set apart as specifically theological.

But that is only to say that Americans participated in the
general profaning of Western civilization. Whatever the force
of church theology in church circles may have been even as far
back as the time of Edwards, he stands as the last major American
religious thinker who fully espoused an orthodox Christian
world-view in all he thought and did. And even so, as we have
seen, he made this world-view support a novel kind of spirituality
that in turn would call for a different world-view. After him
religious doctrines in America became instrumental to a variety
of attitudes and activities — to morality for Charles Chauncy
and Samuel Johnson, to social reform for William Ellery Channing and Theodore Parker, to revivals for Timothy Dwight and
Nathaniel W. Taylor, to sentimentalized love for Horace
Bushnell and Henry Ward Beecher. More boldly than any of
these, Emerson and then James regarded theological doctrines
as derivative epiphenomena incapable of either accurately describing or reliably evoking holiness.

As doctrine lost its authority in the progression of American
religious thought, so did tradition. But that was a later development. By virtue of the moves James made, neither he nor his
successors could simply and pristinely stand in religious traditions capable of framing their minds and souls. Since James
borrowed from Edwards and Emerson and his father, among

others, of course he stood in a sort of tradition. Their legacy to him, however, was no defining body of doctrine but rather an insistence that each age reconcile its own experiences with the reality it lived out and explicated. Thus James refused to define the religious dimension as a factor or faculty of human existence. What religion might become awaited what people made of themselves and their deities and their worlds. In commerce with higher powers they would change their reality, their selfhood, their sociality, and their ways of being religious.

James made American religion irreversibly voluntary and contingent — completely relative. Religiousness, no longer absolute or fixed, could emerge and change because it responded to strenuous human efforts, aided by "the more." By curing his own acedia, James demonstrated this feat in his own life. By examining the varieties of religious experience, he described the range of spiritual versatility. By developing his radical empiricism and pluralism, he built a partial metaphysic appropriate to emergent religiousness. He set the agenda for interpreting religion in relation to the growing reality that human and divine efforts evinced.

Since James's time, theology in America has been clarifying and systematizing the inherited world-views of the churches and showing how such views may bear upon modern life. It has received certain notable infusions of ideas from Europe. Karl Barth, Martin Buber, and Rudolf Bultmann, for example, injected biblical and existential motifs in a way that tended to disparage what men and women did in the name of religion, humanly speaking. This kind of theology spoke of encounters with God and knowledge of God as over against — at least as remote from — religion. Such theology has not been the main concern of the leading religious thinkers in twentieth-century America who took up James's agenda — men like Walter Rauschenbusch, John Dewey, and Reinhold and H. Richard Niebuhr. The last two in particular became rather uncomfortable with the title of theologian, partly because they knew the religious thought of James.

When James's religious thought was taken individualistically,

as we noted, it could be bent into programs of self-help based
on religious make-believe. His more radical theme, however,
bound each person to a society (in fact, to several societies) of
active wills, both within and beyond the margins of human
consciousness. All these powers could cooperatively ameliorate
the shared reality of the plural universe. A similar idea animated
the thought of two younger contemporaries of James. The most
influential exponent of this social theme within the churches
was Rauschenbusch. The same theme, developed within an abiding antipathy toward formal religion, informed the religious
declarations of the aging Dewey.

These men, younger than James, escaped having their lives
and sensitivities scarred, as his were, by the Civil War. But the
First World War, which James did not live to see, sent
Rauschenbusch into a depression and forced him to rethink his
social gospel. The same war convinced Dewey that philosophers
should educate and reform society — led him, as it were, to
turn philosophy into a social gospel.

Rauschenbusch belonged to America's Gilded Age as much
as he belonged to the German-immigrant communities for which
his father trained ministers in Rochester, New York. There
Rauschenbusch lived his whole life except for gymnasium studies
at Gütersloh and for eleven years as pastor to the German Baptist
congregation in a New York slum. The new century found him
a seminary professor at Rochester, whence he issued the
immediately popular *Christianity and the Social Crisis* (1907).
Thereafter he gave the social gospel its most convincing churchly
articulation.

In that gospel the Kingdom of God meant two things. First,
it meant a spiritual reality willed by God and chartered on earth
by Christ. Second, it meant the goal of human societies. When
it meant a nation in pursuit of justice and equality, American
society looked better than other forms of community. In one
sense Rauschenbusch made the salvation of individuals await,
and in another sense made it equal, the salvation of societies.

To sin was to resist the emergence of God's Kingdom on earth.
Deliverance was conforming the economic and political orders
to standards of divine justice. Human beings by their own efforts
could shape these orders significantly but only by the criteria
of God's revealed Kingdom would society be made just. Evil
fed evil, but good aims elicited good actions and good deeds
approached good goals.

Rauschenbusch depicted and wanted to build a Christian
utopia on the principle of justice among men. If theologically
he spoke the old political metaphors of God's sovereignty and
man's obedience, his acquaintance with the ideas of Karl Marx
and Henry George, among others, furnished also the ideal-
historical metaphors of the perfect society. He projected goals,
casting his theological themes within a basically teleological
framework, speaking of God's Kingdom instead of God's law.
His appeal to build that Kingdom on earth enlisted thousands
of church members in crusades for democratizing familial, social,
economic, political, and industrial institutions.

The outbreak of war in Europe in 1914 and especially
America's entry in 1917 with the allies against Germany fell
like the curse of an offended Providence on Rauschenbusch's
hopes. Thus his mature statement of *A Theology for the Social
Gospel* (1917) muted his earlier optimism without really changing
his approach. Even revised in light of these events, the chief
goal of religion and the churches remained that of conforming
social orders and institutions to a utopia blending traditional
Christian precepts of justice with typical American ideals of
democracy.

But simply collapsing religious into democratic criteria of justice never crossed Rauschenbusch's mind. For Dewey, on the
contrary, the self-critical and zealous pursuit of democracy constituted religious activity. Only when Dewey had reached the
age of seventy-five did he make pronouncements on religion,
specifically in *A Common Faith* (1934). Moreover, he warned
against searching his earlier books and articles for harbingers

of these declarations. The lectures addressed "those who have abandoned supernaturalism, and who on that account are reproached by traditionalists for having turned their backs on everything religious. The book was an attempt to show such persons that they still have within their experience all the elements which give the religious attitude its value."[61] Dewey counted himself such a person.

Dewey followed Emerson by distinguishing the religious as a quality of human experience from religions as attempts to embody and invoke that quality. But he outdid Emerson, stripping from the religious quality everything noumenous as well as everything strictly supernatural. Dewey, like Edwards and James, tested religion by its effects instead of its causes. But he outdid them both when he measured the religious value of an experience purely by the degree to which it helped people master their environment.

Any experience, according to Dewey, had religious value so far as it eventuated in "a better, deeper and enduring adjustment in life" (CF, p. 14). The key to this formula was the notion of adjustment. It differed both from passive accommodation of life to circumstances and from active adaptation of circumstances to life. Adjustment, at once voluntary, outgoing, ready, glad, and active, meant imaginatively harmonizing oneself with the universe, with "the totality of conditions with which the self is connected" — specifically, the conditions of physical nature and human society (CF, p. 19). Strenuous efforts toward such adjustment accrued religious value in proportion not to their emotional intensity (here Dewey follows Edwards) but to the degree the emotions were "actuated and supported by ends so inclusive that they unify the self" (here he follows James) (CF, p. 22). Dewey's spirituality consisted in the act — not the motive, not the goal, but the act — of the whole self's coming to be at home in the universe. So far, he added nothing original to a central tradition in American religious thought. His original idea was to hold the universe, or the physical and social realities with which persons were related, open to improvement by critical examination and positive reconstruction via the scientific method.

In these relations and realities, to be sure, evil stubbornly persisted. But for Dewey religious value attached to the active, imaginative, intense, social, cooperative promotion of certain concrete and experimental goods: "the values of art in all its forms, of knowledge, of effort and of rest after striving, of education and fellowship, of friendship and love, of growth in mind and body" (CF, p. 51). These goods latently awaited the exercise of mankind's common faith to actualize them. Being at home in the universe meant accepting certain liberal goals — liberal in the sense that they would set men and women free from traditional restraints. Dewey wanted to build social institutions that would serve individual freedom. Devotion to building them was his religion.

Thus Dewey followed Henry James, Sr., by insisting that "The community of causes and consequences in which we, together with those not born, are enmeshed is the widest and deepest symbol of the mysterious totality of being the imagination calls the universe" (CF, p. 85). To be at home in such a universe meant, for Dewey, to occupy an abode of natural and social relations analyzable by scientific study and reformable by positivistic construction. The only mystery commanding his wonder, in the last analysis, was our awesome capacity to dedicate ourselves to making both nature and society — and with them the symbols of the soul and of deity — utterly *un*mysterious. Mastery of the universe became the mystery of the universe.

To this positive reconstruction of religiousness and to the naturalistic philosophy undergirding it, nobody took more vehement exception than Reinhold Niebuhr. As pastor of a Detroit congregation for thirteen years, Niebuhr tested the workability of the social gospel, taken over largely from Rauschenbusch. Then in 1928 he began a lifelong professorship in applied Christianity at Union Theological Seminary in New York City, dedicating his preaching and social philosophy to contrasting the absolute commandments to love God and neighbor with the ineluctable selfishness of the person's life in human groups — the more complex, the more selfish! Freedom and finitude tore men and women in an unending, insoluble dialectic.

Religion helped expose and answer our need to be reconciled to the awful predicament Niebuhr diagnosed. Human sin (pride) tempted us, however, to undo the tension. We could sin either by exaggerating our freedom (optimism) or overemphasizing our limitations (pessimism). Still, the freedom and the finitude, fundamental to the human condition, remained, unmasking the lies of both optimism and pessimism. As long as history endured, this irreconcilable opposition would stand.

Niebuhr expressed this double dialectic through innumerable analyses and applications, the most influential of which dealt with American political life (domestic and international) from the Great Depression through the New Deal to the Second World War, whose entry by America Niebuhr early advocated, and into the Cold War that followed. The liberal Protestants to whom he addressed his theological criticisms stressed human freedom, against which Niebuhr hurled the ominous events of his era. Jeremiah redivivus proved human finitude and sin by citing current troubles.

Indeed, for Niebuhr religion turned primarily (not exclusively) on our coming to grips with the subtlety and pervasiveness of our pride. Niebuhr translated the doctrine of original sin into a kind of good news. This emphasis, of course, was a strategic move against regnant liberalism in theology, optimism in ethics, and utopianism in politics. What Niebuhr called Christian realism corrected these large hopes while affirming an unquenchable human thirst for their fulfillment. The nub of his religious thought, then, was dialectical — a two-part yes-and-no that he identified as the central teaching of the Bible. In a typical statement, "the biblical view of life . . . affirms the meaning of history and of man's natural existence on the one hand, and on the other insists that the centre, source, and fulfilment of history lie beyond history." [62]

With remarkable consistency Niebuhr applied this dialectic to every feature of personal and social life, always crediting simple human relations, like those of the family, with innocence and damning the imperialism of complex societies like nations. Perhaps less consistently, he made this dialectic the linchpin of biblical and traditional Christian faith. In fact, he dealt with Bible and historic Christianity selectively as to sources and analogically as to meanings. These very approaches show Niebuhr's large measure of agreement with Dewey's conviction that for modern scientific man the traditional supernatural entities had lost their objective, literal existence and with it their mysteriousness. Yet Niebuhr clung tenaciously to the noumenous and transhuman qualities of religion that Dewey discarded. He rejected what he called the secondary myths, the content of the old doctrines, and recast their meanings or lessons into what he called the primary myths. So creation, fall, incarnation, resurrection, Last Judgment, and the rest became the coinage of his rhetoric without being the content of his thought. All such doctrines symbolized a tragic universe, full of irrepressible hopes incompletely fulfilled, to which religion attuned men and women by cultivating in them a tragic sensitivity.

In Niebuhr's most important theological work, the Gifford Lectures of 1939, he eloquently preferred the Christian teaching on bodily resurrection to the notion of the soul's immortality. Resurrection, he said, implied "that eternity will fulfill and not annul the richness and variety which the temporal process has elaborated," yet at the same time it taught emphatically that God, not man, would solve the human predicament. In subsequent correspondence, Niebuhr's host at Edinburgh, Norman Kemp Smith, twitted him for giving comfort to the fundamentalists by defending the notion of bodily resurrection. "I must have expressed myself badly," Niebuhr replied, "for I have not the slightest interest in the empty tomb or physical resurrection but only in resurrection as a concept of immortality. Particularly the idea that the fulfillment of life does not mean the negation and destruction of historical reality (which is a unity of body-soul, freedom-necessity, time-eternity) but the completion of this unity." [63]

For Niebuhr, then, the essence of religion consisted in seizing by its horns the human dilemma: the aspirations of humans under the conditions of history can be fulfilled only when history and its conditions no longer prevail. On the political side, for example, such is the meaning of the famous aphorism, "Man's capacity for justice makes democracy possible; but man's inclination to injustice makes democracy necessary." [64] Niebuhr's saint overcomes the actual workings of tragedy — leaps, in the words of the title to one of his books, "beyond tragedy." By cultivating the tragic sense, this saint corrects utopianism on one side and defies despair on the other. By living in the tragic mode or mood, this saint attunes himself to the profoundest meanings of life and masters his destiny by accepting its limitations and frustrations.

Because the *moods* of their two saints (not the content of their religiousness) differed so starkly, Niebuhr hurled polemical bolts against Dewey, as "the most typical and greatest philosopher of American secularism"; he accused Dewey of holding that "religious loyalties . . . will gradually disappear with the general extension of enlightened good will" and thus of looking "forward to the cultural unification of the community upon the basis of . . . the characteristic credos of bourgeois liberalism." [65]

However, Dewey also believed mankind would always be struggling against evils that could not finally be overcome but must be resisted with efforts that were religious in quality. So the animus of Niebuhr against Dewey is of very subtle origin. Both men wished to avoid optimism and despair alike, but they chose different detours. Dewey called for the courageous mood, Niebuhr called for the tragic. Courage befitted Dewey's teleological ethics of seeking an ideal goal, just as tragedy befitted Niebuhr's deontological ethics of obeying an absolute command. Dewey stood in awe of man's capacity to master the awesome universe. Niebuhr reverenced man's capacity to go beyond tragedy by means of the tragic sense.

To shift from the religious thought of Reinhold Niebuhr to that of his younger brother, Helmut Richard Niebuhr, is to move from the sense of tragedy to the sense of fate and to move from both goal-ethics (Dewey) and command-ethics (Reinhold Niebuhr) to the ethics of responsibility. It is also to shift to a person who critically and self-consciously studied American religious thought in order to appreciate and appropriate and refine it. Although strongly influenced by German theology, especially through Ernst Troeltsch (on whom he wrote his doctoral dissertation at Yale) and Barth, Richard Niebuhr established his scholarly reputation with two studies of American religion: *The Social Sources of Denominationalism* (1929) and *The Kingdom of God in America* (1937).[66] Fascination with the institutional and intellectual expressions of American religion never abated, and in the mid-1950s Niebuhr directed a study of theological education in the United States and Canada, stating his own conclusions in *The Purpose of the Church and Its Ministry* (1956).

But church theology and its preoccupation with an ideology he sometimes called "Christism" (or christomonism) evaded, he believed, the rock-bottom questions: How and why do men and women join into their own histories and accept their own fated existence in a universe of fixed history and order? How and why do men and women hold themselves ultimately accountable for their daily decisions? How and why do men and women, with no option of neutrality, trust or distrust the universe and its gods? By identifying these questions as the seminal ones for himself and his generation, Niebuhr showed striking kinship with the tradition of American religious thought with which we have been dealing. In spite of his standing as a theologian and his theological leaning toward the European tradition, there are good reasons to construe him as a religious thinker and a summarily American one.

The givenness of each person's identity in history and society surrounded Niebuhr's religious thought like the atmosphere, having no special location. Persons first had to discover who and what they had become if they would become what they wanted to be. This brooding stress on fate, destiny, providence, fixity, and order led Niebuhr to explain his own interest in Christ and Christianity as something decided for him by his history. But that was only half of it. Also he voluntarily consented to the values and causes and interests that gave him his personhood. Fate needed faith in the double movement of life — receiving and deciding, accepting and acting.

Had Niebuhr referred this double sense of destiny and freedom to an organically related nature and supernature he might have become another Bushnell; he might even have agreed with his brother. Instead, he steeped himself in the thought of Edwards: fate and fixity underscored the will and its freedom. Within the limits of one's selfhood and moment and place, one chose what one would be and become — consented to his fate and accepted his future. Niebuhr wrestled with Edwards' conundrum of finitude and responsibility in terms of interpersonal and social existence. In that context the unavoidable and historical givenness (even the fated "giftedness") of the self, together with the irresistible agency, the unavoidable decision-making function, of the self, became powerful themes of his religiousness. Niebuhr seriously questioned whether one could terminate his own selfhood. Granting, of course, the possibility of biocide (ending one's life), he suggested that a person may not have the power of suicide (ending one's self).

All this preoccupation (and it was just that) with destiny and choice and selfhood pointed Niebuhr, as it had earlier led Edwards, to relish the subtle, indefinite ramifications of every decision a person made. "To be a Christian is simply part of my fate," Niebuhr's posthumous book on ethics put it, but while "I cannot get away from his [Christ's] influence," it was equally certain that "I do not want to get away from it." In sum, "I call myself a Christian more because I have both accepted this fateful fact and because I identify myself with what I understand to be the cause of Jesus Christ" (RS, p. 43). Moslems or Hindus or Communists (or whatever) were what they were by the same process. Fate and freedom made life whatever it became, and the interplay between them went on intricately, endlessly, perhaps even beyond the grave.

This fate-freedom nexus led Niebuhr to challenge the adequacy of any ethics built either on the model of man-the-maker who pursued good goals or on the model of man-the-servant who obeyed good commands. He proposed to correct deficiencies in the technical and the legislative metaphors of religious ethics with an ethics built on the model of man-the-answerer who acted responsively and responsibly to all his relations with the universe. This metaphor of responsibility is, as we used the term in reference to Edwards and Emerson and James, esthetic: "the *fitting* action, the one that fits in the total interaction as response and as anticipation of further response, is alone conducive to the good and alone is right" (RS, p. 61). What a person is commanded to be and what he rightly takes as his goal of becoming are one and the same. Religious persons respond now to the concatenation of relations — including past and future, nature and society — in which they stand, so as to be in harmony with what those relations are, what they have come to be, and what they will become. In this spirituality persons seek appropriateness, order, symmetry in their relations with all beings and with being in general. In a word, they find the beauty of being at home in the universe of nature, man, and God. Niebuhr wanted to hold to Edwards' translation of saintliness into esthetic terms and in turn to redevelop from this holiness of beauty an ethics of fittingness and a religion of trusting the universe to be hospitable.

For Niebuhr as for Edwards the great universe and one's particular spot in it formed the fixed arena where the self may find being in general trustworthy and lovable. It is fitting to labor similarities between Niebuhr and Edwards, upon whom he confessed heavy (and always critical) dependence. And, without implying explicit reliance, it is also fair to compare Niebuhr with Emerson for their shared emphasis on freedom and fate and for their larger treatments of human selfhood. In a manner distinctly reminiscent of Emerson's teaching on self-reliance, Niebuhr had each man and woman receiving and holding his own self as a gift, in temporal compresence with past and with future and in social companionship with all other beings. By way of correcting an interpreter on this point, Niebuhr sounded like Emerson when he wrote, "I do *not* wish to maintain that there is value in the self's relation to itself (or to its potential self) apart from its relation to others"; rather he held persons to be fated to exercise freedom — as it were, destined to choose responsibly — within their sociality as well as their life and their reason, their humanity and their culture (*RM*, p. 105 n.).[67]

In brief, Niebuhr held personhood — a received gift — inescapably responsible for its existence as well as its thought and its action. The exercise of that responsibility made self-reliance the equivalent of relying upon the universe. The fundamental knowledge of the self (*I am* and *I am I*) arose for Niebuhr, to be sure, from *I think* and from *I act*, but most profoundly from *I respond*; I belong and I respond to nature and society and deity as the response of myself to my selfhood in its inextricable relations with nature and society and deity.

To underscore the soul's responsibility for its self-enlistment in the causes it espoused, Niebuhr borrowed a concept of loyalty from James's philosopher-friend Josiah Royce. The ultimate manner in which a person belonged and responded to the totality of beings, in space and in time, became for Niebuhr "the religious element in our responses . . . , meaning by the word, religion, in this connection man's relation to what is ultimate for him — his ultimate society, his ultimate history" (RS, p. 109). The self was responsible for the entire range of its selfhood-in-relation, and events brought with them their own basic significance instead of being instrumental to some delayed, mediated meanings.

Niebuhr, moreover, insisted as radically as ever did James on the inevitability of a person's finally trusting or distrusting his own universe of history and society, of nature and deities. "Faith as trust or distrust," he wrote, "accompanies all our encounters with others and qualifies all our responses." Again, "The inscrutable power by which we are is either for us or against us. If it is neutral, heedless . . . , it is against us, to be distrusted as profoundly as if it were actively inimical" (RS, pp. 118, 119).[68] Ever partial, ever halting, ever broken, this radical faith, when lodged with the God beyond the gods, set a person on the road of repentance: "Beginning with that faith[,] life is involved intellectually and morally in a continuous revolution" (RM, p. 125).

Thus the soul's relation with the higher powers (the henotheist's many deities) that called it into being constantly undergoes renewal, rethinking, reconstruction, refinement, reenlistment, even revolution. New incursions of distrust come about as the objects of our trust prove themselves untrustworthy, driving us to go beyond them in loyalty to the powers that empower them; we hope to find a truly trustworthy object of loyalty, a God beyond the gods, a One beyond the many. So far Niebuhr's saint, so to speak, clearly resembles the saint, so to speak, of James. And indeed Niebuhr was following James's agenda: to discover and describe and test man's deities by examining and reflecting and entering upon man's religious experience.

But then Niebuhr took one more step. In a way it looks like a step back to Edwards in that it arrived at one highest power as man's truest deity, or maybe a step back to Emerson in that it derived the many from the one instead of the one from the many. By another reckoning we may see Niebuhr — or at least may usefully employ his religious thought — as recapturing a feature of Edwards' and Emerson's insights in a way that denied nothing of James's pluralism but only achieved a very high degree of unification on the basis of it. In this way, Niebuhr's spirituality recapitulated and summarized the tradition of American religious thought with which we have dealt.

The saint tries to trust one higher power, then another: now nature and then the past, again the future and then the nation, the family, even the divine commandment. But we find we cannot break off relations with one higher power by shifting our loyalty to another of the same or similar order. All things and all our companions remain ever compresent with us. By trying to trust the several powers serially we find that a still higher power is revealing the untrustworthiness of each of them. We cannot trust only a part of the reality that presents itself to us in an intricate, interconnected set of relations. We cannot break one power out of these relations unless we forfeit our own responsibility by breaking the unifications of our own selfhood. If a person is to be one self, there must be one highest power — at least, the highest accessible to that person. To have radical faith in any being means to declare faith in the general system of beings. To be fully loyal to a given cause means to enlist in the ultimate aims and values of that cause and in all its related embodiments. To have radical faith is to have faith in a radical deity beyond and above and around and below all the lesser deities. In a word, if the self is to be *one* self, then to try to trust "the more" leads to trusting "the most."

Niebuhr borrowed and gave rich texture to the definition of religion advanced by Alfred North Whitehead, the "transition from God the void to God the enemy, and from God the enemy to God the companion" (*KGA*, p. 192; *RM*, pp. 123–24). This God is not the God of attributes and decrees and punishments and chosen people about whom Edwards thought; it is nonetheless the deity of Edwards, construed as being in general, lovable for its own sake. Nor is it really the absolute monistic unity of Emerson's philosophy; it is nonetheless the deity of Emerson, the God who left a crack in everything He made. It is also the deity of James, with magnificence and majesty certified — enough like us to share our interests, enough unlike us to command our loyalties.

Niebuhr himself had neither neat definitions nor precise names for this deity. "We may call it," he wrote, "the nature of things, we may call it fate, we may call it reality" (RM, p. 122). Whatever we call it, at first encounter it stands over against us like an unknown void. Then like an enemy it reveals the emptiness and pettiness of our little loyalties and transitory trusts. At last, glimpsed but never comprehended, it becomes our companion. We trust or distrust, we are loyal or disloyal, we are fated to choose freely between these fixed options. To trust, to be loyal, is to respond to an invitation to be at home in a majestically hospitable universe.

Thus Niebuhr summarized a great legacy of American religious thought: to be religious is not to feel but to be, not comfortable but at home, not in one's particular world but in the universe.

Notes

<table>
<tr><td>1</td><td>Prelude:</td><td>The End at the
Beginning</td></tr>
</table>

1.   Daniel B. Shea, *Spiritual Autobiography in Early America* (Princeton: Princeton University Press, 1968), p. vii.

2.   See, for example, A. N. Kaul, *The American Vision, Actual and Ideal Society in Nineteenth-Century Fiction* (New Haven: Yale University Press, 1963).

3.   R. J. Kaufmann, "Seeking Authority," *Concourse* (published by National Humanities Faculty, Concord, Mass.), 1, no. 1 (Spring 1972): 14, 22.

<table>
<tr><td>2</td><td>The Sensible Spirituality
of Jonathan Edwards</td></tr>
</table>

4.   Hopkins, *Conv.*, pp. 4–5, testifies that seven of Edwards' eight great-grandparents came out of England, and implies that the wife of John Warham did too.

5.   Like most students of Edwards' MSS., I am indebted to the typed transcriptions that Thomas A. Schafer prepared in connection with the forthcoming Yale edition of these notebooks. I have checked my quotations from the miscellanies with the originals, modernized punctuation and spelling, and lengthened Edwards' abbreviations.

6.   Perry Miller, "The Marrow of Puritan Divinity," *Errand into the Wilderness* (1956; New York: Harper Torchbooks, 1964), pp. 50, 98. Conrad Cherry, *The Theology of Jonathan Edwards, A Reappraisal* (Garden City, N.Y.: Doubleday, 1966), pp. 107–23, treated Edwards as a theologian concentrating on justification by faith, and took Miller to task for his points. To find in Edwards a consistent covenant theology, Cherry appealed to "Edwards' 'better moments'" (p. 122). Even on theological grounds, Edwards succeeded rather well in making the repenter's faith both a promise (of God's covenant with Christ) and a condition (of the dependent covenant of Christ with the church). The faith proffered by men and women as a condition of the latter covenant was thus not their own but something bought for them by Christ's righteousness and accounted in their favor. Thus man brought nothing of his own merit, Edwards concluded, to

the saving transaction. In effect, Edwards' scheme of justification had God imputing to the believer not only the righteousness of Christ that was the only condition of God's covenant with Christ but also the faith that was a promise of that covenant. See Misc., #617, 825, 919, 1091, 1118. Also see Thomas A. Schafer, "Jonathan Edwards and Justification by Faith," *Church History* 20 (December 1951): 55–67.

7.   Harriet Beecher Stowe, *Old Town Folks* (Boston, 1897), p. 229, as quoted by Perry Miller, *ISDT*, p. 144 n. 52.

8.   "For the least sin against an infinite God, has an infinite hatefulness or deformity in it; but the highest degree of holiness in a creature, has not an infinite loveliness in it" (*WY*, 2:326). Against God, the finite creature's sin is infinite, but although the gift of holiness is from an infinite giver it is given to a finite creature and remains finite. See *Conv.*, 37, and Shea, pp. 205–7.

9.   Cherry, p. 25. Edwards followed Augustine in arguing that the Trinitarian God must *be* what creatures made in His image *have*, but Edwards refined the anagogue (as indeed he purified many another trope) by arguing from man's conversion experience to God's nature.

10.   Williston Walker, *The Creeds and Platforms of Congregationalism* (New York: Scribner's, 1893), p. 328.

11.   Williston Walker, "Jonathan Edwards" (*Conv.*, p. 107).

12.   A brief, clear account is in Edward M. Griffin, *Jonathan Edwards*, Pamphlets on American Writers, no. 97 (Minneapolis: University of Minnesota Press, 1971), pp. 10–14. Extraordinary perception and detailed learning inform the story in Perry Miller, *Jonathan Edwards* (New York: William Sloane Associates, 1949), pp. 196–233. Ola Elizabeth Winslow, *Jonathan Edwards 1703–1758, A Biography* (New York: Macmillan, 1940), pp. 215–67, provides a judicious appraisal. Edwards in his own account did not hold himself blameless; see *WD*, 1:298–427.

13.   The works cited above in note 12 tell also of Edwards' life and work at Stockbridge, where he produced the great treatises on free will, original sin, true virtue, and God's end in creating the world, and where he recorded that he had conceived of Christian theology anew in a historical mode. (What he may have meant still tantalizes his interpreters.) Then in January 1758 he took office as president of the College of New Jersey (now Princeton University). A few weeks later he died of smallpox contracted from inoculation against the disease.

14.   White, pp. 5, 10, 29, 33–36, 49–55, 70, 80–82, 143, 168–69, 291–92 — to add "et passim" seems gratuitous — construed Edwards' "sense of the heart" or "new spiritual sense" as an addendum to the five natural senses and as a particular, independent source, alongside them, of understanding and knowledge. But throughout *Religious Affections* Edwards portrayed this "sense" not as separable from or in addition to, rather as a reinvigoration and reorientation of, the natural senses — attuning them to see, touch, feel, smell, taste the loveliness of divine things, and transforming the understanding quite as much as redirecting the will. It placed a new and transcendent object at the center of all understanding and all knowledge. It was comparable to the five "senses" only in analogical, perhaps no more than in allusive, ways.

15.   This person "was converted above twenty seven years ago." Sarah Pierrepont was born January 9, 1710. The experiences under consideration occurred in 1742. The account referred to other experiences that "began about seven years ago." Sarah, then, knew the climax of these recorded spiritual raptures at the age of thirty-two. They had begun when she was twenty-five. Her conversion came "when a little child of about five or six years of age" (*WY*, 4:334, 333, 335).

16.   Miller, *Jonathan Edwards*, p. 287; James Carse, *Jonathan Edwards & the Visibility of God* (New York: Scribner's, 1967), p. 136.

17.   Miller, p. 291.

3   Interlude: *From Edwards to Emerson*

18.   White established continuities between Edwards and Emerson (and on through Chauncey Wright and Charles Sanders Peirce to the early thought of William James) in part by saying all of them lodged belief in the heart instead of the head. (See above, chap. 1, n. 12.) While this reading strikes me as inadequate, I gratefully invoke White's other arguments for these connections. His book appeared just when mine had been fully enough formed to withstand reexamination, for which his became the instructive occasion. On my reading, Edwards and Emerson and James form a stream of religious thought in America intent on distinguishing the head from the heart in order to use the head for learning what goes on both in the head *and* in the heart, as well as to hear what the heart may have to say about the limits of the head. White seems to restrict legitimate philosophizing to the working of the head on the workings of the head on experience.

"From Edwards to Emerson," of course, is Perry Miller's title for his provocative essay (1940), included with new comments in *Errand into the Wilderness* (New York: Harper Torchbooks, 1964). What I call the esthetic mode in which Edwards, prompted by God's Spirit, enjoyed God and the universe and the soul, seems to me comparable with the mode in which Emerson, gazing into the mirror of nature, enjoyed the universe and the soul and God. This way of linking these seminal religious thinkers suits me better than stressing the fact that both meditated on nature. If I have managed to improve the demonstration of Miller's thesis, I am all the more grateful for his having advanced it in the first place.

19.   Sidney Earl Mead, *Nathaniel William Taylor, 1786–1858, A Connecticut Liberal* (1942; Hamden, Conn.: Shoestring Press, Archon Books, 1967), p. 101.

20.   See Taylor's famous sermon, "Concio Ad Clerum" (1828), in Ahlstrom, pp. 213–49; cf. Mead, pp. 108–27.

21.   Mead, p. 124.

22.   *KGA*, pp. 187–95, set down several ways in which "The dynamic liberalism of which Channing and Emerson were the great American protagonists was more akin in spirit to the Evangelical movement [launched by Edwards] than to this earlier rationalistic liberalism [of men like Chauncy]" (p. 186) and placed considerable weight (p. 195) on Hopkins as the connecting link.

4   *The Hospitable Universe of Ralph Waldo Emerson*

23.   To paraphrase Emerson is to risk distorting him, but copious quotation would bloat this essay into a book. About halfway between these pitfalls is the course I steer, proof-texting paraphrases with brief quotes. Before faulting me, let the reader follow

the parenthetic reference of each quote to its source, asking how badly I bruise Emerson's meanings.

24.   Ovid, *Fasti*, 6:5: "*Est deus in nobis, agitante calescimus illo* [var.: *ille*]" (*JMN*, 3:12, 139; 4:29; *YES*, p. 200). Emerson recorded the phrase in 1826, 1828, 1832, and 1833. Later he preferred his own castings of the idea, which were alternately humanistic and theological.

25.   Charles J. Woodbury, *Talks With Emerson* (1890), ed. Henry LeRoy Finch (New York: Horizon Press, 1970), p. 107.

26.   Edward Waldo Emerson's note (*W*, 1:437). Taken together, these essays make a fair start: "New England Reformers," "Historic Notes of Life and Letters in New England," "Ezra Ripley, D.D.," "Mary Moody Emerson," "Historical Discourse at Concord," and "Boston."

27.   George Ripley, Review of James Martineau, *The Rationale of Religious Enquiry* in *The Christian Examiner* 21, no. 177, 3d ser., no. 8 (November 1836): 253–54. The sentence was quoted by Martin E. Marty, *The Modern Schism*; *Three Paths to the Secular* (London: SCM Press, 1969), p. 138.

28.   Cf. *W*, 10:220; var.: "idolatry prevails."

29.   *W*, 7:443. A "page . . . from an old lecture," noted Edward Waldo Emerson (*W*, 10:442).

30.   Robert C. Pollock, "A Reappraisal of Emerson," in *American Classics Reconsidered, a Christian Appraisal*, ed. Harold C. Gardiner, S.J. (New York: Scribner's, 1958), p. 25. Pollock had Emerson seeking to combine Platonism (actually it was neo-Platonism) with Stoicism after the fashion of medieval Catholicism. The endeavor was demolished by R.W.B. Lewis, *Trials of the Word, Essays in American Literature and the Humanistic Tradition* (New Haven: Yale University Press, 1965), pp. 102 ff.

31.   See René Wellek, *A History of Modern Criticism: 1750–1950*, vol. 2, "The Romantic Age" (New Haven: Yale University Press, 1955), *ad loc*. See also René Wellek, "Emerson and German Philosophy," *New England Quarterly* 16 (1943): 41–63.

32.   The first phrase was repeated in "Spiritual Laws" (*W*, 2:131).

33.   Marty, p. 126.

34.   A.C. McGiffert, Jr., *YES*, p. xxviii; Charles Ives, *Essays Before a Sonata* [*1920*] *and Other Writings*, ed. Howard Boatwright (New York: W.W. Norton, 1961 [1962?]), p. 16; Warner Berthoff, introduction to Emerson, *Nature, A Facsimile of the First Edition* (San Francisco: Chandler, 1968), p. lx; Bishop, p. 217.

35.   The other essay called "Character," which Emerson himself published in *Essays Second Series* (*W*, 3:87–115), is quite another matter.

36.   *W*, 2:282; var.: "universal soul."

37.   Stephen Emerson Whicher, "Emerson's Tragic Sense," *Emerson, A Collection of Critical Essays*, ed. Milton R. Konvitz and Stephen E. Whicher (Englewood Cliffs, N.J.: Prentice-Hall, 1962), p. 43.

38.   See the comment of Merton M. Sealts, Jr., ed., *JMN*, 5:xv: "Emerson had now come to believe that God, or the One, is not personal but impersonal, that evil is not absolute but merely privative, and that the moral constitution of man rather than historical Christianity must provide the basis for a modern religion." On my view "merely," which Emerson used regarding evil (*W*, 1:124) ill describes any one of these moves.

39.   See almost any commentator — for a start, Ahlstrom, pp. 293–94, and

Mark Van Doren, ed., *The Portable Emerson* (New York: Viking Press, 1946), p. 17. On prudential ethics in America, see William A. Clebsch, *From Sacred to Profane America, the Role of Religion in American History* (New York: Harper & Row, 1968), pp. 139–74.

40.   Lewis, p. 103: Emerson thus became "America's most knowing and moving portrayer of the failures of connection in human experience — of the appalling lack of context, in modern times, for action and for judgment."

41.   Whicher, p. 41: "Self-reliance, in the oft-cited phrase, is God-reliance, and therefore not self-reliance." I think it more accurate that self-reliance involves God-reliance and opposes other-reliance. But so far as God is alien, thus far God-reliance differs from self-reliance.

5   Interlude: From Emerson
                                  to James

42.   See Conrad Cherry, "The Structure of Organic Thinking: Horace Bushnell's Approach to Language, Nature, and Nation," *Journal of the American Academy of Religion* 40 (March 1972): 3–20.

43.   Horace Bushnell, *Christian Nurture* (New York: Scribner's, 1861), p. 204. But in the "New Edition" revised by Luther A. Weigle (New York: Scribner's, 1923 [first ed. 1916]), p. 172, the second infinitive, "pass," is made into a verb, "passes," and thus the last assertion is not governed by the qualifying "tends." Weigle intended to delete only a few controversial passages, but this unintentional change remained in the "Centenary" edition introduced by Weigle (New Haven: Yale University Press, 1947), p. 172. For the meaning of the statement in the context of Bushnell's thought, see Hilrie Shelton Smith, *Changing Conceptions of Original Sin, A Study in American Theology Since 1750* (New York: Scribner's, 1955), pp. 137–63.

44.   *Faust*, line 3456; cf. William James, "Reflex Action and Theism" (*WB*, p. 136), where for James the apothegm illustrates the point that the theist's "insight into the *what* of life leads to results so immediately and intimately rational that the *why*, the *how*, and the *whence* of it are questions that lose all urgency." In Coleridgean terms, James has feeling speaking through reason, shortcutting the understanding but profoundly engaging the reason.

45.   See Cross, pp. 145–51. Cross took no note of the fact that it was Henry James who in the *North American Review* castigated Bushnell for his theory of love and "thus assaulted the last outpost of Bushnell's truce with common sense" (Cross, p. 147). The quotes of James are from *North American Review* 102 (April 1866): 565, 569. James's authorship of this review is attested (*LR*, p. 471); see Frederic Harold Young, *The Philosophy of Henry James, Sr.* (New York: Bookman Associates, 1951), p. 323.

46.   *North American Review* 102:570.

47.   Striking parallels between Bushnell and Beecher were traced by William G. McLoughlin, *The Meaning of Henry Ward Beecher, An Essay on the Shifting Values of Mid-Victorian America, 1840–1870* (New York: Knopf, 1970). The quotations in this paragraph are, respectively, from pp. 254, 60 (quoting Beecher), 85 (quoting Beecher), 90, 241. According to McLoughlin, "While Emerson provided exceptional young people with a philosophy of self-governed, self-realizable freedom, Beecher offered the average, middle-class churchgoer a philosophy of (in his words) 'regulated Christian

liberty.' However, the starting point for both was the conviction that man must go through Nature to God" (p. 68).

48.   Henry James (the elder), *The Social Significance of Our Institutions* (Boston: Ticknor and Fields, 1861), p. 42.

6   *The Human Religiousness*
                                       of William James

49.   Henry James (the elder), New York, March 3, 1842, to Ralph W. Emerson, quoted by F. O. Matthiessen, *The James Family, Including Selections from the Writings of Henry James, Senior, William, Henry, & Alice James* (New York: Knopf, 1947), p. 39. Matthiessen reprinted most of William James's introduction to his father's *Literary Remains*. Since our interest in the elder James is as background to William, citations of the father's works are from the son's summary and copious quotations (*LR*).

         Quotations from whole passages that are italicized in the sources are sometimes put in roman type in this chapter.

50.   Alice James, *The Diary of Alice James*, ed. Leon Edel (New York: Dodd, Mead, 1934), p. 217.

51.   John Wild, *The Radical Empiricism of William James* (Garden City, N.Y.: Doubleday, 1969), p. 292; see also p. 281.

52.   Herbert W. Schneider, *Religion in 20th Century America* (Cambridge: Harvard University Press, 1952), in order, p. 207, p. vi.

53.   The earlier version, although prepared especially for the book, appeared in *Mind* 14 (July 1889):321–52. The footnote (*PP*, 2:283) dating the article "1869" contains a typographical error.

54.   MS. diary, April 30, 1870, Houghton Library, Harvard University, quoted by permission of the Harvard College Library. Most of the sentence (down to "delight") was published (*L*, 1:147), and "Grübelei" in the MS. was transcribed as "*Grübelei*."

55.   Of course, James knew Edwards' *Religious Affections* and regarded it as "an elaborate working out" of the empirical thesis, "By their fruits ye shall know them, not by their roots" (*VR*, 20). James obviously borrowed Edwards' emphasis on God's moral rather than metaphysical attributes as proper objects of the religious affections. In a notebook for 1862–63 James abstracted several important books, including Edwards' *Original Sin* (*TC*, 1:215).

56.   J. Seelye Bixler, "William James as Religious Thinker," in *William James, the Man and the Thinker*, ed. George C. Sellery and Clarence A. Dykstra (Madison: University of Wisconsin Press, 1942), p. 135 (see *VR*, pp. 196–98, 232–36). "The most important consequence of having a strongly developed ultra-marginal life . . . is that one's ordinary fields of consciousness are liable to incursions from it of which the subject does not guess the source" (*VR*, p. 234).

57.   Ibid., p. 129.

58.   Wild, p. 253.

59.   George Santayana, *Character and Opinion in the United States* (New York: Scribner's, 1921; paperback, Norton, 1967), pp. 76, 77.

60.   For the pervasive influence of James, see Louis Schneider and Sanford M. Dornbusch, *Popular Religion, Inspirational Books in America* (Chicago: University of Chicago Press, 1958).

7   *Postlude:*   *After James*

61.   John Dewey, "Experience, Knowledge and Value: A Rejoinder," in *The Philosophy of John Dewey*, ed. Paul Arthur Schilpp (New York: Tudor, 1939, 1951), p. 597; see also pp. 594–97.

62.   Reinhold Niebuhr, *Beyond Tragedy* (New York: Scribner's, 1955), p. ix.

63.   Reinhold Niebuhr, *The Nature and Destiny of Man, A Christian Interpretation*, 2 vols. (New York: Scribner's, 1941, 1943), 2:295. Reinhold Niebuhr, undated [1943?], to Norman Kemp Smith, TLS, Edinburgh University Library, quoted by permission of the Keeper of Manuscripts.

64.   Reinhold Niebuhr, *The Children of Light and the Children of Darkness* (New York: Scribner's, 1944), p. xi.

65.   Ibid., p. 129.

66.   For European influences on Niebuhr's thought, see Hans W. Frei, "Niebuhr's Theological Background," in *Faith and Ethics: The Theology of H. Richard Niebuhr*, ed. Paul Ramsey (New York: Harper, 1957).

67.   See also Helmut Richard Niebuhr, *Christ and Culture* (New York: Harper, 1951), p. 250. That each self is destined to choose was a theme Niebuhr shared not only with James but also with the existentialists. But for a biting critique of Søren Kierkegaard's individualism in connection with this insight, see *Christ and Culture*, pp. 241ff., and Niebuhr's own formulation of the point: "the decisions we make in the freedom of faith . . . are made . . . on the basis of relative insight and faith, but they are not relativistic. They are individual decisions, but not individualistic. They are made in freedom, but not in independence; they are made in the moment, but are not nonhistorical" (*Christ and Culture*, p. 234). As to Emerson, perhaps it is enough to point out that one of his most perceptive modern biographers made the entire intellectual and spiritual struggle turn on the interpenetration of freedom and fate; see Stephen Emerson Whicher, *Freedom and Fate, An Inner Life of Ralph Waldo Emerson* (Philadelphia: University of Pennsylvania Press, 1953). See also Helmut Richard Niebuhr, "Emerson, Ralph Waldo," *Die Religion in Geschichte und Gegenwart*, 3d ed., ed. Kurt Galling et al., 6 vols. (Tübingen: J.C.B. Mohr, 1958), 2:454–55.

68.   I am asserting Niebuhr's kinship with James's thought only concerning these themes. Niebuhr did not always leave clear tracks of dependence upon thinkers he studied. His library is said to have been well stocked with James. His liking for many of James's leading ideas is obvious.

Suggested Readings

The most thorough bibliography of American religion is Nelson R. Burr, *A Critical Bibliography of Religion in America*, 2 vols. (Princeton, 1961). More recent and more selective is the same author's contribution to the Goldentree Bibliographies in American History, called *Religion in American Life* (New York, 1971). Specialized lists of writings on Catholicism are John Paul Cadden, *The Historiography of the American Catholic Church, 1745–1943* (Washington, 1944); John Tracy Ellis, *A Guide to American Catholic History* (Milwaukee, 1959), and Edward Vollmar, *The Catholic Church in America, An Historical Bibliography*, 2d ed. (New York, 1965). On books on American Judaism, see Moses Rischin, *An Inventory of American Jewish History* (Cambridge, 1954). The old standby in this general field, still useful, is Peter G. Mode, *Source Book and Bibliographical Guide for American Church History* (Menasha, Wis., 1921).

The sections in all the above works listing books and articles and theses that deal historically with religious thought and theology are instructive, partly by reason of their brevity. Other perspectives on religious thought can be gained by reading general histories of American religion, theology, and philosophy.

For a study of religion with neatly balanced attention to Catholicism and Judaism as well as Protestantism, Winthrop S. Hudson, *Religion in America*, rev. ed. (New York, 1973), serves well and provides useful bibliographical guides. The most encyclopedic work by a single author is Sydney E. Ahlstrom's mammoth and remarkably detailed book, *A Religious History of the American People* (New Haven, 1972). It, too, generously displays sources and offers a long list of selected readings on many topics, including religious thought. The history of American Protestantism is narrated without references referring to sources by Martin E. Marty, *Righteous Empire, The Protestant Experience in America* (New York, 1970). The series to which it belongs bars footnotes and references and includes John Cogley, *Catholic America* (New York, 1973). This is also the subject of John Tracy Ellis, *American Catholicism* (1956; Chicago, 1969) and of Philip Gleason, *Catholicism in America* (New York, 1970). The most helpful brief story of the Jewish religious experience in American history is by Nathan Glazer, *American Judaism* (Chicago, 1957).

Turning to the history of theology in America, two works by Sydney E. Ahlstrom are edifying, especially when taken together. Both are called "Theology in America." The earlier is a long essay in *The Shaping of American Religion*, ed. James Ward Smith and A. Leland Jamison (Princeton, 1961). The other is the volume subtitled *The Major Protestant Voices from Puritanism to Neo-Orthodoxy* (Indianapolis, 1967), containing readings from eighteen prominent figures, including many whose religious thought comes into view in the present book, such as Edwards, Channing, Taylor, Charles Hodge, Emerson, Bushnell, Nevin, James, Rauschenbusch, and H. R. Niebuhr. A more elaborate collection of sources by Hilrie Shelton Smith, Robert T. Handy, and Lefferts A. Loetscher, *American Christianity, an Historical Interpretation with Representative Documents*, 2 vols. (New York, 1960, 1963), ranges over the institutional, social, and political as well as the intellectual history of the churches. A book whose title makes it seem to parallel the present work, Frederick Sontag and John K. Roth, *The American Religious Experience, the Roots, Trends, and Future of American Theology* (New York, 1972), romps tendentiously through the past with great zest for the presumed present and future.

Two histories of special themes in religious thought — the nature of human sin and the aspiration for the Kingdom of God — rest on mastery of sources and precision of interpretation that are enviable by any writer in the field; they are Hilrie Shelton Smith, *Changing Conceptions of Original Sin, A Study in American Theology Since 1750* (New York, 1955) and Helmut Richard Niebuhr, *The Kingdom of God in America* (New York, 1937).

Religious thought has been approached through the study of American philosophy in addition to and as well as American theology. Herbert

W. Schneider, *A History of American Philosophy*, 2d ed. (New York, 1963), sees religious thought from this angle. Concentrating on Peirce, James, Royce, Dewey, and Whitehead, a fine book by John E. Smith, *The Spirit of American Philosophy* (New York, 1963), is remarkably sensitive to the religious dimension of these thinkers' philosophies. The same scholar's *Themes in American Philosophy; Purpose, Experience and Community* (New York, 1970) has the same virtue of sensitiveness to religion and also includes a long essay on "The Philosophy of Religion in America." More limited in scope — to James, Peirce, Dewey, and Whitehead — yet more emphatically interested in their religious thought or philosophy of religion, is Robert J. Roth, *American Religious Philosophy* (New York, 1967). This must be the place to mention again Morton White, *Science & Sentiment in America, Philosophical Thought from Jonathan Edwards to John Dewey* (New York, 1972), but why repeat the caveats that recur in my foregoing notes? Surely it is a book to contend with — or against.

Every student of American religious thought should wrestle with the formidable learning and brilliant interpretations regarding spirituality that flowed from the pen of the late Perry Miller. His familiar works on Puritanism and Transcendentalism should not overshadow *The Life of the Mind in America, from the Revolution to the Civil War* (New York, 1965). Miller's literary bent calls to mind the fact that American novels, especially in the middle period, have been shown to have important ramifications into spirituality. See, in this regard, a fine book cited in the notes: A. N. Kaul, *The American Vision, Actual and Ideal Society in Nineteenth-Century Fiction* (New Haven, 1963).

Following these suggestions of books in the general field of American religious thought come periodized proposals for further reading concerning: first, some anthologies and interpretations of Edwards, Emerson, and James, and then some indication of how to study the movements and movers of religious thought that connect Edwards with Emerson, Emerson with James, and James with the reader's own time.

EDWARDS, EMERSON, AND JAMES

The table of abbreviations in the front of this book points the reader to the most important writings by these and some other major figures in American religious thought, as well as to some important interpreters of them. Here some remarks on the published works of the three eponyms may be in order.

Publication of the remaining volumes of Edwards' works, including such important manuscript material as the complete Miscellanies and such crucial publications as the life of David Brainerd, is proceeding at Yale University Press under the general editorship of John E. Smith. As to Emerson, the first volume of a projected new *Collected Works*, text established by Alfred R. Ferguson with introduction and notes by Robert E. Spiller, begins an ambitious project of the Center for Editions of American Authors of the Belknap Press of Harvard University Press. Since this first volume appeared when the present book was already well developed, I give no references to it, but any student can easily trace to it, via *W*, my citations from *Nature* and from the lectures and addresses included in this Belknap Press volume. Although the bulk of James's work continues to be available in paperback reprints, to my knowledge there are no plans for a critical edition of the whole corpus. To be sure, many letters and diaries have never been published. These personal documents would, if made generally available, greatly illumine the relations between James's life and thought.

All these eponyms have been much anthologized, and good selections from each corpus are available in paperback. For Edwards, the *Representative Selections*, an old standby edited and introduced by Clarence H. Faust and Thomas H. Johnson (1935; New York, 1962) still serves very well. So does Brooks Atkinson's edition of Emerson called *The Complete Essays and other Writings of Ralph Waldo Emerson* (New York, 1940); this somewhat misleading title means that the two volumes that Emerson himself put out as "Essays" are reprinted here along with other major essays. Ralph Barton Perry selected meaty morsels by James for *Essays on Faith and Morals* (1943; Cleveland, 1962).

Many of the chief secondary writings about the spirituality of these three figures have been mentioned in the notes and abbreviations. Some notable works, however, remain to be mentioned, such as, with respect to Edwards, Roland A. Delattre, *Beauty and Sensibility in the Thought of Jonathan Edwards, an Essay in Aesthetics and Theological Ethics* (New Haven, 1968), as well as Edward H. Davidson, *Jonathan Edwards, the Narrative of a Puritan Mind* (Boston, 1968). From the veritable library of writings about Emerson, of the titles not cited already, one should mention Vivian C. Hopkins, *Spires of Form, A Study of Emerson's*

Aesthetic Theory (Cambridge, 1951). For James, too, many works help bring him into the focus of religious thought. Two older books are Karl August Busch, *William James als Religionsphilosoph* (Göttingen, 1911) and Julius Seelye Bixler, *Religion in the Philosophy of William James* (Boston, 1926); a newer one is John K. Roth, *Freedom and the Moral Life, The Ethics of William James* (Philadelphia, 1969). There is penetrating appreciation of the Americanness of James's contribution to religious thought in an old essay by Ernst Troeltsch, "Empiricism and Platonism in the Philosophy of Religious Experience," *Harvard Theological Review*, 5 (1912): 401–22 (see Troeltsch, *Gesammelte Schriften*, 2:364–85).

BETWEEN EDWARDS AND EMERSON

The best treatment of the liberalization of New England theology is Herbert W. Schneider, *The Puritan Mind* (1930; Ann Arbor, 1958). The particular relation of rationalism and Arminianism to Edwards, especially in the thought of Samuel Johnson, D.D., is helpfully delineated by Claude M. Newlin, *Philosophy and Religion in Colonial America* (New York, 1962). On the tendency of Puritanism to fall over into moralism, see Joseph G. Haroutunian, *Piety versus Moralism, the Passing of the New England Theology* (New York, 1932). The more extreme rationalism, torn from Puritan soil, became the basis of a new American religion or religiousness, according to Gustav Adolf Koch, *Republican Religion: The American Revolution and the Cult of Reason* (1933; New York, 1964).

The religious awakening which Edwards both promoted and criticized comes to life in Edwin Scott Gaustad, *The Great Awakening in New England* (1957; Gloucester, Mass., 1965). For the more radical side of that movement, see Clarence C. Goen, *Revivalism and Separatism in New England, 1740–1800, Strict Congregationalists and Separate Baptists in the Great Awakening* (New Haven, 1962). There are many local and regional studies of the later, and especially of the western or "frontier," awakenings, for which both a general picture and much concrete detail can be gained from perusing the source materials collected by William Warren Sweet, *Religion on the American Frontier*, 4 vols. (New York and Chicago, 1931–46).

The way that Timothy Dwight's work in the "second awakening" pointed toward and came to issue in the theological revisions of N. W. Taylor is laid out in detail by Sidney E. Mead, *Nathaniel William Taylor* (Hamden, Conn., 1967). For a different kind of modified Calvinism see Daniel Day Williams, *The Andover Liberals, a Study in American Theology* (New York, 1941). The best general study of later revivalism in America is William G. McLoughlin, Jr., *Modern Revivalism, Charles Grandison Finney to Billy Graham* (New York, 1959).

The more strictly theological heritage of Edwards, down to the last Edwardean, is surveyed in Frank Hugh Foster, *A Genetic History of the New England Theology* (Chicago, 1907). The rival theology of Unitarianism, of course, had its own tradition going back in America to Edwards' own day, as is shown by Conrad Wright, *The Beginnings of Unitarianism in America* (Boston, 1955), covering the period 1735–1805. The man who mediated this older Unitarianism to Emerson and combined it with an esthetic piety, drawn in important respects from Edwards, is the subject of Arthur W. Brown, *William Ellery Channing* (New York, 1962). And the man who carried Unitarianism into social moralism instead of the esthetic spirituality of Emerson is the subject of Henry Steele Commager, *Theodore Parker: Yankee Crusader* (1936; Boston, 1947). For the theological side of Parker, see John Edward Dirks, *The Critical Theology of Theodore Parker* (New York, 1948). Commager has collected a fine anthology of Parker's writings.

FROM EMERSON TO JAMES

The more theologically inclined thinkers who are treated in this second "Interlude" have been studied in great detail, but the full range and variety of religious thought during Emerson's lifetime and down to the beginnings of pragmatism have yet to be surveyed in a reliable volume. The theology of Emerson and the Transcendentalists, of the Princeton and Mercersburg theologians, and of Bushnell is woven into the history of Continental and British theological movements by Claude Welch, *Protestant Thought in the Nineteenth Century*, vol. 1 (New Haven, 1972), which also reckons with other Americans such as Lyman Beecher, Brownson, Channing, Dwight, Edwards, Finney, Hopkins, James, Parker, Schmucker, and, at some length, Taylor.

In the order of treatment in my chapter, the Princeton theology comes first. There are old biographies that record the life and work of Archibald Alexander and of Charles Hodge, whose teachings are the point of departure for Lefferts A. Loetscher, *The Broadening Church, A Study of Theological Issues in the Presbyterian Church Since 1869* (Philadelphia, 1954). Nevin and Schaff are historically placed by James Hastings Nichols, *Romanticism in American Theology, Nevin and Schaff at Mercersburg* (Chicago, 1961), and the same author excerpted and introduced the writings of these two men in *The Mercersburg Theology* (New York, 1966). The most systematic study of these leading romantic religious thinkers is Luther J. Binkley, *The Mercersburg Theology* (Manheim, Pa., 1953). Their counterparts in other denominations are subjects of an old book by Peter Anstadt, *Life and Times of Rev. S. S. Schmucker* (York, Pa., 1896), and of a new one by Alvin W. Skardon, *Church Leader in the Cities, William Augustus Muhlenberg* (Philadelphia, 1971).

On the Catholics who proposed to adapt the Roman Church to American life and ways, the general work to be consulted is Thomas T. McAvoy, *The Americanist Heresy in Roman Catholicism, 1895–1900* (Notre Dame, 1963). Individual studies of key figures are Theodore Maynard, *Orestes Brownson, Yankee, Radical, Catholic* (New York, 1943), and Joseph McSorley, *Father Hecker and His Friends* (St. Louis, 1952). The Jewish "Americanists" mentioned later in my chapter may be studied by consulting Mordecai M. Kaplan, *Judaism as a Civilization, Toward a Reconstruction of American-Jewish Life* (1934; New York, 1957), and James G. Heller, *Isaac M. Wise, His Life, Work, and Thought* (New York, 1965).

The handiest single volume on Bushnell (now out of print but available in many libraries), emphasizing the more strictly theological side of his thought, is *Horace Bushnell*, ed. Hilrie Shelton Smith (New York, 1965), which may be supplemented, but not substituted for, by William R. Adamson, *Bushnell Rediscovered* (Philadelphia, 1966). For selections from writings of the major advocates of the social gospel during its heyday, see Robert T. Handy, ed., *The Social Gospel in America 1870–1920* (New York, 1966), containing pieces by Gladden, Ely, and Rauschenbusch, and a historical introduction. The origins of the social gospel are connected with the revivals by Timothy L. Smith, *Revivalism and Social Reform in Mid-Nineteenth-Century America* (New York, 1957), and the standard history of the movement at its flowering is Charles Howard Hopkins, *The Rise of the Social Gospel in American Protestantism 1865–1915* (New Haven, 1940). Suggested readings about Rauschenbusch fall in the next section of this note.

AFTER WILLIAM JAMES

The thinkers treated in the postlude flourished in the first half of our century, for which the broadest survey of religious thought is Herbert W. Schneider, *Religion in 20th Century America* (1952; New York, 1964). For the theological milieu of Rauschenbusch and Dewey, which the Niebuhr brothers (each in his own way) sought to correct, see Lloyd J. Averill, *American Theology in the Liberal Tradition* (Philadelphia, 1967). The social-gospel movement is defended against conservative political as well as radical theological critics by Frederick Ernest Johnson, *The Social Gospel Re-examined* (New York, 1940). Several books present selections from Rauschenbusch's works; see Robert D. Cross, ed., *Walter Rauschenbusch, Christianity and the Social Crisis* (New York, 1964), and *A Rauschenbusch Reader, the Kingdom of God and the Social Gospel*, comp. Benson Y. Landis (New York, 1957).

The histories of American philosophy by Roth, Smith, and White that are mentioned above deal specifically with the thought and religious sensibilities of Dewey, whose religious position was hotly debated in *The Christian Century* just after the publication of *CF*.

The contributions of Reinhold Niebuhr to American life and thought are still being evaluated and some of them reevaluated. Penetrating appraisals by people who knew him well can be found in Harold R. Landon, ed., *Reinhold Niebuhr, a Prophetic Voice in Our Time, Essays in Tribute* by Paul Tillich, John C. Bennett, and Hans J. Morgenthau (Greenwich, Conn., 1962). His life and thought, sympathetically interwoven, are surveyed by June Bingham, *Courage to Change, an Introduction to the Life and Thought of Reinhold Niebuhr* (New York, 1961). His critics and admirers had their say, and he his in response, in Charles W. Kegley and Robert W. Bretall, eds., *Reinhold Niebuhr, His Religious, Social and Political Thought* (New York, 1956).

Published works about H. Richard Niebuhr are far less plentiful than those about the more famous brother. An incisive dissertation that systematizes his thought more than he ever did is by Jerry A. Irish, "Revelation in the Theology of H. Richard Niebuhr" (Yale University, 1967). For the European background of Niebuhr's

philosophy and theology, see the fine essays by Hans W. Frei in Paul
Ramsey, ed., *Faith and Ethics, The Theology of H. Richard Niebuhr* (New
York, 1957); in *RM*, Niebuhr made some explicit responses to these
interpretations by his former students. The implications and repercus-
sions of his achievements as a religious and ethical thinker are the
starting-point for a suggestive appraisal of American spirituality in
the decade of his death — an essay whose mention appropriately ends
this list of suggested readings. It is by Sydney E. Ahlstrom, "The
Radical Turn in Theology and Ethics: Why it Occurred in the 1960s,"
Annals of the American Academy of Political Science, 387 (January 1970):
1–13.

Index

Detailed subject-entries fall under main entries for Edwards, Emerson, and James, for whom a single subject, e.g., Christ or religion, often signified very different things.

Adamson, William R., 203

Adventists, 112

Agassiz, Louis (1807–73), 138

Ahlstrom, Sydney E., ix, 59, 114, 191, 192, 197, 198, 205

Alexander, Archibald (1772–1851), 113, 126, 203

Allen, Gay Wilson, 138–39, 145

Anstadt, Peter, 203

Antirevivalists, 19, 23–24, 33–36, 42. See also Revivalists

Arminians, 19, 21–22

Asbury, Francis (1745–1816), 6, 60–61, 63

Augustine, Saint (354–430), 17, 83

Averill, Lloyd J., 204

Barth, Karl (1886–1968), 173, 181

Bartlet, Phebe, 47

Beecher, Henry Ward (1813–87), xi, 6, 121–22, 172, 193

Beecher, Lyman (1785–1863), 62–63, 112, 114, 202

Bellamy, Joseph (1719–90), 6, 55, 64

Bennett, John Coleman, 204

Berkeley, George (1685–1753), 60

Berthoff, Warner, 192

Bingham, June, 204

Binkley, Luther J., 203

Bishop, Jonathan, 75–77, 93

Bixler, Julius Seelye, 194, 201

Boehme, Jacob (1575–1624), 83

Brainerd, David (1718–47), 38, 45–47, 200

Brown, Arthur W., 202

Brownson, Orestes A. (1803–76), 114, 202, 203

Buber, Martin (1878–1965), 173

Bultmann, Rudolf (b. 1884), 173

Bunyan, John (1628–88), 140

Burr, Nelson R., 197

Busch, Karl August, 201

Bushnell, Horace (1802–76), 6–7, 65, 114–23, 172, 182, 193, 198, 202, 203

Cadden, John Paul, 197

Calvin, John (1509–64), 17

Calvinism, 18–19, 81–83, 87, 126–32, 202. See also Edwardean theology; New Haven theology; Princeton theology

Carse, James, 191

Carlyle, Thomas (1795–1881), 83, 90, 113

Cartwright, Peter (1785–1872), 60

Catholics, 85, 112–14, 123

Channing, William Ellery (1780–1842), 66–68, 83, 119, 172, 198, 202

Chauncy, Charles (1705–87), 35, 59–60, 119, 172

Cherry, Conrad, 189, 190, 193

Clebsch, William A., 193
Cogley, John, 198
Coleridge, Samuel Taylor *(1772–1834)*, 83, 90, 115–16
Colman, Benjamin *(1673–1747)*, 32
Columbia University, 59, 144
Commager, Henry Steele, 202
Confucius, 76, 84
Congregationalists, 31–32, 62, 201
Cousin, Victor *(1792–1867)*, 90
Cross, Barbara M., 115–16, 119–20, 193, 204

Darwin, Charles *(1809–82)*, 113
Davidson, Edward H., 200
Delattre, Roland A., 200
Dewey, John *(1859–1952)*, 173–81, 195, 199, 204
Dirks, John Edward, 202
Doctrine. *See* Theology
Dornbusch, Sanford M., 194
Dwight, Timothy *(1752–1817)*, 6, 61–65, 172, 201–2

Edwardean theology, 6, 14–16, 55, 64–65, 202
Edwards, Jerusha *(daughter of Jonathan; d. 1748)*, 38, 45
Edwards, Jonathan *(1703–58)*
    affections, 15–20, 23–28, 32, 42, 48, 54, 64, 190
    baptism, 13, 25, 27–32, 47
    being in general, 23, 50–55
    and Bushnell, 115–16, 120
    Christ, 13, 17, 20, 29–30, 33–37, 44, 47, 49
    church, 17, 47–48, 55
    church membership, 13–16, 25, 28–37, 47–48
    conscience, 5, 22, 50–53, 64
    conversions, 5, 17, 21–23, 30–38, 43–44, 53–54
    covenants, 17–20, 29, 189–90
    and Dewey, 176
    and Emerson, 6–7, 68, 135, 162, 168–71, 182–86, 191
    esthetics, 7, 15, 18, 43–44, 49–58, 64–66, 118, 182–86
    experiential method, 14–18, 20, 24, 27–28, 32–36, 42, 45–49
    God (nature of), 17–24, 43, 50–58, 66

God (operations of), 13–28, 32–36, 39–43, 47–58, 64–66
holiness, 35–38, 43, 46–49, 53–58
humility, 20, 22, 44, 48
hypocrisy, 25, 28, 31, 48
and Henry James the elder, 128
and William James, 7, 39, 135, 162, 169–73, 182–86, 191
life of, 25–38, 46–47, 49, 190
Lord's Supper, 13, 29–33, 37
love of divine things, 20, 23, 28, 39–43, 50–58, 65
religious thought of, x–xii, xv–xvi, 12, 15, 19–22, 58, 112–13, 119, 122, 172, 182–86, 198–202
sainthood, 14–17, 20–58, 64–66
sainthood (signs of), 38–49, 54, 64
salvation, 21, 27, 35, 38, 50
Satan, 33–34, 41–42
Scripture, 17, 19, 32, 35–36, 42, 49
self-interest, 43, 50–55
sin, 16–17, 20–22, 49, 63, 190, 194
theology, 5, 19–24, 65
Trinity, 17, 23, 190
the understanding, 38–40, 43
virtue, 15, 22–23, 49–55, 66
will, 38–40, 49
world-view of, 5–6, 12–21, 63
writings of
    "Account of His Conversion," 25–26, 189, 190
    Distinguishing Marks, 33–34
    Divine and Supernatural Light, 27–29, 32
    Faithful Narrative, 32–33, 60
    Freedom of the Will, 59
    God Glorified, 27
    Life of Brainerd, 38, 45–47, 200
    Miscellanies, 189–90, 200
    Nature of True Virtue, 23, 49–53, 63–65
    Religious Affections, 27, 36–45, 49, 51, 190, 194
    Some Thoughts, 34–36
    "Sinners in the Hands of an Angry God," 16

Edwards, Jonathan, Jr. *(son of Jonathan; 1745–1801)*, 55
Edwards, Sarah Pierrepont *(wife of Jonathan; 1710–58)*, 26, 35, 38, 47, 190

Edwards, Timothy *(father of Jonathan; 1669–1758)*, 25, 46

Ellis, John Tracy, 197, 198

Ely, Richard Theodore *(1854–1943)*, 123, 203

Emerson, Charles Chauncy *(brother of Ralph W.; 1808–36)*, 94

Emerson, Ellen Tucker *(wife of Ralph W.; 1811?–31)*, 69, 71, 104

Emerson, Lydia Jackson *(wife of Ralph W.; 1802–92)*, 70–71

Emerson, Mary Moody *(aunt of Ralph W.; 1774–1863)*, 82, 192

Emerson, Ralph Waldo *(1803–82)*
  and Bushnell, 115–16, 120, 121
  and Carlyle, 113
  compensation, 70, 74–76, 84, 87, 92, 95, 99, 102–6, 110
  and Dewey, 176
  and Edwards, 6–7, 67–68, 135, 162, 168–71, 182–87, 191
  epistemology, 75–79, 88–91, 96, 101–3
  esthetics, 70, 74, 104–6, 182–87
  and Henry James the elder, 128, 131
  heroism, 73, 83–85, 88, 98
  history, 85–87, 102, 106
  holiness, 88, 98–99
  human solidarity, 72, 80, 89, 102, 109–11
  individualism, 71, 79–80, 101
  institutions (religious), 71–72, 76–86, 91–93, 126
  Jesus, 76, 81, 84, 91, 102, 110
  life of, 69–73, 112, 115
  modern spirituality, 71–79, 82, 93–94, 109–11
  monism, 75, 100–101, 123
  moral sentiment, 76, 78–79, 86–87, 95–97, 105
  nature, 69–78, 89–91, 94–95, 99–111
  optimism, 75, 103–4, 195
  Over-Soul, 70, 72–80, 88–104, 108–11
  poetry, 88, 105
  poets, 76–78, 85–86
  reformers, 76, 83–87
  religiousness, 72–85, 88–111, 124–25

religious sentiment, 82–88, 93, 95–97, 105

religious thought of, x–xii, xv–xvi, 3, 69–111, 119, 192, 198–200

reverence, 79–82, 84–85, 92, 95

self-reliance, 76, 84–85, 92, 99, 106–10, 193

theology, 74, 77–78, 81–85, 172

and William James, 7, 103, 105, 124, 135, 162–63, 168–73, 182–87, 191

writings of
  "Boston," 192
  "Character," 95, 192
  "Divinity School Address," 71, 80–83
  "Ezra Ripley, D.D.," 192
  "Historical Discourse at Concord," 192
  "Inspiration," 89
  Journals, 72–73, 88
  "Life and Letters in New England," 192
  "Mary Moody Emerson," 192
  Nature, 69–71, 94, 112
  "New England Reformers," 192
  "Perpetual Forces," 97
  "Religion," 99
  "Thoughts on the Religion of the Middle Ages," 83

Emerson, Waldo *(son of Ralph W.; 1836–42)*, 71, 77, 94, 125

Enthusiasts. *See* Revivalists

Episcopalians, 59–62, 113

Evolution. *See* Progress

Finney, Charles Grandison *(1792–1875)*, 6, 55, 60, 63, 112, 202

Fiske, John *(1842–1901)*, 115

Foster, Frank Hugh, 202

Fox, George *(1624–91)*, 83, 98–99

Franklin, Benjamin *(1706–90)*, 59

Frei, Hans W., 195, 205

Freud, Sigmund *(1856–1939)*, 113

Gaustad, Edwin Scott, 201

Gautama, 76

George, Henry *(1839–97)*, 175

German Reformeds, 114

Gibbons, James Cardinal *(1834–1921)*, 114, 123

Gladden, Washington (1836–1918), 122–23, 203
Glazer, Nathan, 198
Gleason, Philip, 198
Goen, Clarence C., 201
Graham, Billy [William Franklin] (b. 1918), 15, 60, 202
Great Awakening, 5, 25, 27, 32–36, 54, 60, 112, 201
Griffin, Edward M., 190

Halfway covenant, 29–31
Harvard (University, College, Schools), 71, 80–83, 137, 141, 143–44
Handy, Robert T., 198, 203
Haroutunian, Joseph G., 201
Hecker, Isaac Thomas (1819–88), 114, 203
Heller, James G., 203
Hodge, Charles (1797–1878), 113, 126, 198, 203
Holbrook, Clyde A., 14
Hopkins, Charles Howard, 203
Hopkins, Samuel (1721–1803), 6, 55, 64–68, 189, 202
Hopkins, Vivian C., 200
Hudson, Winthrop S., 197
Hutchinson, Abigail, 47

Ireland, John (1838–1918), 114, 123
Irish, Jerry A., 204
Ives, Charles (1874–1954), 93, 192

James, Alexander Robertson (son of William; 1890–1946), 143
James, Alice (sister of William; 1848–92), 194
James, Alice Howe Gibbens (wife of William; 1849–1922), 143, 144, 160–61
James, Henry the elder (father of William; 1811–82), 7, 121, 125–37, 172–73, 177, 193, 194
James, Henry, Jr. (brother of William; 1843–1916), 129, 137, 140–41, 144
James, Henry, II (son of William; 1879–1947), 143
James-Lange theory of emotions, 103, 137, 164

James, Margaret Mary [Porter] (daughter of William; 1887–1947), 143
James, Mary Robertson Walsh (mother of William; 1810–82), 129, 143
James, William (1842–1910)
  acedia of, 138–48
  belief, 136–52, 155–58, 162–70
  and Bushnell, 115–16
  choice, 135–37, 145, 148–50, 162, 164–67
  conversion, 155
  and Dewey, 176
  doubt, 145–46, 150–51, 166
  and Edwards, 7, 39, 135, 162, 169–73, 183–87, 191, 194
  and Emerson, 7, 103, 105, 124–25, 135, 162–63, 168–73, 183–87, 191
  empiricism, 137, 153, 163
  esthetics, 147, 157, 159–61, 169–70, 183–87
  ethics, 135–36, 139, 151–54, 157–62, 167–69
  experience, 144–45, 149–53, 161–64
  experience (religious), 135, 140, 143, 146, 154–61
  God, 135–36, 140, 142, 148, 151–53, 156–70, 193
  good and evil, 105, 140, 147, 154
  healthy-mindedness, 154–55
  and Henry James the elder, 125, 134–37, 140–43, 172–73
  life and travels of, 125, 129, 137–38, 143–44
  monism, 135–36, 148, 158–59, 164, 168–69
  philosophy of, 135, 140, 150–52, 160–62
  pluralism, 125, 135–36, 149–52, 156–58, 161, 163–74, 185–87
  psychology, 135–37, 141–50, 157–63, 167
  reality, 136, 140, 143–51, 157–70
  religion, 135–37, 146, 159–60, 162, 165–68
  religiousness of, 136–37, 140–41, 144–48, 153, 160, 165, 169
  religious thought of, x–xii, xv–xvi, 113, 124, 134–70, 198–202

saintliness, 156, 168–69
the self, 137, 140–41, 146, 150–57,
    161, 167–70
sick soul, 142, 146, 154–55
theology, 136, 166–68, 172
will, 136–43, 145–48, 152, 158–59,
    162–66
worth of life, 135, 138–42, 145–47,
    161–62
writings of
    Essays in Radical Empiricism, 144
    Literary Remains of Henry James, 143,
        194
    Pluralistic Universe, 144
    Pragmatism, 144
    Principles of Psychology, 143–49, 194
    Psychology: Briefer Course, 143
    "Psychology of Belief," 144–49,
        194
    "Reflex Action and Theism," 193
    Some Problems of Philosophy, 144
    Varieties of Religious Experience, 143–
        44, 146–47, 153–58, 161
    Will to Believe, 143, 165
James, William (grandfather of William;
    1771–1832), 125
James, William (son of William; 1882–
    1961), 143
Jews, 13, 123–24
Johnson, Frederick Ernest, 204
Johnson, Samuel (1696–1772), 59–60,
    172, 201

Kaplan, Mordecai M. (b. 1881), 124,
    203
Kaufmann, R. James, 7, 189
Kaul, A. N., 189, 199
Keane, John Joseph (1839–1918), 114,
    123
Kierkegaard, Søren (1813–55), 195
Koch, Gustav Adolf, 201

Lewis, R. W. B., 192, 193
Liberal theologians, 120–23, 178–79
Locke, John (1632–1704), 18, 57
Loetscher, Lefferts A., 198, 203
Luther, Martin (1483–1546), 76, 83–
    85, 94, 98–99, 110, 142
Lutherans, 114

McAvoy, Thomas T., 203

Machen, J. Greshman (1881–1937), 114
McGiffert, Arthur Cushman, Jr., 93, 192
McIlvaine, Charles P. (1799–1873), 112
McLoughlin, William G., 193–94, 202
Marx, Karl (1818–83), 113, 175
Marty, Martin E., 92, 192, 198
Mayhew, Jonathan (1720–66), 59–60
Matthiessen, F. O., 194
Maynard, Theodore, 203
Mead, Sidney Earl, 62, 191, 202
Mercersburg theology, 114, 198, 202–3
Methodists, 60–61, 85, 113
Miller, Perry, 6, 20, 55, 189–90, 191,
    199
Miller, William (1782–1849), 112
Milton, John (1608–74), 83, 110
Moody, Dwight Lyman (1837–99), 55,
    60, 63
Mode, Peter G., 197
Moralism. See Esthetics; Puritanism
Morgenthau, Hans J., 204
Mormons, 112
Muhlenberg, William Augustus (1796–
    1877), 114, 203

Nevin, John Williamson (1803–86),
    114, 198, 203
New Haven theology, 61–63, 115
Newlin, Claude M., 201
Nichols, James Hastings, 203
Niebuhr, Helmut Richard (1894–
    1962), xv, 6, 165, 168, 173, 181–
    87, 191, 195, 198, 203–4
Niebuhr, Reinhold (1892–1971), 173,
    177–81, 195, 203

Park, Edwards Amasa (1808–1900), 6
Parker, Theodore (1810–60), 7, 67, 83,
    119, 172, 202
Pascal, Blaise (1623–62), 115
Peale, Norman Vincent (b. 1898), 55
Peirce, Charles Sanders (1839–1914),
    199
Perry, Ralph Barton, 134–35, 145, 163,
    166
Pollock, Robert C., 192
Pragmatism, 113–14
Presbyterians, 85, 113
Princeton theology, 113–14, 126, 202–3
Progress, 86–87, 113–15, 121–22

Puritanism, x, xvi, 11–15, 19–21, 24,
31, 53–58, 86, 107, 116

Quakers, 84–86

Rationalists, 19, 22, 58–60, 118
Rauschenbusch, Walter *(1861–1918)*,
122–23, 173–75, 177, 198
Renouvier, Charles *(1815–1903)*, 140
Revivalists, 6, 19, 22–24, 42, 55, 58,
60–65, 112–13, 118, 172, 201–2
Riesman, David *(b. 1909)*, 107
Ripley, George *(1802–80)*, 85, 192
Rischin, Moses, 197
Roth, John K., 198, 201
Roth, Robert J., 199, 204
Royce, Josiah *(1855–1916)*, 184, 199

Santayana, George *(1863–1952)*, 165,
194
Schafer, Thomas A., 189, 190
Schaff, Philip *(1819–93)*, 114, 203
Schelling, F. W. J. von *(1775–1854)*,
90, 116
Schilpp, Paul Arthur, 195
Schmucker, Samuel S. *(1799–1873)*,
112, 114, 202–3
Schneider, Herbert W., 194, 199, 201,
204
Schneider, Louis, 194
Separatists, 19, 24
Shakers, 112
Shea, Daniel B., 189, 190
Skardon, Alvin W., 203
Smith, Hilrie Shelton, 193, 198, 203
Smith, John E., 199, 204
Smith, Joseph *(1805–44)*, 112
Smith, Norman Kemp *(1872–1958)*,
179, 195
Smith, Timothy L., 203
Social gospel, 114, 120–23, 133–34,
174–75, 177–78, 203–4
Sontag, Frederick, 198
Spencer, Herbert *(1820–1903)*, 121
Stanford University, 144
Staupitz, John *(1468–1524)*, 142
Stoddard, John *(son of Solomon, d. 1748)*,
31, 37
Stoddard, Solomon *(1643–1729)*, 26–
32, 40, 55

Stowe, Harriet Beecher *(1811–96)*, 21,
190
Strong, Josiah *(1847–1916)*, 122–23
Sunday, Billy [William Ashley] *(1863–
1935)*, 60
Swedenborg, Emanuel *(1688–1772)*,
83, 127, 129, 131, 132
Swedenborgians, 85, 131
Sweet, William Warren, 201

Taylor, Nathaniel William *(1786–
1858)*, 62–65, 119, 172, 191, 198,
202
Temple, Minny *(d. 1870)*, 139
Tennent, Gilbert *(1703–64)*, 6, 60
Theology, ix–x, xv, 171–73
Tillich, Paul *(1886–1965)*, 204
Tradition, authority of, 87, 113–15,
172–73
Transcendentalists, 65, 71, 83, 85–86,
112, 118, 202
Troeltsch, Ernst, 181, 201

Unitarians, 58–59, 62, 81–82, 85–86,
202

Walker, Williston, 190
Warham, John, 189
Warfield, Benjamin *(1851–1921)*, 113
Welch, Claude, 202
Weld, Theodore Dwight *(1803–95)*, 112
Wellek, René, 192
Wesley, John *(1703–91)*, 60
Whicher, Stephen E., 96, 192, 193,
195
White, Morton, 6, 116, 190, 191, 199,
204
Whitehead, Alfred North *(1861–1947)*,
186, 199
Wild, John, 135, 164, 167, 194
Williams, Daniel Day, 202
Winslow, Ola Elizabeth, 190
Wise, Isaac M. *(1811–1900)*, 123–24,
203
Wordsworth, William *(1770–1850)*, 140
Woodbury, Charles J., 192
Wright, Conrad, 202

Yale (University, College, Schools), 25–
26, 33, 61, 65, 115, 181
Young, Frederic Harold, 193